Texas Auto Trails

The Southeast

D0499297

Texas Auto Trails
The Southeast

by Myra Hargrave McIlvain
Illustrated by Virginia Adams Erickson

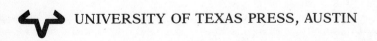 UNIVERSITY OF TEXAS PRESS, AUSTIN

First Edition, 1982

Requests for permission to reproduce material from this work
should be sent to Permissions, University of Texas Press, Box
7819, Austin, Texas 78712.

LIBRARY OF CONGRESS CATALOGING IN PUBLICATION DATA
McIlvain, Myra Hargrave.
    Texas auto trails.
    Bibliography: p.
    Includes index.
    1. Automobiles—Road guides—Texas. 2. Texas—Description
and travel—1981– —Guide-books. I. Title.
GV1024.M42   917.64   82-6908
ISBN 0-292-78050-8 (pbk.)   AACR2

Contents

Preface

History is an account of people in action. This guidebook intends to make those events come alive for the modern traveler by exploring the cradle of Texas history, welding together past lore with present accomplishments. Each community offers a unique quality for tourists—unusual buildings, special restaurants, impressive industries, tours and folk festivals, fine shops, restored hotels, varied agriculture, or natural beauty.

The format of this book calls for reading the stories ahead of time or while traveling to each locale (a navigator is necessary for the latter). Highway directions are included in the narrative. Admission rates change so often that they are not included in the book; however, it will be noted if admission is free or if a charge is made. Operating hours for sites are included, but be aware that these are also subject to change. Occasionally a very interesting book will be mentioned in the text; however, this guide is intended for a popular audience and scholarly references to sources have not been included. A listing of some of the sources is given for travelers who want to pursue in-depth reading.

These short, gasoline-saving holidays offer an opportunity to see "the treasures" that lie just off the interstates. The trails are not written to conform to a specific time schedule. Some folks will hurry and meet their predetermined time for getting back home. Others will savor their trips, tarrying at many sites, and come away enriched by each experience.

Texas Auto Trails

The Southeast

1. Ports Trail

The coastal route skims a collage of industry next door to scenic beauty, rich heritage blended with the latest in space technology. At the center of this maze of history and present-day phenomena nestles the incredible story of men and women who have dared to strike out on new adventures and have molded the unique character of the communities they have touched.

Leave Houston via U.S. Interstate 10 headed east. Immediately after crossing the San Jacinto River, exit on Farm Road 2100, Crosby Lynchburg Road. Continue south to the Lynchburg Ferry for the trip across the Houston Ship Channel.

San Jacinto Battleground

With the laying out of the town of Lynchburg in 1822, this ferry served as a major crossing of the San Jacinto River on the road to Anahuac. In 1836, during the Texas war for independence from Mexico, the crossing served as a strategic point. On the south side, the two armies met: Antonio López de Santa Anna, the Mexican general who considered himself the "Napoleon of the West," led approximately 1,200 (authorities disagree on the number) while Sam Houston, commander of the Texan army, tried to hold together about 700 men (again authorities disagree), who were considering mutiny at every turn. Sam Houston had done the unthinkable among this group of rugged frontiersmen. He had run in the face of danger, or so it seemed. On March 11, when he got word in Gonzales of the fall of the Alamo, Sam Houston helped to begin what became known as the "Runaway Scrape." He retreated east across Texas, avoiding battle encounters and rounding up new recruits. Terrified settlers stumbled behind the army, dragging what few possessions they could carry along the mud-filled trails. Houston sent word to James Fannin at Goliad to join him. Fannin had 400 men, the largest force in Texas, but he delayed his departure from Goliad for six days. The Mexican army, under General José Urrea, soon overtook Fannin's men. They fought until dark, and the following morning Fannin's men raised the white flag in the face of the superior forces. Thinking they were being taken prisoners of war, the 234 nonwounded marched back to Goliad, while about 50 wounded were returned the following day. Santa Anna sent orders to execute the "perfidious foreigners." On March 27, the nonwounded were marched in three groups in opposite directions from the Presidio La Bahía and executed. Fannin and about 40 wounded Texans were executed inside the fort. Sam Houston's motley crew of fighting men now had two slogans that helped to fuel their anger, "Remember the Alamo" and "Remember Goliad." Still, their leader seemed to betray them by not facing the enemy.

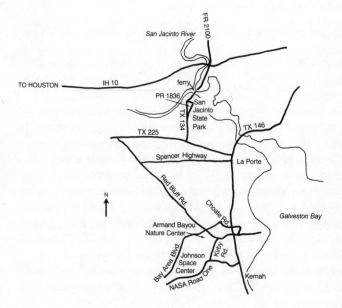

Just down the road from the ferry landing is the San Jacinto Inn Restaurant, an old-time landmark, famous for all-you-can-eat servings of seafood. The restaurant is open Tuesday through Saturday, 6:00 P.M. to 10:00 P.M.; Sunday, 1:00 P.M. to 8:00 P.M.; closed Monday; call 713/479-2828.

The battleship U.S.S. *Texas*, veteran of World Wars I and II, is permanently moored in this state park. The vessel served as the flagship in the 1944 D-Day invasion of Normandy. The ship is open daily: May 1 through August 31, 10:00 A.M. to 6:00 P.M.; September 1 through April 30, 10:00 A.M. to 5:00 P.M. Admission charge.

Immediately beyond the battleship *Texas* lies the campground the Texan forces used preceding the Battle of San Jacinto, the eighteen-minute skirmish that gave Texas independence from Mexico. And, barely a rifle shot away, just beyond the monument, nestled among moss-draped trees, is the site of the Mexican encampment (markers show the layout of the camp).

When the Texans arrived here on April 20, 1836, the area lay in knee-high prairie grass. The Texans' presence cut off retreat across the ferry. Santa Anna's overconfidence had placed the Mexican army in a bad position militarily: their backs to a wide marshy area with the San Jacinto River on their right. Their leader had driven imperiously across Texas, confident of smashing Texas' shaky ad interim government, which had hastily retreated to Galveston Island.

Santa Anna believed himself to be a lady's man. When his army passed through New Washington, present Morgan's Point, he took a beautiful young mulatto indentured servant named Emily Morgan as his captive. Having women in an army camp to cook, forage for food, and tend to the personal needs of the men held a respected place in the Mexican army. Apparently, Emily Morgan became Santa Anna's camp woman. Santa Anna did not travel lightly. He moved his entourage with a three-room octagonal marquee (tent) decorated in gaudy colors. His accessories included silk sheets, crystal stemware, silver serving dishes, and a mounted sterling silver chamber pot.

Sam Houston, after living for years with the Cherokees, knew patience and waited for the right moment. About 3:30 P.M. on April 21, 1836, Houston led the charge, riding his white stallion. Knowing that the Mexicans were in their tents entertaining their camp women, Houston shouted for his men to kneel and shoot low. Some historians credit Santa Anna's delay at ordering retaliatory measures to his dalliance with Emily Morgan.

The slaughter came swift and sure. In their fury the Texans resorted to knives, rifle butts, and clubs. Houston is reported to have tried to stop the carnage. However, he received a painful ankle wound from a musket ball when his horse was shot from under him. He passed command to Thomas Rusk, who encouraged the slaughter by saying, "If we stop, we are cut to pieces."

Juan Linn, a Victoria merchant (see Chap. 5) who arrived with the first shipment of supplies after the battle, said that the pockets of the dead had all been turned in search of plunder. He even saw a dentist pulling the dead men's teeth to get the gold in them. It is estimated that 630 Mexicans were killed, 208 wounded, and 730 taken prisoner. The Texans suffered 2 killed in battle, 7 who died later, and 30 wounded.

Santa Anna disappeared after the battle. The following day a scouting party found him cowering in a marshy area. He was masquerading in slave's clothing but kept his diamond-studded shirt underneath. His captors did not recognize him, knew only that he looked important. As they rode into camp, Mexican prisoners began shouting, "El Presidente." It is said that Emily Morgan went back to New Washington, told her master, James Morgan, of the events, and later returned to her family in New York. It is James Morgan who continued to tell her story. Many believe that the song "Yellow Rose of Texas" was written as a tribute to the yellow-skinned Emily Morgan.

The San Jacinto Monument and Museum of History, a memorial to the men who fought here, was constructed in 1936–1939. The museum is divided into two main halls, the Anglo-American and the Spanish-Mexican. The exhibits are arranged in chronological periods that begin with the Indian occupation and proceed through early statehood (1846–1865). Displays range from a sword found in present-day Kansas and believed to have been carried on Coronado's expedition in 1541 to a lock of Andrew Jackson's hair, which an admiring lady asked Sam Houston to secure for her. Sam Houston's beautifully beaded Indian breechcloth, moccasins, and pouch are displayed next to his gold writing pen and spectacles of later years. Life in early Texas is well documented here.

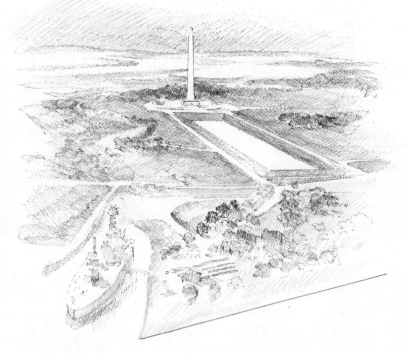

The museum rooms are open Tuesday through Sunday, 9:30 A.M. to 5:30 P.M.; closed Monday. No admission charge.

The elevator to the top of the monument is open daily, 9:30 A.M. to 5:30 P.M.; the last ride leaves at 5:15 P.M. When the museum is closed on Monday, the elevator is still in operation. Admission charge; tickets sold until 5:00 P.M. Both the museum and the monument are closed on Christmas Eve and Christmas Day.

The next leg of the trail roams through miles of petrochemical plants, thick forests, vast shipping facilities, and quiet harbors filled with sailboats.

Drive south from the monument on Park Road 1836 to Texas 134 and turn left. After 2.2 miles, turn left on Texas 225 toward La Porte. Take the right fork on Texas 146. At the second exit, Spencer Highway, the traveler has two options. First, country-western fans may want to take a look at Gilley's of Urban Cowboy *movie fame. Turn right and drive for 15.1 miles.*

The recording studio sits on the left, near the road. Drive into the sprawling gravel parking lot. The dance hall is the wooden building with the tin roof. The sign across the entrance makes the perfect spot for a snapshot. The business is open daily for tourists who wish to look around and buy souvenirs; the entertainment starts in the evening. The interior consists of acres of tables, "Texas-length" bars, a dance floor, and mechanical bulls at strategic locations. Open daily 10:00 A.M. to 2:00 A.M. No admission charge. Children may accompany parents.

To exercise the second option, return on Spencer Highway toward La Porte. At the intersection with Texas 146, continue east on Main Street through the city.

La Porte

La Porte is French for "the door," and the community is still "the door" to a variety of images from industries to resorts. Five Points, the intersection at the heart of town where old Texas 146 converges with Main and San Jacinto streets, is the hub of the original town laid out by developers in the early 1890s. The gentlemen planned to build a port facility at the end of this street, and, after many years, their dream came true.

Proceed on Main Street and turn right on Barbours Cut Boulevard.

The containerized docking facility here is part of the Port of Houston. The finger of land from here to the ship channel has been known as Morgan's Point since James Morgan, who held Emily Morgan of San Jacinto fame as an indentured servant, bought the site in December 1834. Even before Morgan, men dreamed of this area being a shipping haven. Morgan laid out the town of New Washington here and opened a store and warehouse. When Morgan came to Texas, he bound all sixteen of his slaves as indentured servants for ninety-nine years, the method that slaveholders used to get around the Mexican prohibition on slavery. When Santa Anna reached this point on his way to San Jacinto, he had the town burned and it never recovered.

To reach the Houston Ship Channel at the end of Morgan's Point, drive south from the port on Vinsonia Avenue and turn left on Bay Ridge Road, which ends at the ship channel.

In the early days this point extended out to the island that is visible in the channel. In 1874, the Galveston Wharf Company made a costly decision and began charging wharfage rates for Commodore Charles Morgan's vast ocean-going fleet. A man not easily pushed around, Commodore Morgan began dredging across Morgan's Point and took his business up Buffalo Bayou to the village called Houston.

Return along Bay Ridge Road. From the intersection with Vinsonia, it is less than a mile to the Sterling Mansion.

Built in 1928 by former Governor Ross Sterling, this structure holds the reputation for being the largest single-family dwelling on the waterfront between Brownsville and Miami Beach. The story is told that the front of the building, which faces Galveston Bay, looks like the White House because Sterling held a $10 bill before the contractor and told him he wanted a house that "looks like that."

Sterling, born across the bay near Anahuac, became

an oil operator and eventually founded the Humble Oil
and Refining Company. During his tenure as chairman of
the Texas Highway Commission in the early 1930s, large
sums of money that had been paid out as kickbacks on
highway contracts during the previous administration under "Ma" (Miriam A.) Ferguson were returned to the state.
Sterling served as governor from 1931 to 1933 but was
defeated in his bid for a second term by none other than
"Ma" Ferguson.

Boys' Harbor, the facility across the road, once occupied the Sterling Mansion, a gift from Governor Sterling to the Houston Optimist Club. However, the club sold
the mansion to private investors because the structure
became too expensive to maintain. Boys' Harbor provides
a residence for underprivileged boys, who live here and
attend La Porte schools.

*When the road forks 0.6 mile from the Sterling Mansion,
take the left fork, Park Drive. In seven blocks turn left on Oak
Grove Avenue. At the bay, turn right and follow Bay Shore
Drive, which becomes Grand View Avenue.*

Beyond Happy Harbor, a Methodist retirement home,
the large church on the right is St. Mary's Catholic
Church. The towering white column on the bay side of
the road is not a rocket, as some have argued, but the
power plant smokestack left from St. Mary's Seminary,
built on this site about 1900. The building was razed in
the early 1950s after severe storm damage. This area is
part of Sylvan Beach, a Harris County park.

Follow the road around the park.

The old depot on the right served Sylvan Beach from
1914 to 1928 when this was a famous night spot for Houstonians who came here in the 1920s and 1930s to dance to
the big bands. Many came on the train, disembarking at
this depot. The old structure, built in La Porte in 1896,
was moved here and served the community until 1928,
when a paved road to Houston was opened. Plans have
been made to restore the building and to open a museum
and art gallery here in 1982.

A possible side trip includes a 1,600-acre wilderness next to Johnson Space Center, a mansion converted into a haven for lunar and planetary scientists, thousands of sailboats, and a sailmaker who welcomes visitors.

Exit from the park on East Fairmont Parkway. Turn left at the second traffic light on Texas 146. Turn right on Choate Road and follow the road as it winds to Bay Area Boulevard. Turn left and drive to the Red Bluff Road intersection. Continue on Bay Area Boulevard for 0.4 mile to the left-turn sign at the entrance to Armand Bayou Nature Center—an amazing wilderness in the midst of this space-age community.

Armand Bayou Nature Center

The quarter-mile trail from the parking lot to the Interpretive Building narrows, occasionally traverses raised boardwalks, and is so quiet that visitors can hear falling leaves. This 2,000-acre haven for wildlife owes its existence to a handful of people. Jimmy Martyn, whose parents bought 84 acres in 1879, lived here until his death in 1964 and refused to sell, even when developers offered him a half-million dollars. His reason: he could not leave his friends, the birds and animals who ate from his hand. After Martyn's death, his heirs sold the land and another man came on the scene. Armand Yramategui, curator at Houston's Burke Baker Planetarium and a nationally recognized conservationist, realized that this area held great ecological value. Armand Yramategui used his considerable influence to get matters moving toward preservation of this site. In early 1970 he had car trouble on the freeway and an unknown person assassinated him. As a tribute to Armand Yramategui, public pressure came to bear, money accumulated, and this refuge and learning center became a reality.

The enthusiasm here is contagious. Skilled naturalists offer programs on Indians of the area, including a reconstructed Indian camp, plant and bird walks, and an owl prowl. Amid all the activity an attitude of "please touch" prevails. The staff wants visitors to experience with their

hands the gifts that are here in this unpolluted area, a site
next door to society's modern miracle—the Johnson Space
Center.

Requirements for enjoying this retreat are mosquito
and chigger repellent, good walking shoes, and a spirit of
adventure. The facility is open Tuesday through Sunday,
9:00 A.M. to 5:00 P.M.; closed Monday. Guided tours are
offered at 10:00 A.M. and 2:00 P.M. on Saturday and Sunday. Or drop in for the owl prowl the first and third Wednesday evening each month. The prowl leaves at 7:00 P.M.
Schedules of events are available from the Interpretive Headquarters, P.O. Box 58828, Houston, TX 77058,

713/474-2551. No admission charge to visit the park or take the guided tours; small fee for the nature classes.

Turn left on Bay Area Boulevard for less than a mile to the Bay Area Park.

Bay Area Park

Picnic and playground facilities are available. An informed guide captains an electric pontoon boat on a one-hour trip along Armand Bayou for a water-side view of the region. Call for reservations, 713/221-6126. No admission charge.

Return to Bay Area Boulevard, turn right, and drive to Red Bluff Road; turn right. It is 1.2 miles to Kirby Road. Turn right, drive to NASA Road One, and turn right again. It is less than a mile to the Lone Star Sailing Center on the left at the edge of Clear Lake Park.

NASA Road One

This sailboat rental business is housed on piers extending into Clear Lake. Dolphins and sunfish, two-person boats, are for rent, April 1 through October 31, open Monday through Friday, 10:00 A.M. to 6:00 P.M.; Saturday and Sunday, 9:00 A.M. to 7:00 P.M.

Cross the bridge that separates Clear Lake and Forest Lake.

The old Jim West Mansion looms on the right. The structure houses the Lunar and Planetary Institute, which is owned by Rice University and serves as a center for research of lunar, planetary, and terrestrial sciences. The scientists who come here to do theoretical work have access to data at Johnson Space Center. The emphasis is on maximum scientific yield from each space program, pursuit of questions raised by the space missions, and research for future missions.

Jim West, owner of a 30,000-acre cattle ranch and game preserve here and father of the flamboyant Silver Dollar Jim West, built this home in 1930. For a time it was

called the most palatial home in Harris County. The sixteen bedrooms have been converted into offices, but the
main hall still has hand-painted mahogany-paneled
beams in the ceiling and hand-carved mantels and windows. The man who lived here was almost a recluse,
while his son, Silver Dollar Jim West, made a name for
himself during the Great Depression by tossing silver dollars to people on the street and handing silver dollars to
whomever he met.

Most of the land that comprises the Armand Bayou
Nature Center originally belonged to West. He sold the
property in 1939 to Humble Oil Company for $8 million in
cash and $30–40 million in royalties. Free tours by ap-
pointment are available if the busy schedule at the institute will permit; call 713/486-2180.

*Continue on NASA Road One for a little over a mile to the
Johnson Space Center visitors' entrance.*

Johnson Space Center

Humble Oil and Refining Company gave this 1,620-acre
site to Rice University on the condition that Rice offer it to
the federal government for a space center. On September
21, 1961, when NASA officials arrived, they found a cow
pasture. Hurricane Carla had torn through the area less
than a week before. Debris filled the ditches along the
country road that cut through here. Construction began
on the multimillion-dollar space program the following April.

A tour of this facility hones an appreciation of what
has been done here and what is planned for the nation's
space future. The cool precision that dominated the TV
screen during earlier space flights and the Shuttle program pervades the place.

Guests are encouraged to visit the Rocket Park near
the entrance and to take the self-guided tour, which begins at the visitors' center and includes a film and a look
at space hardware, Gordon Cooper's Mercury capsule, and
the Apollo 17 spacecraft. The tour continues to the Mis-

sion Simulation and Training Building, where visitors see the equipment the astronauts use to train for Shuttle missions. The last portion of the tour includes the facility where lunar material is being studied.

A guided tour is available with advance reservations. This plan includes a trip to the Mission Control Center and the Space Environment Simulation Laboratory, the largest vacuum chamber in the world. For reservations, write Public Services Branch, AP4, NASA Johnson Space Center, Houston, TX 77058, or call 713/483-4321. These tours are offered Monday through Friday only. Johnson Space Center is open daily, except Christmas, 9:00 A.M. to 4:00 P.M. No admission charge.

When leaving the space center, turn left on NASA Road One. It is almost four miles to Sails, Inc.

This sailmaker does not run an assembly-line operation. Employees crawl around the huge workroom floor, cutting and hand-stitching sails and other custom canvas

products. The business is open Monday through Friday,
8:30 A.M. to 5:00 P.M.; closed Saturday and Sunday. If the
group will include more than five visitors, it is necessary
to call ahead, 713/334-5566. No admission charge.

In about one mile turn right on Texas 146.

A few blocks ahead, a drawbridge crosses Clear Creek.
This waterway lies between Clear Lake and Galveston Bay
and is busy, especially on weekends, with every size sailing, motor, and shrimp boat.

Kemah

Kemah and Galveston County begin on the south side of
Clear Creek. Truck gardens, a few cows, oysters, and crabs
made up the primary income for this area until gambling
came in with Galveston's "open era" (1922–1957). During
this period Houstonians and visitors from all over the
state swarmed in here.

*Continue south on Texas 146. Turn left on Loop 197, which
circles east through Texas City, passing the Industrial Complex on the south side of town.*

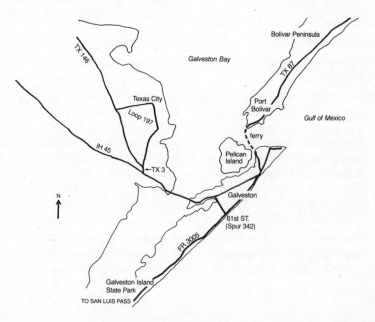

Texas City

On the beautiful spring morning of April 16, 1947, a fire broke out on the S.S. *Grandcamp*, a French ship with a cargo of ammonium nitrate fertilizer meant for Europe. The fire seemed routine and a crowd gathered to watch. Many of the curious were children who were on a split school shift due to overcrowding. A little after 9:00 A.M., the *Grandcamp* exploded. Then a nearby vessel exploded, and fires broke out at the industries along the shore. Over five hundred died and over four thousand received wounds. Loss of property reached about $67 million. The concussion from the explosion was felt as far as sixty miles away in Port Arthur, and a mist of oil fell in Galveston eight miles across the bay.

The nation watched in horror and then in great admiration. Texas City became known as the "city that would not die." Immediately, the rebuilding began. On the corner of Twenty-ninth Street and Loop 197 the Memorial Cemetery contains graves of sixty-three unidentified victims. Many residents still show physical, if not emotional, scars of that day.

The Texas City dike, a natural shell reef, has been extended five miles into Galveston Bay as a protection against storms. Fishing, boat launching, even motel accommodations are available on the barrier.

Turn left on Texas 3 for 0.5 mile and then left again on U.S. Interstate 45.

Galveston

Galveston Island is twenty-seven miles long and three miles wide. By all practical standards, this once-marshy strip of sand should still be a sun-bleached site where fishermen come to drink beer and swap tales of adventure. Instead, due to the phenomenal effort of residents and outsiders who loved the island, Galveston has prospered after tragedies that would have destroyed other settlements. People have made Galveston special and the residents today are again making the city a unique spot on the Gulf coast.

Until recent years, the beaches, fine restaurants, and entertainment houses brought tourists to the island. Now travelers are also finding depth and beauty in the architecture and history of the city.

The city limits begin on the causeway, but the town really starts with the oleanders that line the boulevard. The beauty of these shrubs, which are not native to this area, is symbolic of the color that lies ahead. Oleanders first appeared on the island in 1841. They came from Jamaica and grew in a private yard. After the grade raising, which will be discussed later, all the vegetation on the island died. Mrs. Fred M. (Margaret Sealy) Burton led the project to plant oleanders along Broadway.

In 1911, as Galveston emerged from the horror of the 1900 storm and the years of rebuilding, the Galveston-Houston Electric Railway, or Interurban, began operation. The electric overhead wires and track ran down the middle of the esplanade on Broadway. This rapid service encouraged Houstonians to come to Galveston's beaches after work, returning home late the same evening.

The cemetery on the right at Forty-third and Broadway is similar to others in town. Although the grade raising after the 1900 storm placed the city several feet above sea level, most families choose burials in mausoleums or above ground. The huge amount of water that accompanies storms can cause bodies to pop out of ordinary graves.

Turn left on Twenty-fifth Street (known also as Rosenberg Avenue—some Galveston streets are known by three different names) and drive eight blocks to The Strand. Turn right and drive along the former "Wall Street of the Southwest." Park near the corner of Twentieth Street to begin a walking tour of this unusual area.

The actual Strand consists of five blocks of restored nineteenth-century commercial buildings. Some were designed by fine architects; others have good designs that were mail-ordered from catalogs, a common practice in

that era for home designs as well. Many of the buildings
are decorated with stylish iron façades. These structures,
which housed the wealthy businessmen who made Galveston hum as the "New York of the Gulf," are being opened
as superb restaurants, antique shops, artists' studios and
galleries, medical offices, and private apartments.

The Hendley Building (northwest corner of Twentieth
and The Strand) is actually four structures, three of which
are the oldest surviving commercial buildings (1855–
1859) in Galveston. During the Civil War, Confederate
troops used a cupola on top of the Hendley Building as a
watchtower. From this vantage they could observe Union
gunboats blockading the harbor. In early October 1862,
this vital port fell to Union forces. During the brief occupation, the Union forces controlled Hendley's Wharf,
which ran out over the bay behind the building.

On New Year's Day, Confederates, using cotton bales
as bulwarks on two small vessels, sailed into the harbor
from the bay. They rammed one Union ship and boarded
it. In a few hours, the Union forces surrendered. Confederates had won the Battle of Galveston, and for the duration
of the war the bay stayed under Confederate control. For
years, the Hendley Building showed scars from the heavy
artillery bombardment.

Demolition of the west section of the structure was
begun in 1969. The Galveston Historical Foundation, concerned about preserving the city's heritage, moved into
action and eventually acquired the building for its new
headquarters. The Visitors Center occupies the lower floor.
This is where information is available about all of Galveston's historic sites. This is also the point of departure
for forty-five–minute walking tours that the foundation
conducts. Well-informed docents share lively details
about the buildings and their original occupants. The
tours, which take about an hour, begin on Saturday at
noon; Sunday, 2:00 P.M. No admission charge.

The huge granite stones in the floor of the Visitors
Center came to Galveston on sailing ships from Boston.
The stairs leading up to the foundation offices are worn
from years of use.

Parades, patent medicine men, strolling show people with trained monkeys and bears, a man who ate glass, and gamblers frequented The Strand during the last half of the 1800s. To reenact that early-day frivolity, the Galveston Historical Foundation sponsors an annual Dickens's Evening on The Strand, the first Saturday in December. There are street vendors, musicians, carolers, and free entertainment. The shops are open and feature Victorian merchandise. The event connects London's Strand of Dickens' time with the Galveston era. The gaslights glow and costumed characters from Dickens' *A Christmas Carol* are everywhere, even Scrooge and Tiny Tim. Special selections from *A Christmas Carol* are presented by local actors.

In the second block to the west, the Old Strand Emporium (2114 Strand) occupies one of the oldest iron-fronted buildings in Galveston. The iron façade was prefabricated in Baltimore and shipped to Galveston in 1866. Diners listen to the antique nickelodeon while enjoying sandwiches and imported wines and cheeses. Open daily, 10:00 A.M. to 6:00 P.M.

In the nineteenth century, ladies came to The Strand only when it was necessary to meet or board ships or trains. The businessmen, however, exchanged thousands of dollars daily as wholesalers received merchandise for most of the Southwest and slave traders auctioned their human chattel. Five of the state's largest banks did business here; commission merchants (brokers) and cotton factors (agents) had offices on the street.

The earlier buildings were made of wood and erected on pilings that stuck out over the bay. Cargo from ships could be received directly into the buildings, which backed up to the harbor. Employees often fished from the second-floor windows. In later years, sand was filled in behind the buildings and Avenue A was completed.

In the midst of the important transactions lay Strand Street, a quagmire of mud. Many of the buildings sat on·a continuous pool of stagnant water, and yellow fever plagued the city, especially the occupants of these buildings. No one realized that the horrible disease, which

caused victims to vomit black bile and bleed from their gums, was carried by mosquitoes. When word spread of the first case of yellow fever, residents began leaving the city. Ships lay quarantined in the harbor for weeks with great loss of revenue. People isolated themselves and tried to avoid the dead and dying, while mosquitoes flew in and out of the unscreened windows. Then, the north wind blew and the pestilence disappeared as suddenly as it had come.

The worst yellow fever epidemic, which spread inland several hundred miles, occurred in 1867, affected 8,000 people, and took 1,150 lives in Galveston. With the filling in of low spots and ridding the area of the filthy marshy land, yellow fever abated. The turn of the century came before Dr. Walter Reed discovered that mosquitoes carried yellow fever and the disease became a terror of the past.

Turn right at the next corner, Twenty-second Street, and walk down to Pier 22.

The *Elissa*, an authentic sailing ship built in 1877 at Aberdeen, Scotland, is anchored here. The *Elissa* visited

Galveston in 1883 and 1886. The Galveston Historical Foundation purchased the vessel and, after extensive structural renovation and restoration in Greece, brought it to Galveston for the finishing and rigging work. Plans call for opening the *Elissa* to the public in the summer or fall of 1982.

Return to The Strand.

The old Colonel W. L. Moody Building on the Northwest corner houses the Strand Surplus Senter. Designed by architect Nicholas Clayton, the structure was erected in 1884 with cast iron columns on the first floor. The American National Insurance Company, which became the largest life insurance company west of the Mississippi, was organized in 1905 in a small upstairs room by the colonel's son, W. L. Moody, Jr. The business occupying the building today deals in authentic government surplus. Shoppers looking for surplus from armies all over the world will enjoy the neatly stacked and sized merchandise in this store. Closed Sunday.

Nicholas Clayton designed eight buildings that are still standing in this five-block row, but his designs are all over the city; although eighty-six have been razed, thirty-four remain. Clayton came to Galveston in 1872 to build the First Presbyterian Church and the third Tremont Hotel. One would expect that a genius of design, who built such a large number of elegant structures, would become quite rich. In fact, Clayton, according to his descendants, knew little about business. He charged very low fees, often did not collect his full price, continued to work even when money had run out, and loved church design so much that he often worked without compensation.

Sometime around the early 1890s, Nicholas Clayton put up his personal bond of $80,000 cash for the construction of a new county courthouse. While he was out of town, according to family members, someone changed his specifications without his knowledge and the commissioner's court canceled his contract. Forced into bankruptcy, Clayton could no longer secure a bond, which came as a terrible blow to his integrity. Many who owed him money refused to pay, and he could no longer get work. His beautiful Beach Hotel, whose fine carpentry has never been duplicated, burned in 1898. The 1900 storm destroyed many of his greatest architectural achievements. Even Sacred Heart Church, noted as the most beautiful church building in the Southwest, received such severe damage that it had to be torn down.

Clayton never fully recovered. While he was repairing his chimney, a candle he held set fire to his undershirt. Due to the severe burns, Clayton developed pneumonia and died on December 9, 1916, at the age of seventy-five. His widow worried about a proper monument to him until Rabbi Henry Cohen reminded her that cornerstones on buildings all over town served as monuments to Nicholas Clayton.

In the next block to the west, the Greenleve, Block and Company Building (2310–14 Strand) and the Hutchings, Sealy and Company Building (2326–28) are Clayton's.

The large white building at the end of The Strand is the Shearn Moody Plaza, originally the division home office of the Santa Fe Railroad. The Moody Foundation acquired this structure in 1975 and through adaptive reuse has helped in the economic revitalization of The Strand. On the ground floor, the Galveston Center for Transportation and Commerce operates a railroad museum, which features the depot's original benches and cages and a multimedia history of the railroad. Behind the building is a display of railroad memorabilia, including engines and cars standing under the old railroad canopy. Other floors provide office space for various agencies.

The Moody Foundation, established in 1942 by W. L. Moody, Jr., and his wife, Libbie Rice Shearn Moody, has grown steadily over the years. With the addition of the assets of Mr. Moody's estate in 1959, the annual income had increased by 1980 to $10–11 million. According to restrictions governing this foundation, all the income must be given away each year in the state of Texas. Over $40 million had been given to benefit Galveston by 1980 and $160 million had gone to education, welfare, the humanities, religion, and physical, life, and social sciences elsewhere in Texas.

Return east along The Strand on the south side.

A portion of the sidewalk in the second block is the original brick and stone. La King's Confectionery and Ice Cream Parlour is housed in another Clayton design. Originally, in 1870, this building had a cast iron front on the lower floor. Today it's fun to watch candy being made here and to sample the delicious ice cream. Open Tuesday through Saturday, 10:00 A.M. to 6:00 P.M.; Sunday, 1:30 P.M. to 6:00 P.M.; closed Monday.

The T. Jeff League Building (Twenty-third Street and The Strand) houses The Book Bag, a children's bookstore with a corner for adults, where the Sunday *New York Times* can be bought on Sunday. The Wentletrap Restaurant also occupies this restored structure, serving elegant meals in an opulent Victorian setting. This is not just a tourist haven. Locals come here to dine quietly and businessmen seem to favor the spot for unhurried luncheons. Open daily for lunch and dinner.

Return to Twentieth Street and turn left to Pier 19, the home of the Mosquito Fleet.

The hundreds of refrigerated trucks parked here are loading coconuts, pineapples, and bananas from South America and Hawaii for shipment all over the United States.

About two hundred shrimp boats make up the Mosquito Fleet and they are berthed here, at Pier 7, and in Offatt's Bayou. The name came from the way the boats look as they head out for their day's catch: they swarm across the water with nets bowing out like mosquito legs.

Hill's Pier 19 Restaurant sits on the dock. Choose from the wide range of delicious seafood and then carry it up to the third deck. From this level it is easy to watch the Mosquito Fleet, which docks outside Hill's windows, and the ships from all over the world coming in and out of Galveston's port. Open daily, 11:00 A.M. to 8:00 P.M. or 8:30 P.M.

East of Hill's Restaurant is Galveston Party Boats where excursions are arranged for daily bay or deep-sea fishing. The *Jean Lafitte* also offers a tour around the island. The two-hour, narrated trip is made comfortable by a lounge, upper sun deck, and snack bar. The boat operates Sunday through Friday, 10:00 A.M. and 7:00 P.M.; Saturday, 7:00 P.M. only. For reservations, call Houston, 713/222-7025, or Galveston, 713/763-5423. Tour charge.

Galveston's natural harbor attracted early attention. Jean Laffite, a privateer who will be discussed later, recognized Galveston's assets and chose to set up his headquarters on the eastern end of the island. In 1825 the Mexican government designated this location as a provisional port and point of customs entry. From this headquarters, the Texas Navy effectively aided the Texans in the revolution. By 1836, when Texas emerged as a republic, about one ship a month docked here, beginning a commercial business that is the oldest in the state. In December 1836, Michel Menard bought a portion of Galveston Island from the Republic of Texas and began laying out a townsite.

The next year, Commodore Charles Morgan, the eastern shipping tycoon, established a service between Galveston and New Orleans. By 1854 the dock enterprises had grown so rapidly that they joined together to form the Galveston Wharf and Cotton Press Company. Even after the Civil War blockade and the economic struggle during Reconstruction, Galveston maintained its position as the number-one port in the state.

Galveston did not grow without problems, however. The Galveston Wharf Company became a giant monopoly. Others followed: largest distiller, biggest wholesale hardware dealer, one of the largest plate and iron importers, largest dealer in pianos, ship suppliers, wholesale dry goods and clothing merchants. The monopolies spread from the docks to the newspaper and cotton compress. Monopolies produce business elite who often look to the good of the city with a vision narrowed to what is good for their own enterprises. Despite the problems, Galveston was known as "a city of philanthropists and millionaires."

But then competition to the port developed. Galveston recovered rapidly from the 1900 storm, but the discovery of oil at Spindletop (Chap. 2) in 1901 introduced a new form of shipping: pipelines to handle oil export. Texas City became a deep-water port in 1904, the Houston Ship Channel was deepened, and the Port of Houston became a giant almost overnight. Orange also opened a deep-water facility.

In 1940 the citizens voted to take control of the Galveston Wharf Company out of the hands of private interests and place it with the city of Galveston. Some folks say that Galveston missed out, that it should have been the metropolis and Houston should have played second-fiddle. As the remainder of this tour will show, Galveston has retained a freshness that is perhaps tied to a slower pace—an impossibility for a sprawling giant. Rapid growth often brings destruction of the "old-fashioned" structures or modernization to keep up with the changing times. Galveston's pride now is the preserved and restored beauty from the early days.

The next portion of the tour continues to revolve

around people: Jean Laffite, the man who built a commune of privateers, who shared in the booty taken from ships in Gulf waters; Ashbel Smith, the medical doctor who fought for higher quality in education and for a medical center here; the Sealy family, who endowed a hospital that has grown to be the only multicategorical health referral center in Texas and one of the most important in the Southwest.

Return to the car. Drive one block north on Twentieth Street to Avenue A and turn right for six blocks.

The site of Laffite's fort is on the right (1417 Avenue A). The lot is grown up in weeds and sits behind a high fence. The foundation ruins are from a home built on top of the remains of Laffite's headquarters. When Laffite left in 1821, he burned the fort and all the structures on the island.

Laffite and his activities mystified people in the early 1800s and continue to prick imaginations. He and his brother Pierre, the less flamboyant and more practical of the two, operated a smuggling business off the Louisiana coast, south of New Orleans in 1808 and got into trouble with United States officials. During the Battle of New Orleans in 1815, they redeemed themselves by coming to the aid of General Andrew Jackson. Within two years, however, their piracy caused so many problems that they were asked to leave the area.

Many Central and South American countries were writhing in anger against Spain, their mother country. These countries issued letters of marque (permission to arm a ship and seize enemy vessels and their cargoes), and the Laffites were happy to work for any or all of the countries. On the other hand, when Laffite settled on Galveston Island in 1817, he swore allegiance to Mexico, which was still under Spanish rule. He also made a secret agreement to spy against filibusterers who were constantly working to secure Mexico's freedom from Spain. In several cases, these adventurers came to Laffite seeking his help in their enterprises. Always, he seemed to stay neutral in a sort of courtly and noble fashion. He enter-

tained them here in his lavishly furnished Maison Rouge.
His table boasted the finest linens and silver plate, booty
from his privateering.

Stories abound about what happened to all the treasure Laffite and his men accumulated. They operated
under a communal agreement, which provided that the
men share on a percentage basis in each seizure. Because
of the sharing and Laffite's fair treatment, a broad assort-
ment of characters came to Galveston, which Laffite
called Campeachy. By the end of 1817 the population
reached one thousand. Besides privateering in merchandise, slave trade provided an enormous income. Importing slaves had been outlawed in the United States by 1808,
and by 1818 Jim Bowie, of later Alamo fame, and his
brothers were big slave traders. They bought slaves on
Galveston Island for $1 a pound and took them to New
Orleans. Bowie is said to have earned $65,000 in this man-
ner between 1818 and 1820.

Although Laffite agreed not to harm United States
shipping, some of his men reportedly attacked a U.S. ship.
In 1821, the United States government sent the *Enterprise*
to demand that Laffite leave the island. This is where the
real mystery begins. What did Laffite do with all that
treasure? And, did he die soon afterward as people were
led to believe? It was discovered in 1958 that a man
claiming to be Jean Laffite's great-grandson had preserved
a journal, which disclosed that Laffite lived under the
name "John Lafflin" in various United States cities until
his death in 1854. Further, the journal, which is now in the
Sam Houston Regional Library and Research Center in
Liberty, reveals that Laffite went on to support the cause
and writings of Karl Marx and Friedrich Engels. He says
in the journal that he met the men in Paris in 1847 and
established a bank account to help them in their effort to
form a "pure and simple utopia" for the working man.

Some say Laffite had plenty of time to divide the treasure among his men. Others say he buried it but that his
six cohorts, who decided not to leave the area, had time to
locate all the burial sites. Finally, many like Carroll Lewis,
in *Treasures of Galveston Island*, claim that vast fortunes

still lie hidden on the island and along the bayous and inlets surrounding Galveston Bay.

As challenging as the idea of treasure hunting may be, state law prohibits digging on public land without a permit from the Texas Antiquities Committee. The permits are issued under very careful supervision to protect items that might hold special historic significance from being damaged by inexperienced excavation. Metal detectors on Texas public lands are permitted for searching the surface for items like modern coins, but they may not be used for the purpose of digging for treasure. Antiquities permits are also required for excavation on federal lands.

Return to The Strand and continue east to the fork. Drive straight into the University of Texas Medical Complex.

Old Red, the Ashbel Smith Building, is the enormous red brick structure with the red sandstone columns and red roof. This Romanesque revival structure, a Nicholas Clayton design, opened in 1891 as the only building for the

University of Texas Medical Department (later Medical
Branch). The first year, twenty-three students attended
classes here. In 1949 the building was named in honor of
the pioneer surgeon whose determination to upgrade
Texas education finally gave the push to establish the University of Texas. While serving as the first president of the
Board of Regents, Ashbel Smith became known as "the
Regent who bellowed fire" because of his demand for high
standards. He initiated an examination system for pro-
fessorship candidates and influenced passage of laws reg-
ulating medical practices.

The teaching hospital for the medical branch was
completed in 1889 due to the generous gift of John Sealy,
who stipulated that the facility must serve all Texans re-
gardless of their ability to pay.

John Sealy came to Galveston in 1846 and began work
as a clerk in a dry goods store. After saving his money, he
opened his own dry goods company, then moved into the
commission and banking business. He served as president
of the Galveston Wharf Company, organized the Galveston
Gas Company, and bought into railroad interests. John
Sealy II and his daughter, Jennie Sealy Smith, established
the Sealy & Smith Foundation, which had contributed
$85 million to the hospital by 1980.

*Return west about eight blocks to Nineteenth Street and turn
left to Mechanic Street. Park and take a ride to the top of the
American National Insurance Company Tower.*

This twenty-story building is a symbol of financial
achievement by the Moody family. As mentioned earlier,
the American National Insurance Company began in
a small upstairs room of the old Moody Building on
The Strand. This magnificent structure, opened in 1972,
houses only the home office of the insurance company.
Original investors paid $120 for one share of American
National Insurance stock in 1905. In 1970, each share
reached a value of about $350,000. Dividends, which the
company began paying in 1911, were $66,445 per share
by 1972.

Colonel William Lewis Moody came to Texas from

Virginia in 1852 and moved his family to Galveston after
the Civil War. His son, W. L. Moody, Jr., grew up here, and
after studies at the Virginia Military Institute and the University of Texas Law School he returned to Galveston.
Very soon his genius for financial organization became
apparent. He started as a junior partner in his father's
cotton firm. Soon he added a bank, opened a branch of the
cotton business in New York, and organized the Moody
Compress Company, which grew into one of the leading
cotton factors in the United States. After starting this
insurance company, he branched into banking, hotels,
and ranching.

Huge windows give visitors a 360-degree, thirty-mile
view of Galveston Island, the Gulf, the bay, the port, and
the Houston Ship Channel. Between each pair of windows
hangs an enormous photograph of early Galveston. In the
center of the building, glass walls enclose the multi-
colored mechanical equipment for more than eighteen
hundred tons of air conditioning. The building does not
have a heating system, but, if heat is needed, air is circulated through the five hundred lights on each floor.

American National also displays an art collection all
over the building ranging from pre-Columbian and pre-
historic American Indian to avant-garde contemporary
works of American artists. Art tours are available for
groups by appointment; call 713/763-4661, ext. 216. The
tower is open daily, 2:00 P.M. to 4:00 P.M., June through
August; Monday through Friday only, 2:00 P.M. to 4:00
P.M., September through May. No admission charge.

*Drive south on Nineteenth Street for two blocks to Church
Street.*

The First Presbyterian Church, organized in 1840,
houses the oldest congregation in the city. Nicholas
Clayton came to Galveston as supervising architect for
this building, which was completed in 1876. After the 1885
fire, which destroyed forty city blocks, school classes resumed here until new facilities could be built. Following
the 1900 storm, the building served as a morgue, having
suffered only minor damage.

*Turn right on Church Street and drive two blocks to St.
Mary's Cathedral.*

Built in 1848, this is the oldest religious structure in
the city and the oldest cathedral in the state. During the
Civil War, the structure suffered so much damage that the
bishop complained that bullet holes made it impossible to
say Mass except during dry weather. Nicholas Clayton designed the central tower added in 1878. During the 1900
storm, refugees huddled in this strong building. The two-
ton bell fell, and the remainder of the building, except
the statue of Mary, Star of the Sea, received extensive
damage. Many believe that the survival of the statue of
Mary is an omen: if she ever topples, her demise will
signal the end of the island.

Galveston has had many public servants who had no
wealth. In 1896, one year after being ordained a Catholic
priest, Father James Martin Kirwin came to Galveston as
rector of St. Mary's. Immediately, he gained public appreciation for his help during the 1897 yellow fever epidemic.
Very soon it became clear that his priestly office would
not get between him and daily contact with life. Before
the water had receded after the 1900 storm, Father Kirwin
and a group of citizens met on a street corner in several
feet of water to formulate plans for helping the devastated
city. Looters were already at work and Father Kirwin
wrote the order declaring martial law. It is estimated that
six thousand died in the storm that is still considered the
worst natural disaster in United States history. The dead
lay everywhere. Identification and individual burials
proved impossible. At first, bodies were taken out to sea,
only to wash back to shore with the incoming tide. Although many were shocked at Father Kirwin's suggestion
of mass cremations, the measure proved to be a necessity
to avoid contaminating the rest of the city.

The next year Father Kirwin suffered permanent eye
injury during a rescue attempt in a fire that threatened
the entire city. For the remainder of his life, his vision
was obstructed by dancing black spots. After the fire,
he worked to get adequate city water for fire fighting.

He even helped mediate a Southern Pacific dock workers' strike.

When the Ku Klux Klan began gaining power after World War I, Father Kirwin and many others believed that the Klan hid behind patriotism while violating the rights of others. He and his friend Rabbi Henry Cohen spoke out strongly against the Klan and, despite personal danger, were effective in preventing its members from getting a stronghold in Galveston.

On January 24, 1926, at the age of forty-four, Father Kirwin died suddenly. Galveston and the nation were stunned. Tributes came from everywhere. One that is most symbolic of Kirwin's broad scope of concern came from members of the Harris County Prison Aid Society. They held a memorial service for this Catholic priest at the First Presbyterian Church.

A man who loved Father Kirwin, worked at his side, and paid tribute to him was a tiny Jewish immigrant, Rabbi Henry Cohen. Rabbi Cohen came to Galveston in 1888 to serve the B'nai Israel Congregation and remained in that position for the next sixty-four years.

Rabbi Cohen rode his bicycle all over the island, calling on the sick and imprisoned without regard to their religion. He wore starched white shirts and kept appointments and sermon notes written on the cuffs. When asked why his home always stood open to anyone in need, he replied, "I had heard that when you enter the ministry, you serve the public."

Rabbi Cohen headed the Central Relief Committee after the 1900 storm and he stood up to the Ku Klux Klan with Father Kirwin. From 1907 until World War I, Rabbi Cohen met shiploads of European immigrants arriving at the Galveston docks and helped over ten thousand find homes and work throughout the South and the West. He also helped New York City slum residents relocate in the South. During World War I, he played a big role in influencing Congress to provide Jewish naval chaplains.

As a member of the Texas Prison Board, Rabbi Cohen initiated reforms that separated hardened criminals from first offenders and improved prison medical facilities. Because of his concern and ability to deal effectively with people, many young men were paroled to his care.

On one occasion, Rabbi Cohen received word that an immigrant had come into this country illegally and was about to be sent back to Russia where he would certainly meet death. The little rabbi caught a train to Washington, where, after exhausting all other avenues of help, he finally obtained an interview with President William Howard Taft. After the president declined his help and the rabbi turned to leave, President Taft added, "but I do admire you coming all this way for one of your people." Rabbi Cohen promptly informed the president that the gentleman was Greek Catholic. A stunned president immediately placed a call ordering the immigrant released into Rabbi Cohen's custody.

Turn right on Moody Street, drive one block to Postoffice Street, and turn right to "The Grand" (2020 Postoffice Street).

Galveston's 1894 Grand Opera House and hotel complex, which spread for three blocks, is being restored. Once again, this impressive structure is a live performance hall and cultural center under the supervision of the Galveston County Cultural Arts Council. Around the turn of the century, Sarah Bernhardt, Enrico Caruso, James O'Neill, Anna Pavlova, John Philip Sousa's band, and William Jennings Bryan performed on this stage.

Plans for this elegant structure with hand-painted stenciling on the twelve Victorian boxes include an extension building to be added behind the million-dollar Mary Moody Northen Stage, as well as restoration of the beautiful lobby and the fly-loft atrium.

The hotel serves as artists' studio-apartments, meeting rooms, and a fine restaurant and pub.

Continue to the end of the block, turn left on Twentieth Street, and turn left again on Market Street. Drive to the Galveston County Historical Museum (2219 Market).

An overview of the county's history is documented here. This building, originally the City National Bank, erected in 1919 by W. L. Moody, Jr., was given to the county for a museum by Moody's daughter, Mary Moody Northen. At the time of her father's death in 1954, Mrs. Northen, although past retirement age, took over as president of more than fifty corporations. Today, she chairs the board of trustees of the Moody Foundation. Perhaps her name is most recognized for the Mary Moody Northen stages built across the state and financed by the Moody Foundation. The museum is open daily, but the hours are variable. No admission charge.

Continue west to Rosenberg Avenue and turn left to the Post Office Building (600 Rosenberg).

The U.S. Weather Bureau has facilities on the fifth floor, which are open to the public if there is no major weather threat. Started on April 19, 1871, this is one of the oldest weather stations west of the Mississippi. The radar scans an area up to 250 miles. The building is open to the public Monday through Friday, 8:00 A.M. to 5:00 P.M.; closed Saturday and Sunday. For a party larger than five, please make reservations; call 713/765-9506.

In 1900, the Galveston Weather Bureau knew as early as September 4 that a tropical cyclone in the Gulf was moving westward. Heavy wind and rains arrived on the morning of the eighth. At 4:00 P.M. the city lay under one to four feet of water. At 8:00 P.M. the wind reached an estimated 120 miles an hour, and a four-to-six-foot tidal wave swept across the island. Homes splintered into debris, piled up along Avenue K, finally forming a breakwater that helped to save the rest of the city. After midnight, the wind slackened. Many reported that the damage intensified as the water roared back out to the Gulf. Entire families perished. In some cases, one member survived by clinging to a tree or floating debris while watching one and then another of the family slip into the black swirling water. (John Edward Weems gives a graphic account of this disaster in *A Weekend in September.*) The population in 1900 had reached 38,000. The best estimates say that 6,000 lost their lives that weekend with about $40 million in property damage.

As the death toll mounted, residents became convinced that something must be done to prevent the horror from reoccurring. Many Galvestonians had accepted the theory put forth in the early 1870s by an "expert" in winds and tides who said that Galveston lay out of the hurricane range: hurricanes in the Gulf would hit land either east of Galveston on the Louisiana coast or west on the Texas coast. And, for all the years that Galveston had been a city, that theory held true, until 1900. A board of three engineers, headed by retired Brigadier General Henry M. Robert (author of *Robert's Rules of Order*), recommended building a seawall and raising the level of the city.

The latter suggestion required the actual raising of buildings, roads, streetcar lines, and alleys. This engineering feat took place between 1902 and 1910. Over 2,300 buildings, large and small, were raised from five to eight feet; sand pumped in from the Gulf filled in under the structures. In some cases, owners of buildings of more than one level filled in the first floor and the original second story became the ground level. During this period, a canal cut through the center of the island at Tremont Street facilitated the dredging operation. Catwalks criss-crossed the city to allow residents to get about above the stinking muddy silt from the Gulf bottom. Buildings on The Strand, because of their immense size, were not raised but the grade in that area was increased. The state helped to finance the restoration by returning ad valorem and other taxes.

Turn left at the next corner, Winnie Street, drive three blocks to Kempner Street, and turn right.

Trinity Episcopal Church was the third Episcopal mission established in the Republic of Texas. The 1900 storm severely damaged the structure and Nicholas Clayton designed the restoration. To accomplish the raising, workers placed hundreds of jacks under the building. The workmen sang songs to synchronize the operation and, on designated words, they cranked the jacks one-quarter turn. In this manner, the building was painstakingly lifted five feet. Built in 1879, Eaton Memorial Chapel, next door, is another Clayton design.

Turn right on Ball Street, drive to the end of the block, and turn left on Tremont Street.

Rosenberg Library (823 Tremont) is a cultural center for Galveston. It is noted for its fine archives to which researchers come from around the country. The library provides a maritime collection, a rare book room, and several galleries displaying fine art and Texas history collections. The library was built in 1904 from the residue of Henry Rosenberg's estate. The following year, a branch for blacks opened, the first of its kind in the United States.

Henry Rosenberg came to Galveston from Switzerland in 1843. He began as a clerk, soon owned the largest dry goods business in Texas, organized a bank, expanded into railroads, and served the civic and religious community. Rosenberg built the $80,000 Rosenberg Free School and paid more than half the cost of constructing Eaton Memorial Chapel. Although he was not as wealthy as some of Galveston's benefactors, his careful planning has made his gifts continue to serve the community. He left funds to build the Island City Protestant Orphans' Asylum (now Home), Grace Episcopal Church, a women's home, the YMCA, a monument to the memory of the heroes of the Texas Revolution, and drinking fountains for people and animals.

Turn left at the next corner, Sealy Street, and drive four blocks to the beginning of the East End Historical District.

This area has been placed on the National Register of Historic Places because of the collection of ninety-one homes, variety of styles, and periods represented. This is the most intact grouping of nineteenth-century buildings in the state. The entire area is zoned so that owners cannot demolish or change the exterior of these houses without consulting the Historical District Board. The Galveston Historical Foundation Visitors Center offers a free riding or walking tour-guide pamphlet to this area. It gives details of construction and points out special architectural features of many of the houses. The Galveston Historical Foundation conducts an annual homes tour the

mid-weekend of each May. Many of these homes are open at that time.

Some of the structures date back to the 1850s; however, many of them were built after the terrible 1885 fire, which consumed forty city blocks. The Sonnentheil House (1826 Sealy) is perhaps the most photographed home in this area. The details of design lead many to believe that Nicholas Clayton served as architect of the home, built in 1886–87. However, his office diary does not list the house. The owner declared bankruptcy soon after the home was completed and it may be that Clayton never received payment, which kept the structure off his records.

For an overview of the district, drive to Fifteenth Street and turn left.

A "Pocket Park," developed by the East End Historical District Association, is on the next corner. One of Henry

Rosenberg's drinking fountains has been moved here. The Lockhart House (1502 Ball) is across the street. It is said that, when the city began the grade raising, the owners raised their one-story home and built the present first floor underneath.

Continue to the next corner, Winnie Street, and turn right. Turn right again on Fourteenth Street and drive three blocks to Broadway.

During the 1900 storm, a raft of houses floated to this corner and completely destroyed the Clayton-designed Sacred Heart Catholic Church. Clayton did not draw the plans for the present Moorish-Indian style building, built in 1903, but he did execute the design for the dome, which had to be replaced after the 1915 storm.

Clayton's most famous architectural achievement stands across the street (1402 Broadway). The Gresham House, better known as the Bishop's Palace, took seven years to build. The interior is as grand as the exterior. It is the only house in Texas listed by the American Institute of Architects as one of the one hundred outstanding structures erected in the organization's first one hundred years. The home is also on a list in the Archives of the Library of Congress of fifteen buildings that are representative of early American architecture. This is the only building in the United States included on both prestigious lists.

Walter E. Gresham came to Galveston in 1866 and made a fortune in his law practice, cotton markets, and railroads. He and his artist wife built this twenty-four–room, four-story home for their nine children. After the Gresham family had lived here twenty-seven years, the home was sold to the Catholic Diocese of Galveston in 1923 for the residence of the bishop until his death, which came in 1950.

The Palace is open for tours Monday through Saturday, May 31 through Labor Day, 10:00 A.M. to 5:00 P.M.; Sunday, 1:00 P.M. to 5:00 P.M.; winter tours are daily, 1:00 P.M. to 5:00 P.M. Groups are welcome by appointment; call 713/762-2475. Tour fees are used to maintain the structure.

*Drive west on Broadway about nine blocks to Ashton Villa
(2328 Broadway).*

A showplace upon its completion in 1859, the house is
still a showplace today. "Enthusiastic" describes the attitude of the tour guides who tell the tales that bring to life
the opulent style of the last half of the nineteenth century.
J. M. Brown, the wealthy hardware merchant, president
of Galveston Wharf Company, banker, and civic leader
who built this house, traveled extensively with his family.
On their travels, Brown and his wife selected much of the
material used in the construction.

Part of this home tour includes a twelve-minute slide
presentation of the 1900 storm and Galveston's amazing
recovery. This home graphically portrays the effect of
the grade raising. The cornstalk fence is about three feet
high today. Before the grade raising, the fence rose ten to
twelve feet above the lawn. Soil, pumped onto the property, completely filled the lower level of the home, which
contained the furnace. The guides point out the top of a
window that is visible just to the right of the front steps.

Travelers who have come to Galveston since 1928 remember this structure as the El Mina Shrine Temple. In
the early 1970s, the city of Galveston purchased the home
and it is operated by the Galveston Historical Foundation.
The story of the saving of this grand house is a credit to
farsighted citizens who got busy when they heard that
plans called for razing the building and erecting a service
station. A $200,000 Moody Foundation grant to establish a
revolving fund to save threatened historic buildings and
the opening of Ashton Villa, in June 1974, marked the
beginning of Galveston's historic revival. The stately mansion is open for the Spring Homes Tour, sponsors a July 4
Lawn Party, and in December is decorated beautifully for
the holidays. To begin the festive season a candlelight tour
is offered and donations are accepted. Ashton Villa is open
Monday through Friday, June through August, 10:00 A.M.
to 4:00 P.M.; Saturday and Sunday, noon to 5:00 P.M.;
closed on Tuesday, September through May. Admission charge.

Turn left at the corner on Twenty-fourth Street and drive two blocks to the Sweeney-Royston House (2402 Avenue L).

This home, built in 1885 by J. M. Brown, owner of Ashton Villa, as a wedding gift for his daughter, is one of the outstanding structures in the tiny Silk Stocking Historic Precinct. Information available at the Historical Foundation's Visitors Center outlines this small neighborhood, which is being preserved. This Victorian cottage is another Nicholas Clayton design. Matilda and Thomas Sweeney, for whom the house was built, divorced after a few years and Matilda moved back to Ashton Villa. One bedroom displayed at the villa is furnished for Matilda and her young daughter. The Sweeney-Royston home is open to large groups by appointment, call 713/762-9982.

Turn left on Avenue L, drive three blocks to Moody Street, and turn right to the Galveston Children's Home (1315 Moody).

This facility, which shelters abandoned and neglected children, has been in operation since 1878 because of the love of many people. It all started with George Dealey, an Englishman who came to Galveston in 1870 with his wife and nine children. (Yes, this is the same Dealey whose sons became publisher and editor of the *Dallas Morning News*.) After working for a time as a hospital volunteer, Dealey recognized the need for an orphans' home, secured a director, and rented a house. The Island City Protestant Orphans' Asylum opened with two children. In a year, the enrollment reached forty. Henry Rosenberg, who was childless, served as president of the board of directors and left $30,000 for the construction of a permanent building. The new structure had just been completed, in 1895, when the 1900 storm destroyed it. Although the children remained in the building, no one was injured. Word of the dreadful destruction spread around the world. When newspaper publisher William Randolph Hearst heard of the loss of the new orphanage, he hosted a charity bazaar at the Waldorf Astoria Hotel in New York City and raised $50,000 for the construction of the present building.

Continue south on Moody Street toward Seawall Boulevard,
the hub of Galveston's early twentieth-century tourist mecca.

The Galvez Hotel, one of the city's legends, has been
restored. The main entrance to the hotel, as in the early
years, is on Bernardo de Galvez Avenue, the street behind
the hotel. Parking is easier on Seawall and the east side of
the hotel; however, the main entrance, the north porte
cochere, affords visitors the first grand view of the lobby
and it's worth parking and walking around the hotel.

Before the 1900 storm, Galveston held the title of
cosmopolitan business center of the Southwest. Efforts at
establishing hotels had been successful for businessmen
and their families, but a real resort atmosphere, although
attempted, had never developed. With the construction
after the storm of the causeway to handle five railroads,
the Interurban, and the highway for automobile traffic, a
group of businessmen in 1910 challenged the Galveston
Business League to meet their subscription of $50,000

each toward the construction of a first-class beach-
front hotel.

After the storm, an esprit de corps developed among
the populace, especially the business community, which
literally worked miracles to bring Galveston back to life;
the seawall (to be discussed later), the grade raising, and
the rebuilding of the port and business community—all
represented Herculean tasks. And then, this idea: develop
the island's tourist potential. In less than two months a
half-million dollars had been raised. One year and three
months later, June 10, 1911, the Galvez opened to guests
from all over the world. The construction cost reached $1
million.

The Galvez, restored to its early-day ambience at a
cost of about $13 million, has earned its place on the Na-
tional Register of Historic Places. The first floor retains
the original oak-beamed ceilings tinted with gold and
beautiful column capitals. The promenades on each side
of the lobby provide the same open air that made them
favorite "strutting spots" (thus the name Peacock Alley) in
the early days. The main floor and the exterior are all that
remain of the original Galvez, which offered rooms beginning at $2.00 ($2.50 with bath). The renovation required
gutting the building from the second floor up. Only the
exterior walls, structural columns, stairs, and elevators
remain. The 224 rooms and 4 suites enjoy completely new
furnishings and mechanical, electrical, and plumbing
equipment.

The Galvez has made a major contribution to Galveston's role of "playground of the Gulf." In 1915 the hotel
also served as a refuge for thousands who received warning to take cover on high ground behind the seawall. For
two days the hotel fed the refugees at no charge. The
building stood up mightily against the ravages of the
wind, sustaining only roof, glass, and water damage.

Once again Galveston moved into a heyday of flour-
ishing business and wealthy tourists who, accustomed to
hotels all over the world, chose the Galvez for as long as
six weeks to six months each year. In 1937, the Galvez
served as the temporary White House while President

Franklin D. Roosevelt went deep-sea fishing. During President Roosevelt's visit here, he met, for the first time, a freshman Texas congressman, Lyndon B. Johnson.

The Galvez celebrated its modern opening as a first-class hotel on June 10, 1980, the hotel's sixty-ninth anniversary. Reservations are available by calling 713/765-7721 or, toll-free, 800/228-9290.

Soon after the Galvez opened, a young Italian immigrant named Sam Maceo operated a barbershop in the hotel. He and his brother Rose expanded into the nightclub business. By 1922 Sam Maceo was kingpin of what some call Galveston's "sporting era," which lasted until 1957. The Maceo brothers added gambling houses to their nightclub business, finally moving to the pier across from the Galvez. The club became the Balinese Room and brought in big-name bands and entertainers.

Gambling operations flourished, with only occasional raids from the Texas Rangers. At the Balinese Room, it is said, word always spread ahead of the Rangers and the gambling equipment was folded up into hidden wall compartments. Finally, after strong complaints from local citizens, the gambling houses were permanently closed as were the bawdy houses that made Postoffice Street notorious. Some say that Galveston did not "become" an open city. They say it was always a frontier town and that, when turn-of-the-century morality was ushered into this part of the country, it simply did not cross the causeway. Today, the Balinese Room remains a fine restaurant and bar.

Across the street, the Moody Civic Center, a $3 million gift from the Moody Foundation to the city of Galveston, offers meeting, convention, and entertainment facilities as well as the Visitor's Information Bureau. Passengers board the Galveston Sightseeing Train here at the Moody Center for a one-and-a-half-hour, seventeen-mile commentated tour around Galveston. The summer schedule begins in May with trips at 9:00 A.M., 11:00 A.M., 1:30 P.M., and 3:30 P.M., seven days a week in good weather. June through August another trip leaves at 5:30 P.M.; September 1 to

December 1 and March 1 to May 1, closed Monday. Special group rates for this sixty-four–passenger train can be arranged; call 713/765-9564 or 713/744-1826 or write 66 Lebrun Court, Galveston, TX 77551.

The Galveston seawall is one of the great engineering feats of its time. The solid concrete wall rises seventeen feet, spreads sixteen to twenty feet at the base, and is three to five feet wide at the top. Known as the world's longest sidewalk, it stretches nearly ten miles. In July 1904, at the completion of the first phase, the wall, founded on wooden pilings, protected 3.3 miles of waterfront.

The 1915 hurricane gave the wall its first test. The 1900 storm had produced sixty-mile-an-hour winds for seven hours, while the 1915 storm lashed the island with sixty-mile-an-hour winds for nineteen hours and then increased to seventy miles an hour for another nine hours. The tide in 1915 rose three and a half feet higher than in 1900, yet only twelve people lost their lives and the property damage was far less. The wall paid for itself in that first storm and has continued paying since then. The fourteen granite-covered jetties, which protrude five thousand feet into the Gulf between Tenth and Sixty-first streets, are called groins and are there to control the Gulf currents, protecting the beaches and the seawall from erosion.

Drive west along the seawall to Rosenberg Avenue. Turn right and continue to Avenue O. Turn left for two blocks to Garten Verein (2714 Avenue O).

German residents formed a social club, laid out this octagonal-shaped pavilion (1876), bowling alleys, tennis courts, and croquet grounds in the midst of a garden. Stanley Kempner purchased the property in 1923 and gave the site to the city for a public playground. Some residents believe the delicate detailing on the pavilion is indicative of a Nicholas Clayton design.

Continue west about six blocks to the Powhatan House (3427 Avenue O).

This structure was originally part of a hotel built in 1847 on Twenty-first Street by John Sydnor, one of the major slave dealers and an early Galveston mayor. Many refugees rode out the 1900 storm in this home. Instead of raising the house, the owners partially filled in the basement, which left the structure three feet above ground instead of the original nine feet. Careful observation will reveal other buildings sitting above ground level a few feet, yet not high enough for a full basement underneath. The Galveston Garden Club now occupies the home. The facility is open Tuesday, Friday, and Saturday only, 1:00 P.M. to 5:00 P.M. Donations are accepted for the tours.

Retrace the route on Avenue O to Thirty-first Street and turn left; turn left again on Avenue K and drive to St. Patrick's Cathedral (Thirty-fourth and Avenue K).

Built in 1872–1878, this Nicholas Clayton design, which was elevated several feet, is the largest building lifted during the grade raising.

Continue west on Avenue K to Thirty-seventh Street and turn left. Drive to Avenue P and turn left to the Samuel May Williams Home (3601 Avenue P).

Built by one of Texas' outstanding citizens, this is one of the oldest homes still standing in Galveston. The structure does not face the street because when it was erected, 1839–40, it sat out in the country and Avenue P did not exist. Samuel May Williams immigrated in 1824 to San Felipe, the capital of Stephen F. Austin's colony, to serve as Austin's secretary. He carefully recorded the Mexican land grants in Spanish. Later, Williams went into a mercantile partnership with Thomas F. McKinney. During the Texas Revolution, their business, the largest commission-merchant firm in Texas, advanced the Republic of Texas more than $150,000. In 1935, when no heirs remained to claim the payment, the state of Texas finally repaid the debt.

Careful on-site investigation indicates that portions of the building were prefabricated in New England and shipped to Galveston for final construction. Early photos show the home about five feet higher above the ground than it is today. The grade raising filled in a kitchen and storage room originally built under the structure.

The Galveston Historical Foundation purchased the home and, after extensive restoration to its pre–Civil War period, opened it to the public in 1981. Half of the museum features the original Williams family furniture; the balance of the furnishings include antiques of the pre–Civil War period. Check at the historical foundation's Visitors Center for hours and tour fees.

The next portion of the tour touches what probably are the most frequented attractions on the island.

Continue on Avenue P to Thirty-fifth Street, turn right, and drive south to Seawall Boulevard. Turn right for a drive out to the west end of Galveston Island.

Gaido's Restaurant (Thirty-ninth and Seawall) is a well-known landmark. San Jacinto Gaido came from Italy in 1888 at the age of two. By the time he was eleven, he was working in restaurants. He owned three small restaurants before opening the original Gaido's on Murdock's Pier in 1920. Gaido's serves excellent seafood in large dining rooms. Prepare to wait in line or enjoy a drink in the bar on most evenings.

Continue west on Seawall Boulevard.

Fort Crockett, built in 1897, is visible from Forty-fifth to Fifty-third streets. Some of the later defense bunkers are still in position along this route, although the fort has been closed since 1947.

Continue west on Seawall Boulevard to Ninety-first Street.

At Sea-Arama Marineworld dolphins and sea lions perform, guests watch animal-training workshops, and rare aquatic specimens are on display. Other shows include a Bengal tiger, spotted leopard, and black panther, as well as king cobras, pythons, and rattlesnakes. Open daily year round, 10:00 A.M. until dark. Sea-Arama has special rates for groups of fifteen or more; call 713/744-4501 or Houston 713/488-4441 for more information.

Seawall Boulevard becomes Farm Road 3005. Drive about ten miles to 13-Mile Road and turn right at the entrance to Galveston Island State Park.

This birdwatcher's paradise spreads from the Gulf to West Bay and is made up of marsh areas that can be observed from boardwalks and observation platforms. Reservations are advisable for overnight camping; call 713/737-1222. The usual state park entrance fee is required. Travelers planning to use several state park facilities may find it economical to purchase an annual entry permit, which allows access to most state parks. Inquire at any state park headquarters.

The Mary Moody Northen Amphitheater is within the park. Performances of a Broadway show alternate with Paul Green's *The Lone Star*. This historic production depicts early Texas history, including the burning of San Felipe during the Runaway Scrape (Chap. 4). Texas barbecue dinners are served each evening before the performance, 5:30 P.M. to 8:00 P.M. Performances are held May 1 through August 31, 8:30 P.M., except Monday. For reservations, call 713/737-3442 or Houston 713/486-8052.

It is about twelve miles west on Farm Road 3005 to the toll bridge at San Luis Pass.

In early days a stagecoach from Galveston to Velasco (Chap. 6) carried passengers to a mule-drawn ferry at the pass.

Return to town on Farm Road 3005 to Seawall Boulevard. Turn left on Sixty-first Street (also called Butterowe) and drive to U.S. Interstate 45; turn left. Take the Port Industrial Boulevard exit to the right. It is about one mile to the Galveston Ship Building Company site on the left.

Ocean-going barges are constructed here. They reach sixty feet high and are able to go anywhere in the world. The operation can be observed from the fence. To obtain a better view of how the huge vessels are launched (sideways), drive to the next gravel road and turn left. This is private property, and visitors need to remain on the road.

Continue east on Port Industrial Boulevard to Fifty-first Street (also called Seawolf Parkway). Turn left and drive across the bridge that spans the ship channel to Pelican Island.

The Texas A&M University at Galveston, a marine science and maritime resource institution, is situated on Pelican Island. Although the training ship *Texas Clipper* is berthed here during the academic year, the cadets are required to take three ten-week summer training cruises with emphasis on maritime activities rather than military. These cadets are preparing for service in the merchant marine.

Drive to Seawolf Park.

Tours of a World War II submarine, U.S.S. *Cavalla*, and a destroyer escort, U.S.S. *Stewart*, are available daily. Admission charge. The island offers an excellent view of ocean-going ships in the Galveston ship channel and of operations at the yacht basin. The impressive white pavilion is on the site of a former quarantine station, established in the mid-nineteenth century. Thousands of immigrants came through this island station as part of the effort to keep such dread diseases as yellow fever out of Galveston.

Return to Galveston Island by the same route and turn left on Port Industrial Boulevard, a road crisscrossed by railroad tracks and pocked with chuckholes. Turn right on Rosenberg Avenue and drive south to Broadway.

The Texas Heroes Monument is in the middle of the esplanade. Dedicated in 1900, the seventy-two–foot monument, a $50,000 bequest in Henry Rosenberg's will, commemorates the Texas struggle for independence from Mexico.

Turn left and drive along Broadway to the intersection with Seawall Boulevard. Turn left and continue to Texas 87. Turn left to the ferry.

Galveston belongs to the state and the nation because the events that occurred here have affected more than just this island—they have touched the world. Galvestonians are revitalizing the unique city, discovering that more than one thousand nineteenth-century homes and commercial buildings are still intact and offer a unique visual image of that era in Texas history that no other municipality can boast.

The last portion of this trail takes the traveler across Bolivar Ferry and along the narrow Bolivar Peninsula to High Island. The trip inland traverses Chambers County: salt marshes, pine trees, rich rice land, stories of pioneer settlement, and murder.

The ferry, operated by the state Department of Highways and Public Transportation, leaves about every twenty minutes, weather permitting. Travelers who do not plan to continue on the trail will find a round trip on the free ferry very much a part of a thorough look at Galveston.

After boarding the ferry, climb to the observation deck for a better view and a chance to feed the expectant sea gulls. Look to the right, or northeast, while crossing the ship channel. That hunk that looks like cement sticking out of the water is a concrete ship, the *Selma*, built as an experimental vessel during World War I. The ship sank in 1922.

Bolivar Peninsula

In 1820 General James Long arrived on Bolivar Peninsula. Long, a medical doctor and plantation owner turned adventurer, led a force that planned to free Texas from Spain. He came here in a vain attempt to secure the services of Jean Laffite, who occupied Galveston Island. As discussed earlier, Laffite gave verbal allegiance to Spain and to Mexico and to the United States, but he carefully remained aloof from entanglements that might harm his privateering enterprises.

In 1816 James Long married a beautiful debutante from Natchez, Mississippi, Jane Wilkinson, before her seventeenth birthday. When Long headed to Texas in 1819, the couple had one daughter and Jane was pregnant with

a second child. Long agreed that Jane could follow him
after she recovered from the birth. When the baby was
twelve days old, Jane left for Texas with both children
and her slave girl, Kian. Illness forced Jane to stop at her
sister's home in Alexandria, Louisiana. She left the in-
fant there, only to hear some time later that the baby
had died.

The Longs headquartered in Nacogdoches for a time
before General Long came here. Jane followed him to
Bolivar, where they waited for supplies either from Long's
benefactors in Natchez or from Jean Laffite. Finally, without aid from any source, Long and fifty-two men set out to
capture Presidio La Bahía, present Goliad. They held the
fort for four days before being forced to surrender.

Long did not take Jane on this expedition. He left her
at the rude fort with several men to protect her from the
Karankawa Indians roaming in the area. As the winter
grew fierce, the men abandoned Bolivar, leaving Jane,
who was expecting another child, her daughter, and the
slave girl, Kian, alone. In December, in the midst of a
raging storm, they ran out of food. Kian became delirious
from an illness and Jane delivered her own child. The next
morning, she rose, walked along the shore looking for
food, and found frozen fish on the beach.

Jane refused to leave until word came the following
July that her husband had been killed. She lived for a
time in San Felipe, ran a boarding house in Brazoria, and
then opened a boarding house in Richmond (Chap. 5). It is
said that, although she refused all suitors, many men were
taken by her beauty and charm, including Sam Houston
and Mirabeau B. Lamar. The child born here died in 1824.
Because of her heroism, many Anglo-Americans call Jane
Long "the mother of Texas."

According to a story in *Jane Long*, a collection of
Mirabeau B. Lamar's notes, Long's men were constantly
bothered by the Karankawas while they stayed on Bolivar.
Long led twenty-five men to Galveston Island to surprise
a group of one hundred Karankawas. The Indians did not
flee until they had lost forty warriors. The Anglos suffered
two dead and nine wounded. Lamar's account makes his

case for calling Indians "savage" rather difficult to uphold. The Anglos took two Indian boys captive, but one accidentally drowned while crossing the bay. The second became very attached to General Long, calling him father. One of the soldiers, testing the child's sincerity, pretended to fire a musket at the general. The Indian boy threw himself before the gun, crying out in terror. The soldier, believing the musket to be unloaded, continued with his "play." He pointed the gun at the child, saying he would kill him; whereupon, the boy bared his chest and the soldier pulled the trigger, only to discover as the bullet ripped into the child's body that the musket was indeed loaded. Lamar concludes the story with the information that "there was not a dry eye in the whole garrison."

The Karankawas had a bad reputation that survives to this day. They were tall, nomadic people who refused to be tamed by the mission priests. The men wore a piece of cane "two fingers thick" bored through a breast nipple, another length of cane run through their underlip, and long hair to show manliness. They kept mosquitoes, and the rest of society, at a distance by smearing their bodies with alligator grease and fish oil.

The stories of Karankawas being cannibals are not completely accurate. They did, on occasion, consume human flesh during special ceremonies, but not as a regular practice. Some scholars believe that they learned cannibalism from the Spanish. The Karankawas suffered defeats in battles with Austin's colonists in the 1820s and 1830s. They supported Texans during the Texas Revolution, but by the mid-1840s the few remaining Karankawas escaped into Mexico.

About one mile from the ferry exit at Port Bolivar, take the road that goes up to the old fort site on the right.

Plans are underway to develop the area into a park. During the Civil War, the Confederate army occupied this location, calling the outpost Fort Green. Then, in 1898, the federal government built Fort Travis. The ruins are still here.

The Bolivar Lighthouse is another historic site on this point. The first lighthouse was built in 1852 of cast iron and was torn down by the Confederates during the Civil War. Apparently the material served the war effort. The present structure was not completed until 1872. During the 1900 storm, 125 people took shelter here, and during the 1915 storm, the water rose shoulder deep as 60 refugees huddled on the tower steps. The keeper hand-turned the revolving machinery through the night, using the last of the oil supply to guide ships to safety. In 1933 the Lighthouse Service discontinued use of the structure, which is now on private property.

Continue east along Texas 87 on the peninsula.

Since the beach is not protected by a seawall, very few structures remain after each storm. Shell collectors will enjoy exploring these Gulf beaches, especially after a winter "norther." Ask at a community grocery for direc-

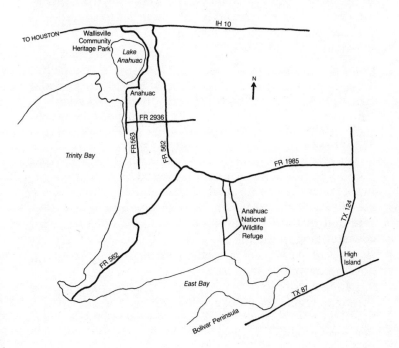

tions to the best areas. Rollover Pass, a very narrow cut through the peninsula, is a good wade-fishing spot. The name comes from the days when freebooters "rolled" barrels of their booty and supplies from the Gulf "over" to the safety of Galveston Bay.

Turn left on Texas 124 to High Island.

High Island

This community took its name from the elevation here. Refugees often seek shelter on this forty-seven–foot salt dome, the highest point between Port Bolivar and Sabine Pass.

There is an oral tradition that, during early exploration for oil at High Island, a young A&M graduate believed strongly that oil would be found under this salt dome. When the crew reached the agreed-upon depth and planned to call the operation a dry hole, the Aggie rushed to Beaumont, got Frank Yount, the well-known oil operator, out of a party and convinced Yount not to stop the drilling. Sure enough, oil came in, just as the young engineer had believed.

Continue north on Texas 124.

The high bridge spans the Gulf Intracoastal Waterway. This inland route for tugboats, barges, and small craft extends from Carabella, Florida, to Brownsville. Within Texas the waterway spans 421 miles with many feeder and tributary channels added over the years. When the United States government proposed building this bridge over the intracoastal, the Santa Fe Railroad was asked to split the cost with the highway department. It is said that the Santa Fe promptly produced a picture of a cow standing in the middle of Mud Bayou, the waterway that ran along here, supposedly proving that this could not be a navigable stream.

In late summer and early fall, there are many fires in this area. Often, the smoke will be visible for miles. The marsh grass is burned to allow the tender young shoots to develop for winter grazing.

*Turn left on Farm Road 1985. In 10.6 miles turn left on the
park road into the Anahuac National Wildlife Refuge.*

The 9,836-acre refuge is a bird watcher's haven with
good dirt roads along the coastal marshlands. Maps and
fishing information are available at the headquarters
building.

*At the intersection of Farm Road 1985 and Farm Road 562,
take the right fork, north on Farm Road 562, toward Anahuac. It is 4.3 miles to Farm Road 2936. Turn left and drive
3.4 miles to the T intersection. Turn right and continue toward Anahuac. Turn left into Fort Anahuac Park.*

Anahuac

This site played an important role in the beginning flur-
ries that led to the Texas war for independence. The Mexican government passed the Law of April 6, 1830, which
inflamed Texas residents because it aimed at stopping the
flow of emigrants from the United States and halted the
introduction of slaves into Texas. In an effort to enforce
the law, the Mexican government had a fort and customs-
house built here in 1831 or 1832 and at Velasco (Chap. 6).

The government sent Juan Davis Bradburn to command the garrison. Bradburn, a Kentucky-born Mexican
army officer, immediately made enemies with his over-
bearing tactics. Finally, when he arrested William B.
Travis, of later Alamo fame, and others in 1832, local citizens demanded release of the prisoners and drew up the
"Turtle Bayou Resolutions." The document officially supported the Mexican constitution and denounced the exist-
ing autocratic government under Anastasio Bustamante.
The group at Anahuac, like other Texans at the time,
leaned toward Santa Anna, who appeared to be a liberal
and a champion of the Mexican constitution. In less than
four years, they would realize how wrong they were.

*Circle through the park and exit at the north gate on Main
Street; turn left. Turn left again at the first caution light and
drive one block to the corner of Washington and Cummings
streets.*

An unsolved mystery surrounds the house on the southwest corner. In an upstairs room of this home, in 1865, General Thomas Jefferson Chambers, for whom the county was named, sat holding his six-month-old baby girl while he visited with his wife and daughter. Suddenly a shot rang out and the sixty-three–year–old man, one of the largest landowners in Texas, slumped forward, dying in his wife's arms. The killer rode quickly away on horseback and was never apprehended.

Chambers had many enemies, even men in high places, because he loudly argued with anyone who did not meet his high standards of truth, justice, and integrity. He acquired vast landholdings in payment for his services as superior judge of the Judicial Court of Texas. His salary in land the first year reached about 133,000 acres.

Chambers became involved in a bitter newspaper fight with David G. Burnet, who had served as president of the ad interim government. Chambers denounced Sam Houston for sexual misconduct and rowdiness. And, he laid claim to land in Austin on which the capitol was to be built, tried to force squatters from the site, and ended up with the case dragging through courts for the next twenty years. Many say that plenty of people had good reason to want him dead.

In 1845 Chambers built this home, which he called Chambersea. The house is open by appointment; call the Chambers County Historical Commission, 713/267-3543. No admission charge.

The building behind Chambersea is the Dr. Nicholas Schillings home, which includes his office. Dr. Schillings came to the Cedar Bayou area (across Trinity Bay in southwestern Chambers County) in 1874 to practice medicine and served as one of the few doctors in the area until his death in 1929. His home was moved to this site and is operated by the historical commission. It is also open by appointment. No admission charge.

Drive to the end of the block and turn right on Bolivar Street. At the end of the second block, just beyond Miller Street, is the Lone Star Canal.

Recognizing the need for fresh water for rice crops, local farmers began buying land in 1902 and building this irrigation canal. Mules pulled barges loaded in the fields with sacks of rice. When they reached the end of the canal, here at the mouth of Lake Anahuac, the bags of rice were tossed down a zinc-lined chute kept slick with corn meal. The rice bags were then loaded onto sailboats for the trip across the bay to Galveston.

In dry seasons, salt water backed into the bay and then into the canal and killed the rice crops. To prevent the damage, a dam and locks were built here at the mouth of the bay. Today, this canal provides water for both agricultural and industrial use.

Turn right and drive east along Miller Street to Farm Road 563. Turn left and cross the canal.

The Chambers County Historical Museum is on the left. County genealogical records, archeological reports, and other historical data are displayed here. The facility is open Monday through Friday, 8:00 A.M. to noon, 1:00 P.M. to 5:00 P.M.; closed Saturday and Sunday. If more than two make up the group, call for an appointment, 713/267-3543. No admission charge.

Continue north on Farm Road 563 for 6.1 miles.

The pasture on the left just before the intersection with U.S. Interstate 10 is filled at various times of the year with registered Texas Longhorns: bulls, cows, and heifers. James Taylor White, who settled in Chambers County in 1819, introduced Longhorn cattle to this area. By 1840 he owned eight to ten thousand head, which grazed on 100,000 acres along both sides of the Trinity River and south to the Gulf. When he died in 1852, he was known as the cattle king of Southeast Texas, with $150,000 on deposit in New Orleans banks. White's ranch home, which is just east of here, is the site where the Texans met to draw up the "Turtle Bayou Resolutions."

Turn left on the south access road of U.S. Interstate 10. It is 2.5 miles to the Wallisville Community Heritage Park.

Wallisville is a town that is being reborn from nothing. As part of a 1960s plan to construct the Wallisville Reservoir and Saltwater Barrier, downstream on the Trinity River, the Army Corps of Engineers relocated or tore down all the buildings in the town. The Wallisville Heritage Park Foundation and Chambers County Historical Commission are carefully documenting and restoring this early Texas community, first settled in 1825. By the 1830s Wallisville had become an organized village. The 1869 schoolhouse has been restored and serves as a well-documented area museum and headquarters for the park.

Future plans call for rebuilding, on the original foundations, the 1886 courthouse and nearby jail with its hanging tower. Other structures will be returned to the community, restored, and furnished in period pieces. The Army Corps of Engineers operates a ranger station here to help visitors. The Wallisville Heritage Park is open Monday, 1:00 P.M. to 5:00 P.M., Wednesday, 8:00 A.M. to noon; Tuesday, Thursday, Friday, and Saturday, 8:00 A.M. to 5:00 P.M.; closed Sunday. No admission charge.

Across the interstate from the Heritage Park is the site

of an Indian settlement that dates back about 3,500 years. Over two hundred aboriginal occupation sites, or shell middens, have been found. The Indian "refuse heaps" are being examined by archeologists. The site has been placed on the National Register of Historic Places and is called "El Orcoquisac Archeological District" in honor of the Orcoquisac Indians who lived here. Plans include displaying the artifacts in interpretive centers at the Heritage Park.

This is also where the Spanish built Presidio San Agustín de Ahumada and Mission Nuestra Señora de la Luz in 1756. The Spanish abandoned the mission in 1771 when they gave up hopes of completing their dual purpose: Christianizing the Orcoquisac Indians and keeping the French from moving into the area.

Return east on the access road to the Farm Road 563 intersection. Turn left under U.S. Interstate 10 and then turn west on the interstate toward Houston. The five o'clock traffic on weekdays is very heavy on this route. To avoid some of the congestion, exit about five miles beyond the Trinity River on Texas 146. Drive through Baytown and cross the Houston Ship Channel through the Baytown tunnel. Turn right at Texas 225 and return to Houston on La Porte Road.

This trail has wound through the Texas coastland, which looked so promising to the far-sighted early settlers. They had dreams of magnificent shipping lanes, and those dreams came true. They imagined thriving cities, and they are here. Some envisioned personal empires carved from this land, and many of their descendants are still business giants. Each of the pioneers who moved across this land gave his or her personal touch to life here. And, today, this area thrives in the midst of diversity: a space center next to a wildlife refuge, historic restoration beside international shipping lanes, commercial fishing beside sport fishing, and business people alongside vacationers.

2. Industrial Trail

This trail cuts through a section of Southeast Texas where cattle graze, rice elevators dot the horizon, and some of the largest petrochemical plants in the world have changed the face of the prairie. The three major cities in this area—Port Arthur, Orange, and Beaumont—have produced such wealth that the geographic region they form is known as the "Golden Triangle."

Leave Houston, driving east on U.S. Interstate 10. At Winnie, take the Texas 73 exit toward Port Arthur. After crossing the intersection with Texas 124, continue east on Texas 73 about 7.5 miles to Jap Road. Turn left and drive 1.4 miles to the green 7UP sign, which points left to the Boondocks.

This is a genuine bayou-based catfish restaurant. Not only is the catfish very good (served cayenne-pepper hot, medium, or plain) but also the entertainment is unusual. Alligators and turtles vie for spots on the banks of Taylor Bayou, the canal that edges the restaurant. These creatures are visible from the restaurant and diners enjoy the after-dinner diversion of tossing hushpuppies to the creatures from the safety of the porch. Since alligators hibernate during the winter, they are visible only in the spring, summer, and fall. The Boondocks is open Tuesday through Friday, 4:00 P.M. to 10:00 P.M.; Saturday, noon to 10:00 P.M.; Sunday, noon to 8:00 P.M.; closed Monday.

Retrace the route to Texas 73 and continue east.

Port Arthur

Billed as "Energy City USA," Port Arthur began as a dream and became an inland port with rail connections to the Midwest, a resort town for wealthy northern investors, and the center of a vast petrochemical industry. The town also holds proud title to a school for severely physically handicapped children and young people. This unusual institution has drawn the attention of such celebrities as Bob Hope, for whom the high school is named, and Bum Phillips, who sponsors an annual golf tournament to finance construction of an adult training school.

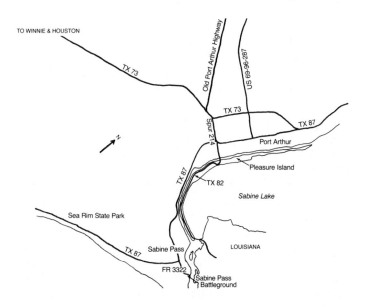

By 1840 a few settlers had moved to this site on Sabine Lake, just nine miles from the Gulf of Mexico. After enduring a harsh freeze and a hurricane without medical attention in 1890, the inhabitants abandoned the community.

Five years later Arthur E. Stilwell, president of a midwestern railroad, had a "vision" of extending travel from Kansas City to the Gulf of Mexico. Stilwell organized the Townsite Company, which laid out the village of Port Arthur and erected a hotel, pleasure pier, and loading docks. By 1899 a twenty-five–foot canal had been dug in the shallow lake, which permitted ocean-going vessels to reach the dock.

Stilwell's vision paid off. On January 10, 1901, Spindletop, the world's biggest oil discovery at that time, blew in just a few miles north, near Beaumont, and Port Arthur already had docking facilities for shipping out the crude oil.

After entering the city limits, drive to the intersection with Spur 214 and turn right (south).

This route passes through the largest oil refining and petrochemical complex in the world: Texaco, Inc., on the left and Gulf Oil Company on the right. Eleven percent of the petroleum used in the United States is refined here.

This is Texaco's largest plant in the United States, employing over 5,300. Within three months after Spindletop blew in, the Texas Fuel Company formed with a capital investment of $50,000. Within a year the company rechartered as the Texas Company and capitalized at $3 million—the main reason that it, and a handful of others, survived out of the almost two hundred oil companies that began after Spindletop. The first year, the company built thirty-six storage tanks and lay twenty miles of pipeline to move the crude from the oil fields to the Port Arthur harbor.

Gulf Oil Company also began with Spindletop. Anthony F. Lucas and his two partners in Guffey Petroleum Company borrowed $300,000 from Pittsburgh bankers T. Mellon & Sons to finance the first Spindletop well. Their business became the Gulf Refining Company of Texas the following November. The refinery began operation to produce kerosene from the Spindletop oil. From that limited beginning the company has continued to expand, making this facility Gulf's largest refinery in the world, producing more than six hundred products.

Gulf offers a free group tour of the refinery. Visitors board an air-conditioned, forty-six–passenger bus, complete with a public address system. The guide points out the cannon used in the days before the invention of foam for putting out storage tank fires. The bus passes the largest crude processing unit in the world; the largest catalytic reformer, built to process unleaded gasoline; as well

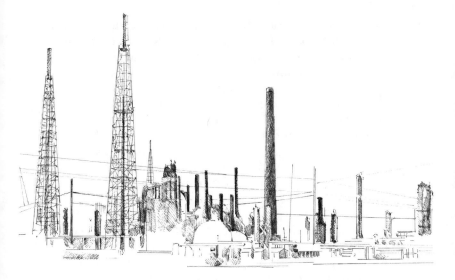

as the harbor and turning basin, which accommodate six ocean-going vessels. The one-hour tour is offered Monday through Friday only, 8:00 A.M. to 5:00 P.M. Gulf requires reservations two weeks in advance. This service is available to groups of not less than ten and no younger than eleven years. For reservations and directions to the plant, write Jim I. Gatten, Area Director Public Affairs, Gulf Oil Corporation, Box 701, Port Arthur, TX 77640.

In 2.1 miles, at the intersection with Texas 87, turn left and drive into town.

The evacuation route signs on many Port Arthur corners are posted in case of flooding. The U.S. Corps of Engineers is undertaking the construction of a $70 million hurricane protection system, which includes a vast levee complex to hold back storm-driven water.

The prospect of storms and flooding did not cloud Arthur E. Stilwell's ideas, or "hunches" as he referred to them. Raised in a wealthy family who later lost its money, Stilwell ran away from home and joined the Travelers Insurance Company. By the time he was twenty-seven years old, his "hunches" had served him so well that he followed another, quit Travelers, and formed a trust company in 1886 to build a railroad from Kansas to the Gulf of Mexico. Stilwell possessed a phenomenal ability to raise enormous sums of money through the force of his ideas, personality, and extreme honesty.

Stilwell's new railroad, the Kansas City Southern, laid plans for this city, built in 1895 on the northwest bank of Sabine Lake with a seven-mile-long canal to the Gulf of Mexico. Stilwell "saw" this landlocked harbor as safe from the frequent Gulf storms and as a much more profitable place for midwestern farmers to ship their grain exports than the East Coast. The railroad reached Port Arthur in 1898.

In a short time, however, John "Bet-a-Million" Gates found opportunity to buy into the Kansas City Southern Railroad, and in even less time (January 1900) Stilwell found himself ousted as president of the company.

John W. Gates, who grew up in poverty on an Illinois farm, amassed his first million in the barbed-wire business by his twenty-fifth birthday. He and his family built a fine summer home in Port Arthur in 1899, and Gates became a moving force in the development of the town and a major investor in the Texas Company. Gates fought to get the Intracoastal Waterway dug between Sabine Lake and Port Arthur. During this period the shipping business grew rapidly with the coming of oil at Spindletop and the refineries that grew up on Port Arthur's outskirts. John W. Gates died suddenly in 1911. More about his important contributions to Port Arthur will be included later.

Drive east on Texas 87 to Woodworth Boulevard and turn right; go approximately thirteen blocks to Procter Street or detour to the Hughen Center.

This school for severely physically handicapped children and adults has, through the power of love, welded Port Arthur and the surrounding communities together in an amazing operation that has changed the lives of countless young people.

For the drive to Hughen Center, turn left on Woodworth,
travel to Twenty-fifth Street, and turn right. Drive to Ninth
Avenue and turn left. (Port Arthur has numbered streets,
which run east and west, and numbered avenues, which run
north and south.) It is three blocks to the intersection with
Twenty-eighth Street on the right and Bob Hope Street on
the left. Bob Hope Street is actually the driveway into the
Hughen Center parking lot and the Bob Hope Vocational
School.

This school's story includes a long list of outstanding
accomplishments. Just as Port Arthur began as a dream,
Hughen Center developed from a 1922 dream of the local
Rotary Club. A committee organized the Port Arthur Society for Crippled Children in 1933 and opened the Spastic
School in 1936 with five students and a staff of three. The
following year, local residents contributed one day, from
sunup to sundown, and built a one-room school on this
property. The community has continued its support; volunteers are plentiful, including retirees. When the local
labor unions go on strike, the workers spend their free
time here performing volunteer building and mainte-
nance projects.

Perhaps the most dramatic story of community support occurred in January 1980. Bob Hope and others were
scheduled to be here to dedicate the new Bob Hope Vocational School and the Sertoma Club planned to present its
annual Service to Mankind Award to Hope and to honor
those who took part in the telethon that raised money
to build the vocational school. The only building large
enough to feed such a gathering was the Oil, Chemical,
and Atomic Workers Union Hall. At that time the union
was deeply immersed in a long and heated strike. The
hall served as union headquarters, and pickets paraded
around the site. Naturally, representatives of management
planned to be part of the big Hughen Center celebration.
Gulf had provided the school's food service area and Texaco had built a dormitory. And, Hughen Center students
often visited the refineries. Preparations ground forward
hesitantly. The night of the banquet, the pickets volun-

tarily disappeared and the program went off without a
hitch. The next day, the pickets resumed their march.

Young people from all over the world who have been
unable to communicate are learning to use computers to
write, speak, and perform tasks. Some students must use
pointers attached to football-type helmets to operate the
machines; others control the sensitive devices with their
chins, noses, feet, or eye movements. When they graduate,
they are ready for the work force or college. The out-
patient physical therapy program serves an age span from
five and a half to eighty years.

The bank of computers that have opened the world
to the bright minds of the Hughen students has been donated by civic clubs. The heated indoor pool is a gift from
Jimmy Durante. The annual Bum Phillips Golf Tournament, the last weekend in May, benefits the construction
of an adult vocational center next door and provides
scholarships.

Visitors are welcome at Hughen Center but are asked
to make arrangements in advance to ensure a staff member being available for a tour; call 713/983-6659 or write
2849 Ninth Avenue, Port Arthur, TX 77640.

*Turn right from Bob Hope Street; drive south on Ninth Ave-
nue about twenty-two blocks to Procter Street and turn right;
go four blocks to the 3300 block of Procter.*

The unusual conch shell fence on the left borders Eddingston Court, Port Arthur's first large apartment building project, built in 1929. Captain A. T. Eddingston had
conch shells loaded onto two ships in the Grand Cayman
Islands and delivered here. A Hispanic family from San
Antonio used six thousand of the shells to build this fence.

*Continue to Woodworth Boulevard and turn left. (This is
where the trail rejoins the alternate route for travelers who
did not go to the Hughen Center.)*

In 1909 Rome H. Woodworth, an early Port Arthur
mayor and founder of the First National Bank, built Rose
Hill Manor (100 Woodworth). The family deeded the mansion to the city in 1948 for use as a civic and social center.

Turn right on Lakeshore Drive and drive to the pink Pompeiian Villa (1953 Lakeshore).

In addition to John W. Gates, Arthur Stilwell attracted two other business tycoons to Port Arthur: Isaac Ellwood, developer of barbed wire and wholesale hardware dealer, and James Hopkins, president of the Diamond Match Company. Gates, Hopkins, and Ellwood bought the land in this long block between Richmond and Lake Charles avenues with plans to build adjoining winter "cottages." Gates erected a twenty-room Virginia-style colonial mansion east of here, and Ellwood built this smaller, exact version of a villa in Pompeii. Both homes cost $50,000 to build.

Although Hopkins never built on his land, which is the present Masonic Temple site, he bought this villa from

Ellwood. However, the story goes that, when Mrs. Hopkins and their two daughters arrived, they found Port Arthur sweltering. Mrs. Hopkins took one look at the villa and the mud and mosquitoes and refused to leave her carriage. Hopkins rented the home for a time to officials of Guffey Petroleum Company, present Gulf Oil. Then, in 1903, land developer and banker George M. Craig offered to give Hopkins 10 percent of the stock in a new oil business called Texas Company as the purchase price for the ten-room villa. That little dab of stock, in what is today Texaco, is presently worth more than $657 million.

The Port Arthur Historical Society owns the Pompeiian Villa and offers tours of the beautifully decorated home by appointment: Monday through Friday, 9:00 A.M. to 4:00 P.M.; Sunday, 1:00 P.M. to 4:00 P.M.; closed Saturday; call 713/983-5977. Donations accepted.

Continue west on Lakeshore Drive.

In the early days, this street faced beautiful Sabine Lake. The wealthy and their children romped under these shade trees and swam in the lake, bordered by sandy beaches. Rue des Soldats, "street of the soldiers," was dedicated in 1932 and ran alongside the ship channel. The street skirts the top of the storm levee, part of the Corps of Engineers program of storm protection for the city. The Rue des Soldats still offers a lovely view of the city and the ship channel on the other side. Yes, those masts belong to ocean-going tankers moving along the Intracoastal Waterway just beyond the levee. They look as though they are on the next street.

Woodrow Wilson Junior High School is the impressive English colonial-style building on the left (1500 Lakeshore Drive). The dome is covered with 1/2,000-inch-thick gold leaf.

The Ruby Ruth Fuller Building across the street serves as the chapel of Lamar University at Port Arthur. In 1909, seeing the need to attract business to this rapidly growing region, John Gates founded Port Arthur College, a nonprofit, private business school. He gave the facility to the Methodist Church in 1911, and, finally, Lamar Univer-

sity of Beaumont accepted the deed in 1975 and opened
the Port Arthur branch. The school boasts the oldest radio
college in the world.

Across the street is the Gates Memorial Library, dedicated in 1918 as a gift from Delora R. Gates in memory of
her husband, John W., and son, Charles G. Gates, who died
two years after his father. The impressive structure served
as the city library until 1980. Presently, it houses the
Lamar Branch Library and the Heritage Room, the Port
Arthur Historical Society Museum. The museum offers a
wide range of material significant to Port Arthur's development. It is open Monday through Friday, 10:00 A.M. to
2:00 P.M. The library is open Monday, Thursday, and Friday, 9:00 A.M. to 5:30 P.M.; Tuesday and Wednesday, 9:00
A.M. to 7:30 P.M. Both the museum and the library are
closed Saturday and Sunday.

*Continue west on Lakeshore Drive to Savannah Avenue just
beyond Woodrow Wilson Junior High School. Turn left for
the 1.5-mile drive along the top of Rue des Soldats. At the end
of the route, make a U-turn and retrace the route west along
Lakeshore Drive. After returning to Savannah, take the right
fork in about one block on Fourth Street when Lakeshore
Drive goes to the left.*

After crossing Beaumont Avenue, watch for the enormous murals painted on the rear of buildings to the right.
The murals are part of the city's bicentennial celebration
and depict important events in Port Arthur's and the
country's history.

*Turn right on Dallas Avenue, drive to Fifth Street, and turn
left. Turn left again in two blocks on Houston Avenue. It is
about three blocks to the entrance to the Port of Port Arthur.*

Stilwell's dream of an inland port connecting the
Midwest and the Gulf has grown into a modern ocean
port. The seventy-five–ton gantry crane, "Big Arthur," lifts
cargo from some of the world's largest ships. The port is
open to visitors daily, 10:00 A.M. to 2:00 P.M. Tours may be
arranged by calling 713/983-2029.

Return to Houston Avenue and drive north to Seventh Street. Turn left, and proceed to Texas 82, and turn left for the drive across Gulfgate Bridge to Pleasure Island.

Pleasure Island

Gulfgate Bridge, completed in 1970, spans the Sabine-Neches Ship Channel, the twenty-mile canal through which tankers move to the Port of Port Arthur and the Port of Beaumont. It is also part of the Gulf Intracoastal Waterway. (It is said that the red wolf ranges into the marshes beside the bridge.)

Pleasure Island is a 3,500-acre slip of land between the ship channel and Sabine Lake. The dredging of the canal parallel to the lake formed the island. Facilities here include picnic grounds, a golf course, campsites, sailboat and charter fishing boat marina, and the world's longest fishing piers. One levee reaches five miles into the lake and the other stretches six miles. Sabine Lake is the largest saltwater lake in East Texas, and spots are available along the levees for excellent fishing.

Drive on T. B. Ellison Parkway; turn right at the marina.

Googan's Restaurant is at the end of the boulevard overlooking the lake. Googan's specializes in seafood and exotic fruity drinks. It is open in the summer, Tuesday through Friday, 11:00 A.M. to midnight; Saturday and Sunday, 3:00 P.M. to midnight; closed Monday. In the fall-winter season, open Tuesday through Thursday, 5:00 P.M. to 11:00 P.M.; Friday and Saturday, 5:00 P.M. to 1:30 A.M.; Sunday, noon to 9:00 P.M.; closed Monday.

Return to T. B. Ellison Parkway and turn right to the first road beyond the marina.

This is one of the fishing levees. A five-day saltwater sport fishing license may be purchased at the convenience store here or at the marina.

Return by the same route over Gulfgate Bridge on Texas 82, continue north to Texas 87, and turn left. It is 10 miles to

*Sabine Pass, a former seaport. From there it is another 1.4
miles to Dick Dowling's Battleground, site of one of the most
decisive encounters in Texas during the Civil War. It is 9.4
miles from Sabine Pass to Sea Rim State Park, which fronts
the Gulf and is an animal and water-fowl sanctuary.*

Sabine Pass

In 1836, when Sam Houston and Philip A. Sublett laid out
the town, it took the name Sabine City. The founders expected great things of this ideal port city sitting strate-
gically on the waterway dividing the United States and
Texas. In fact, the population reached six thousand before
storms in 1886, 1900, and 1915, along with the challenge of
Arthur Stilwell's new city of Port Arthur, spelled doom for
the town.

*After entering Sabine Pass, watch for Sartin's Restaurant in
the second block on the left. The big crab marks the spot.*

Seafood is the order of the day here, and "lots of it" is
the motto. Boiled crab legs are piled on a platter-size
plate; nut crackers and lots of napkins are handy. With
plenty of time for the operation, lunch is a fun and
tasty treat.

*Texas 87 goes to the right out of Sabine Pass. Continue south
on Farm Road 3322 to Sabine Pass Battleground State Historical Park.*

During the Civil War, an earthen fortification called
Fort Griffin, and sometimes Fort Sabine, protected this
vital entrance to the mouth of the Sabine and Neches
rivers. Richard W. (Dick) Dowling, a twenty-five–year–
old Houston saloon keeper, headed a force of forty-six
Irish dockworkers, who had been assigned the inglorious
task of defending Sabine Pass because the Confederates
believed that Union forces would invade farther east on
the Louisiana coast. On September 8, 1863, Dick Dowling
and his men remained at the fort, ignoring orders from
General John Magruder to withdraw. Dowling's men
watched four Yankee gunboats pass over the bar into the

channel, while transports loaded with more troops waited to come ashore. A shell reef lined the middle of the channel, allowing passage of one ship on the Louisiana side and one on the Texas side of the pass.

As the gunboats moved into the channel, Dowling's men began firing all six of the fort's cannons. They struck the *Sachem*'s boiler and it exploded on the Louisiana side. Then the cannon balls hit the *Clifton*'s steering cables and rendered it helpless on the Texas side. Within forty-five minutes the battle had ended and the remaining Union forces made a hasty retreat. Dowling's Texans killed 19, wounded 9, left 37 missing, took 315 prisoners, and captured two Union vessels, with "nobody hurt." The bronze statue of Dick Dowling is located at the approximate site of the old fort.

This fifty-six–acre park offers picnic tables, boat launching ramps, and sheltered fish-cleaning facilities. The four concrete bunkers are leftovers from World War II, when a coastal artillery division of the United States Army manned this battery to protect the petroleum ports of Beaumont and Port Arthur.

The Sabine Pass Lighthouse is across the channel. Built in 1856, this eighty-five–foot tower sent its beacon eighteen miles into the Gulf until it was decommissioned in 1952. The Belgian-constructed lens is on display in the Port Arthur Historical Society Museum at the Gates Memorial Library.

Return to Sabine Pass and turn left on Texas 87 for 9.4 miles to the entrance to Sea Rim's marshlands unit on the right.

Sea Rim State Park

The helicopters on the left, in less than two miles, are used as a lift service to offshore oil rigs. Visitors to the park can rent canoes or take airboat tours. Alligators bask in the sunlight; nutrias, muskrats, raccoons, rabbits, and river otters all live here. In the fall thousands of ducks and geese arrive. In early spring, nesting birds and their babies are visible in the tall reeds. The thirty-minute airboat tour covers an eight-mile round trip. Tours are offered daily March through October, 9:00 A.M. to 7:00 P.M. Special appointments may be made at other times by calling 713/971-2963.

Drive west about one mile to the entrance to the beach, camping sites, interpretive center, and observation platform.

During winter, wave action deposits seashells and other interesting items on the three-mile sand beach. Another two-mile stretch of salt tidal marshland grows right up to the Gulf, providing a nursery for Texas coastal fish. Bird watchers will appreciate boardwalks and photo blinds over the marshes. Take plenty of insect repellent. For further park information, call 713/971-2559.

Return to Port Arthur on Texas 87. Bypass the city by turning left on Spur 214 and right on Texas 73. This highway will rejoin Texas 87 on the east side of Port Arthur.

The twenty-story-high Rainbow Bridge, the tallest in the south, was built in 1938 to allow ships to pass up the Neches River to the Port of Beaumont. The view from the top is spectacular for all but the driver. The two-lane traffic is often heavy and requires a steady hand. Plans are underway for another bridge to ease the heavy congestion.

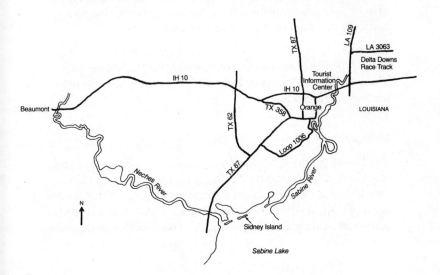

Sidney Island

A one-hundred-acre bird sanctuary, Sidney Island, is off to the right of the bridge at the edge of the Sabine-Neches Ship Channel. Created along with 1,100 islands when the Intracoastal Waterway was dug, this site is so important in the life of migratory and shoreline birds that the National Audubon Society leased the island from the state in 1975. A warden sees that the almost 35,000 adult birds who flock here during the summer, as well as the almost 105,000 baby birds that hatch each year, are protected from human intruders, hungry water moccasins, and alligators.

Visitors are not allowed on the island from March through August while the birds are nesting unless the warden allows a small group to motorboat over for the daily inspection. For further information or arrangements to visit Sidney Island, write Mrs. Sue Bailey, Box 11, Bridge City, TX 77611, or call 713/735-4298.

East of Bridge City, cross the intersection with Texas 62 and turn right on Gaylyn Street. Drive less than 0.4 mile to the end of the street and turn left.

The Warner-Kachtik two–and–one-half–acre Christmas tree farm is one of several in the area. The garden also boasts four hundred rose bushes. Visitors are welcome to walk among the roses and the trees.

Return to Texas 87, turn right, and drive about one mile to Loop 1006, DuPont Drive. Turn right for a three-mile trip along Orange's Chemical Row and into downtown Orange on South Border Street.

Orange

Twelve to thirteen thousand of Orange's thirty thousand population are employed along Chemical Row, making this the most industrialized town per capita in the Southwest. At night, this drive is aglow with the lights from the plants, working around the clock. Many of the petrochem-

icals used here have been piped in from the refineries at
Port Arthur.

The petrochemical industry is the primary support of
the Orange economy today. However, the lumber empire
of the Lutcher and, later, Stark families built the modern
downtown Cultural Plaza: a 1,500-seat theater for the performing arts, a very impressive art museum filled with an
extensive collection of early American art and artifacts,
the Stark family mansion bordering the complex, as well
as the priceless Lutcher Memorial Presbyterian Church.

Orange began as a hamlet in the mid-1800s when
ships sailed down the Sabine River with cotton as their
main cargo. Lumber, cattle, and agriculture also provided
an important base for the economy. Henry J. Lutcher and
G. Bedell Moore founded the Lutcher and Moore Lumber
Company in 1877 and the boom began. Wooden ship
building developed with the dredging of the harbor in
1914, and Orange stood in the forefront, ready for large-
scale ship construction during World Wars I and II.

*Upon entering the downtown area, South Border Street con-
verges into Seventh Street. Drive three blocks to the Cultural
Plaza and park near the corner of Green Avenue or on the
east side of the main plaza in the parking lots.*

Imagine this open parklike area lined with ordinary
small-town commercial structures. Until the late 1970s
this part of the city housed Orange's business district.
Some communities allow their downtown areas to deteriorate, others restore the façades, but Orange did something quite different. Nelda C. Stark, widow of the late
H. J. Lutcher Stark, who owned most of these buildings,
decided that demolishing the business structures and con-
structing this Cultural Plaza would be of more benefit to
the city.

To begin the story of the Lutcher-Stark family, walk
west on Green Avenue to the Lutcher Memorial Presbyterian Church. Henry Jacob Lutcher, the lumber king,
married Frances Ann Robinson in 1858, and they had two
daughters, Miriam (Mrs. W. H. Stark) and Carrie Launa
(Mrs. E. W. Brown).

As a memorial to the Lutcher family, Frances Ann Lutcher began in 1908 to direct and pay for the construction of this church. The three stained-glass windows above the front doors won prizes at the 1893 Chicago World's Fair. These masterpieces were created by a process so time consuming and expensive that similar windows are no longer manufactured. The carvings and decorations in the church are overlaid in gold leaf; the light fixtures and hardware are bronze; the paneling, pews, and piano are all of fine dark mahogany. The dome is topped with copper; the marble for the columns, communion table, and baptismal font was imported from Italy. Upon completion of the building in 1912, every detail had been carefully orchestrated, including enough china, glass, and silver to serve two hundred.

In accordance with Mrs. Lutcher's wishes, the cost of the building has never been disclosed. A brochure is available in the church office detailing the intricate symbolism in the structure. Arrangements can be made for groups to visit the facility during the week by calling 713/883-2097. The church office is open Monday through Friday, 8:30 A.M. to noon and 1:00 P.M. to 4:30 P.M.; closed Saturday. Sunday worship begins at 10:30 A.M.

*Walk east (right) on Green Avenue to the Stark Museum
of Art.*

The Nelda C. and H. J. Lutcher Stark Foundation
built this thirty-thousand-square-foot museum. The facility houses the valuable art collection of the late H. J.
Lutcher Stark, grandson of Henry Jacob and Frances Ann
Lutcher. Stark began his American western art collection
as a continuation of his mother's interest in art.

The American Indian Collection includes about two
hundred Navaho rugs and blankets, examples of Plains
clothing, and many other items crafted by the tribes of
the Southwest and the Great Plains. Rare books, manu-
scripts, paintings, and sculpture make up the western collection, with such notables as Frederic S. Remington and
Charles M. Russell represented, as well as the twentieth-
century artists of Taos, New Mexico. The museum has the
largest known collection, nearly four hundred works, of
William Herbert Dunton (1878–1936), who was one of the
original six members of the Taos art colony. Dunton gave
up his work as an illustrator in New York and moved to
Taos in 1912. He spent the remainder of his career depicting cowboy scenes and western wildlife.

Outside the business community, Stark made a name
for himself in educational, philanthropic, and cultural affairs. The family donated a collection of ten thousand rare
books and art objects valued at more than $4 million to
the University of Texas in 1937. When the university did
not provide proper housing for the art, the family with-
drew that portion of the gift. The books are presently
housed in the Miriam Lutcher Stark Library at the Harry
Ransom Center on the University of Texas campus in Austin. Until the museum's completion in 1976, the art objects adorned the homes, offices, and businesses of the
Stark family.

The Museum Shop offers art books and information
on the collections here for those wishing further information. The postcards are Remingtons and the travel books
are excellent. The museum is open Wednesday through
Saturday, 10:00 A.M. to 5:00 P.M.; Sunday, 1:00 P.M. to 5:00

P.M.; closed Monday, Tuesday, and holidays. Group tours may be arranged by calling 713/883-6661. Children under twelve must be accompanied by an adult. No admission charge.

The Stark mansion, built in 1894 by Miriam Lutcher and W. H. Stark, is across the street. This home reflects the opulent era and the life-style of the family who lived and entertained here. The house was surrounded by elaborate gardens and pastures for the carriage horses. Restoration includes the original furniture, curtains, glassware, and family portraits. This home is listed in the National Register of Historic Sites and is open to adults, Tuesday through Saturday only, 10:00 A.M. to 4:00 P.M. There is a tour fee. Make reservations by calling 713/883-0871.

The Frances Ann Lutcher Theater for the Performing Arts is on the south side of the plaza. This 1,500-seat theater opened in 1980 with a performance by Liberace and continued with such variety as Dickens' *A Christmas Carol* and the Joffrey II dancers. Touring companies of first-rate Broadway shows are scheduled here about every two weeks. For tickets or information, call 713/886-5535.

Retrieve the car now or plan to walk at least twelve blocks. Go east on Front Avenue, the block behind the theater, to the intersection with Third Street.

The offices of Livingston Shipbuilding Company face Front Avenue, but the shipyard, which includes facilities for repairing ocean drilling platforms, lies across the river in Louisiana. From the vantage of Ochiltree Park, beside the river, it is easy to observe the ship building and repair, which is still a major Orange industry. In an effort to straighten out a very sharp bend in the river, the U.S. Corps of Engineers dug a channel on the far side of the ship building company. The site thus became part of Louisiana but now sits on an island in the middle of the Sabine River. Workers check into Livingston's offices and then go to the island in Louisiana to work each day.

Return west along Front Avenue. Turn left on Fifth Street and walk (or drive) to the end of the block at Division Avenue.

The Orange House Inn is the only hotel in the downtown area. Remodeled in 1980, the inn offers a restaurant, which opens at 6:00 A.M., and a disco bar. Members of the Broadway productions that perform at the Lutcher Theater enjoy staying here because of the convenience to the Cultural Plaza.

Turn right on Division Avenue for one block and go to the corner of Sixth Street.

The Farmers Mercantile stocks hay, cattle feed, saddles, and modern fertilizers. Tourists may want to browse, pick up a butter churn like Grandma used, or even buy a few groceries for a picnic at the Louisiana Tourist Bureau or in Ochiltree Park. Farmers Mercantile opened in 1928 and is still run by the same family. Originally, the building housed the Dodge automobile dealership, which explains the very tall, wide doors and the large glass windows.

Continue west to the Heritage House Museum (905 Division).

This 1902 home is furnished to reflect the life of upper-middle-class families in Orange at the turn of the century. The house is open Tuesday through Friday, 10:00 A.M. to 2:00 P.M.; Sunday, 1:00 P.M. to 5:00 P.M.; closed Monday and Saturday. Admission charge. The old Curtis Elementary School building is the next structure on the left. It was remodeled in 1981 to provide apartments for the elderly and the handicapped.

Turn right on Tenth Street. Just before crossing the railroad track, turn left in the driveway to the Old Wood Shop.

In the cabinet shop that opened here in 1914, a steam engine was hooked up to a shaft to operate the second-hand machinery. The business made shrimp boats, church pews, and caskets along with ordinary windows and doors. Electricity replaced the steam engine, but the machinery remained. Today, the old building houses a craft shop. The owner said that the only caskets he makes are for dogs. He builds most anything a child could want, including hobby horses and doll houses. The craft shop is chock-full of items to delight a craftsperson, from silk flowers to clock works. Craft classes are offered. The shop is open Tuesday through Saturday, 9:00 A.M. to 5:30 P.M.; closed Sunday and Monday.

Cross the railroad track and continue north to Green Avenue. Turn right. This is where those who walked pick up their cars. Drive east several blocks to the T intersection with Simmons Drive. Turn left and go about three blocks to a tall chain-link fence enclosing a parking lot on the right. Drive through the gate into the lot, which is on Destroyer Drive.

Each year the International Gumbo Cook-Off is held here with 35,000–40,000 people sampling the gumbo. One of the featured attractions is the crawfish race: the winner gets a kiss and the loser gets dropped in the gumbo pot. The Gumbo Cook-Off is held the first Saturday in May.

Continue through the parking area to Pier Road and turn left.

This is an old naval base. Some of the buildings are used for navy and marine recruiting. The Sabine River is over the embankment to the right.

Turn right immediately after crossing the bridge and drive out on one of the eighteen piers.

Hundreds of ships in the navy's mothball fleet docked here after World War II until other uses could be found for the vessels. The ship berthed at the end of this road belongs to the Corps of Engineers. The housing to the left originally served the naval base, but today it is privately owned rental property. Some of the buildings serve as vocational training facilities for Lamar University at Orange.

Return to Simmons Drive, turn right, and go for three blocks to the next traffic light, Park Avenue. Turn left for a drive across town to the palatial Brown Center.

Afterward, the trail leads on to Beaumont or a thirty-mile round trip into Louisiana, a stroll on a boardwalk over a swamp, and a visit to Delta Downs Race Track.

*Stay on Park Avenue at the intersection with Sixteenth Street
as Park takes a forty-five-degree turn to the right.*

The facilities called Sunday in the Park, on the right,
are part of a public community center. The rail fence on
the left, which runs for over a mile, encloses the Shangri-
La Gardens and Bird Sanctuary. Henry J. Lutcher Stark's
great concern for floral beauty and preservation of wildlife prompted the establishment of this park. However,
when public use became detrimental to the preservation
of the area, the family brought this rail fence in from
other property and closed the park to the public.

*Park Avenue makes a sharp bend to the left and becomes the
Old Beaumont Road. After Strickland Drive joins this road,
it is 0.5 mile to the gates of Brown Center on the left.*

This impressive mansion, sitting so far off the road
amid the towering pine trees, belongs to Lamar University at Orange, a 1976 gift from the late Edgar W. Brown,
Jr., estate. Brown was a Lutcher grandson. Today, the
home is used for seminars, meetings, and conferences. It
is open by appointment only, Monday through Friday, 9:00
A.M. to 3:00 P.M., except holidays; call 713/883-2939. Admission charge.

*To travel directly to Beaumont, continue west on Old Beau-
mont Road to the intersection with U.S. Interstate 10. For the
drive into Louisiana, retrace the route toward Orange for
about 0.1 mile to Fortieth Street. Turn left and drive to the
access road beside U.S. Interstate 10. Turn right and drive
east to Louisiana on the interstate. Take the first exit after
crossing the Sabine River into Louisiana.*

This is the Tourist Information Center. A long boardwalk extends out over the marsh, offering visitors an opportunity to see birds and alligators. It's reported that an
alligator occasionally catches a bird. Fishing is permitted
from the bank, and signs identify the flora and fauna
along the route.

*Continue east on U.S. Interstate 10 for 2.5 miles and turn
right at the Toomey exit. Turn back to the left on Louisiana*

109. When the highway forks, continue north on Louisiana 109 for 2.5 miles to Louisiana 3063. Turn right toward Vinton. It is less than a mile to the entrance to Delta Downs Race Track.

Delta Downs Race Track

This is a parimutual betting racehorse track. No one under eighteen is admitted, and gentlemen must wear coats in the clubhouse. Coats are not necessary in the general admission or forecourt areas.

The regular season is from mid-September to early April; Quarter horses race from April through July. There are usually ten races a day. The gate opens at 5:30 P.M., Thursday, Friday, and Saturday, with post time at 7:30 P.M.; on Sunday, the gate opens at 11:00 A.M., with post time at 1:05 P.M.; closed Monday through Wednesday. On race days, the horses are exercising on the track in the morning and visitors can drive into the parking lot for a closer view. For more details, call the reservations office at 800/551-7142. Greyhound offers charter bus trips from Houston every race day; call 713/222-1161.

Return on Louisiana 3063 to Louisiana 109, turn left and follow Louisiana 109 to U.S. Interstate 10. Head west back into Texas.

Immediately after the interstate crosses the Sabine River, the Texas Tourist Bureau is on the right. There are thirteen bureaus in the state, but this facility registers more visitors than any of the others. Free information, maps, routing, and travel literature are available.

Continue to Beaumont on U.S. Interstate 10.

Beaumont

The size of Beaumont, the largest city in the Golden Triangle, has often been attributed to the Spindletop oil discovery south of town, which literally changed the world. Beaumont boomed, of course, but the community man-

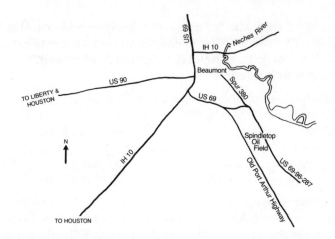

aged to absorb the wild, hurly-burly growth and the glut
of sudden success because the town had grown accustomed to success. Beaumont already thrived from lumber,
cattle, rice, and its port, as well as from the prosperity
brought by being crisscrossed by five railroads.

Travelers see surviving symbols of Beaumont's broad
range of history, from the 1845 trading post to a replica of
the boom town that sprouted on the plains next to Spindletop Oil Field; the art deco buildings, which symbolize
construction during the second oil boom in the mid-1920s;
and the Beaumont Port, where ocean-going vessels from
all over the world can be observed daily.

In 1825, a Tennessean named Noah Tevis settled with
his wife and children on the high banks of the Neches
River. The site became known as Tevis Bluff. Since a trail
to the interior of Texas came through here, Tevis began
operating a ferry, which his wife, Nancy, continued for
many years after his death. A few months before Tevis
died in 1836, he sold fifty acres to Henry Millard. Millard's
property is part of what became Beaumont. Nancy Tevis
stayed here with her nine children and fought to keep
her land. She welcomed Texans fleeing in the Runaway
Scrape during the Texas Revolution but refused to join
them. After the war, Nancy worked with several men to
get Beaumont laid out as a genuine town. In 1838, she

received a franchise for operating her ferry, which authorized her to collect three cents a head for swimming cattle. By 1856, more than forty thousand head crossed
annually at her ferry site.

Enter Beaumont on U.S. Interstate 10. Exit north on the
Eastex Freeway, U.S. Highway 69. Remain in the right lane
and exit immediately on Delaware Street. Turn left under the
freeway, follow Delaware three blocks to French Drive, and
turn right. It is about three blocks to the French Trading Post
on the left, almost hidden in the towering pine and oak trees.

Trees in Beaumont grow especially tall. The trunks
appear to climb forever upward before branches begin to
sprawl across the sky. John Jay French chose this site, and
more land on the river, because he needed the oak bark in
his tanning business. French came to Texas from Connect-
icut and New York in the 1830s and did business from
Brazoria to Louisiana. He settled here and in 1845 built
this two-story frame house for his wife and four children.
This house, one of the few of its age still standing on the
Texas coast, is typical of a prosperous settler's home during that period.

In addition to tanning cow and alligator hides, French
opened a trading post and provided settlers for miles
around with shoes, harnesses, leather goods, calico, mus-
lin, thread, tobacco, flour, and sugar in exchange for their
hides, beef, hogs, barrels of corn, and tallow. It is said that
for many years French and his sons made most of the
shoes worn in East Texas.

Restored to its original state, the facility features
a "swept yard" and rooms decorated in early Texas
and American antiques, some of which belonged to the
Frenches. Beaumont Heritage Society docents guide visitors through the home, pointing out the bubbles in the
original hand-rolled glass windows and the original paint
on the ceiling, which has survived because settlers in that
day mixed the basic pigments with either buttermilk, animal fat, or blood. For some reason that concoction produced very long-lasting paint.

The actual trading post operated from the large up-

stairs room, reached by a narrow, steep inside staircase. The room boasts a bearskin rug that can be touched, delicate handmade clothing, and a quilting frame on which local women prepare quilt tops.

The first Sunday in December, a Candlelite Tour is held here. The entire complex is decorated and there is no admission charge at that time.

Adjacent to the trading post, the Beaumont Heritage Society operates a gift shop, filled with unique selections, such as handmade china dolls, pottery, and other hand-crafted items. The museum and gift shop are open 1:00 P.M. to 4:00 P.M., daily except on Monday and holidays. Park in front of the home and walk back to the gift shop to purchase tour tickets. Group tours can be arranged by calling 713/898-0348.

Go back on French Drive to Delaware Street, turn left, and return to the Eastex Freeway. Drive south, following U.S. Highway 69 when it joins U.S. Interstate 10. Watch for the Washington Boulevard exit, number 850, which comes just before the interchange where U.S. Interstate 10 turns south and U.S. Highway 69 swings east. After leaving the freeway, remain on the access road about one-half block to Don's Restaurant.

Don's serves crawfish in season and other Cajun dishes that add to the uniqueness of this area. This is a family-type restaurant and other menu selections are also available. It is open for lunch and dinner.

The route from here follows U.S. Highway 69 as it travels east, but it is tricky to get to the highway from Don's Restaurant. Drive south on the access road until the road makes a U turn under U.S. Interstate 10. Enter U.S. Interstate 10 and drive north for a short distance. Remain in the right-hand lane and then take the U.S. Highway 69 exit to the right. Exit from U.S. Highway 69 on Florida Avenue. Turn left under the freeway and follow Florida Avenue about thirteen blocks to University Drive. Continue on Florida to the middle of the next block, beyond the baseball diamond. Turn right and drive to the rear of the parking lot to the Spindletop Museum.

In addition to early oil well equipment on display and oil-related exhibits, this museum provides a Geology Room where the salt-dome formation at Spindletop is explained in lay terms. The museum is open Monday through Friday, 9:00 A.M. to 5:00 P.M.; closed Saturday and Sunday. No admission charge.

Turn left on Florida Avenue, drive back to University Drive, and turn left to the Gladys City Museum in the first block.

This complex is a replica of the town that grew up with Spindletop. The fifty-eight–foot granite monument commemorates the oil discovery. In the mid-1880s Patillo Higgins, a local roughneck, lost his arm in a shootout in which he killed a deputy marshal. Since it all happened at night, Higgins' self-defense claim got him out of the scrape. Two years later, he attended a revival meeting, became a born-again Baptist, and never swore, ran with a wild crowd, drank, or even smoked again. A fellow Baptist and wealthy lumberman, George Carroll, hired Higgins, who proved to be a bright and aggressive employee, buying timberland for Carroll all around East Texas. Higgins took his Sunday School class on picnics south of town in the 1880s. He entertained the class by punching cane poles into the ground on "Big Hill" and lighting the gas that escaped.

Although Higgins had only three or four years of schooling, he read extensively and became convinced, despite geologists' theories to the contrary, that oil existed in abundance on "Big Hill." After struggling to convince local businessmen to go in on the venture, George Carroll and two others formed the Gladys City Oil, Gas and Manufacturing Company, with Higgins as the manager. Higgins selected the name Gladys in honor of a seven-year-old girl in his Sunday School class and even carefully drew up the plans for his model industrial city adjacent to the future oil field.

Despite Higgins' insistence that oil would be found at 1,000 to 1,100 feet, deep for those days, drillers never got that far and declared four dry holes in a row. Finally, Anthony Lucas, a mining engineer and the only person left who agreed with Higgins' theory, induced a firm to get financial backing from Dick and Andrew Mellon, sons of T. Mellon of Pittsburgh. Their $300,000 deal cut Higgins out of the operation.

When the Lucas Gusher, called a "geyser of oil," blew in on January 10, 1901, Higgins gained the respect of the community, but Anthony Lucas became the hero. Spindletop was born, the petroleum age had arrived, and Beaumont's population mushroomed from nine thousand to fifty thousand almost overnight.

Oil shot over one hundred feet above the well for nine days, spewing out 800,000 barrels before it could be controlled. The news flashed around the world and get-rich-quickers poured into town, sleeping where they could or not bothering to even try.

By April 18, when Higgins' well came in on his land, six wells had already been gushers. Men made fortunes only to later lose everything. It is said that the derrick floors measured seventeen feet across and the wells sat so close together that a person could walk a mile without stepping on the ground. Swindlers came out of the woodwork and bilked the unsuspecting as well as the tough businessmen. Higgins' Gladys City became a reality but not the settled, ideal community he had envisioned; it became a boom town of frame shanties.

Fires broke out on the wells and burned for days. Overproduction caused a decline by 1903 and, within ten years, the area had become a virtual ghost town. As for Patillo Higgins, he sued Lucas and his partners for $4 million, settled "satisfied" out of court, and continued oil speculating until he died at the age of 92. Some say that Higgins became one of the wealthiest oilmen in the state; however, his grandson said the old man was merely "comfortable." One account tells that Higgins pawned his wife's wedding rings to keep a lease on a place called Barber's Hill. The family still receives royalties from that field.

The reconstruction of Gladys City is the result of a Bicentennial project. The buildings are patterned after those early-day shanties and are furnished in the same fashion. The first building is the information center and gift shop. Special educational tours may be arranged by calling 713/838-8122. A folk festival dubbed Spindletop Boom Days is held here the last weekend in September. The museum is open Sunday through Friday, 1:00 P.M. to 5:00 P.M.; Saturday, 9:00 A.M. to 5:00 P.M.; closed Monday. Admission charge.

Turn right from the parking lot. Drive to the access road and turn right. From here it is two miles out to the Spindletop site. Turn left on Highland Avenue under the freeway. Follow the road when it makes a sharp right. Turn left at the T *intersection on the Old Port Arthur Highway.*

Modern-day drilling is taking place along this road on the right. There were never any metal oil storage tanks at Spindletop. The tanks that appear on the left mark the Spindletop field and are made of wood. The end of the field is designated by the beginning of the tank farm.

Marrs McLean became a 1920s version of Patillo Higgins. He believed that the salt-dome formation at Spindletop would give up more oil along its flank, and he hawked his theory to every oil executive he could corner.

Finally, Frank Yount, president of Yount-Lee Oil Company, began drilling November 13, 1925. The McFaddin No. 2 struck oil at 2,518 feet on the south flank of the dome. This time technology had improved and no geyser appeared. The oil flowed easily at five thousand barrels a day. Spindletop boomed again; production peaked in 1927 at over 27 million barrels and stayed at over a million a year until 1934. This time a few major oil companies controlled the field, speculators did not roar in, and hotel rooms did not bulge. The petroleum industry had grown up.

Retrace the route on Old Port Arthur Highway for 1.8 miles to the expressway. Turn right, enter the expressway, go east to Spur 380, downtown and Lamar University exit. Turn north (left) toward downtown.

Lamar University, on the left, began in 1923 as a technical training school called South Park Junior College. The school became a four-year, state-supported institution in 1951 named Lamar State College of Technology with students from all over the Golden Triangle. A second campus opened in 1969 at Orange and a third in 1975 at Port Arthur. Lying in the heart of the petroleum world, this institution has gained worldwide recognition for its school of engineering. Area petrochemical plants have assisted this outstanding record of growth with financial contributions and scholarships.

Continue toward town until the railroad tracks take over the middle of the street. Angle right on Sabine Pass Street. In about eight blocks, the old Hotel Dieu Hospital is on the corner of Sabine Pass and Bufford Street.

Only part of this structure survives. The facility began when five sisters of the Order of the Incarnate Word came here from Galveston in 1897. They lived in a rundown house nearby and quietly sought funds to build Beaumont's first hospital. There is a story that a local businessman, disbelieving the validity of the sisters' claim of poverty, eavesdropped one night while they had dinner. He heard them discuss saving the few crusts of leftover bread since they did not know if anyone would give them food the following day. Immediately, the man began a campaign that raised money to build the first unit: two private rooms and two wards. The building is owned by the Port of Beaumont and is used as the International Seaman's Center.

Turn left on Emmett Street. Stop at Pipkin Park across the street from the turning basin of the Port of Beaumont.

The chapel here is called Temple to the Brave. The local chapter of the Daughters of the American Revolution and other patriotic organizations had this structure erected in 1932 in honor of all Texas war heroes. The stained-glass windows represent the branches of the military and

the six flags that have flown over Texas. The Daughters of the American Revolution open the chapel on patriotic holidays.

Across the street, on the narrow piece of land between the park and the turning basin, is the walking beam from

the *Clifton*, one of the federal gunboats sunk in Sabine
Pass by Dick Dowling's men during the Civil War. A walking beam is the connection between the steam engine and
the drive shaft, which propels the ship. In 1912 Beaumon-
ters jerked the walking beam from the submerged vessel
and placed it here.

This land along the Neches River, which fronts on the
Port of Beaumont, is the highest point in the city and
the best place for viewing the handling of the cargo at
the port.

*Turn right beside the park on Pennsylvania Street, jog left on
Orleans Street, and drive six blocks to Wall Street. Turn left
and continue four blocks to Jefferson Street.*

The St. Anthony Cathedral is on this corner. After
Spindletop, Beaumont needed a large Catholic church,
and this Italian villa style structure was completed in
1908 at a cost of $60,000. The interior of the cathedral is
magnificent, reminiscent of the finest in Europe. The
building is open Monday through Saturday, 7:00 A.M. to
4:30 P.M.; Sunday 7:00 A.M. to 1:00 P.M.

*Drive around the block by turning right on Jefferson, left on
Forsythe Street, and left again on Archie Street. Drive two
blocks to College Street and turn left.*

Watch for the fire station on the right in the first
block. The old Engine No. 9 is housed in this station. Look
through the windows on the east front of the building.
That is a 1923 American La France tractor and a 1903
ladder truck. Photos are available of this ladder truck
being pulled by horses before the first motorized vehicle
went into service.

*Turn right on Trinity Street and drive to Franklin Street. Turn
left and continue four blocks to Pearl Street. Turn left.*

The Jefferson County Courthouse is on the corner. A
courthouse has stood on this site since 1838. This 1931
building is an example of art-deco architecture, a building style that found popularity in America from 1925 to
1940. This design is an attempt to find a new form. Look

at the stone panels of this building for figures representing the natural resources that made this county an industrial center. This style usually incorporates lots of angles and geometric forms. Several Beaumont buildings erected during the second Spindletop boom were built in this architectural form.

Continue north along Pearl Street.

Railroads have brought great prosperity to Beaumont and plenty of headaches, too. The track that runs down the middle of Gilbert Street usually halts traffic at this corner around 9:00 each morning and about 5:30 each evening. The structure across the tracks (northwest corner of Pearl and Gilbert) is the 1905 Heisig Building, an example of the architecture that followed Spindletop's first boom. The façade is plastered and scored with lines to give the appearance of carved stone.

Beginning at this corner, many of Beaumont's downtown buildings make up the Beaumont Commercial District, which has been placed on the National Register of Historic Places. The structures are representative of a stable nineteenth-century community jolted into sudden prominence in the petroleum age.

Continue on Pearl Street to Forsythe Street and turn right beside the Tyrrell Library in the old First Baptist Church building.

Erected in 1903, this structure is another thanks offering for Spindletop. Captain W. C. Tyrrell bought the building in 1923 and gave it to the city for a public library in memory of his wife. He stipulated that an accredited librarian be hired, that she direct the conversion of the facility into a library, and that blacks be included in the service. Upon completion of the new city library in 1975, this facility underwent conversion and now houses fine genealogy, Texana, and art collections. Enter from the side door on Forsythe Street. The library is open daily, except Monday and Friday, 9:00 A.M. to 6:00 P.M.

Drive to the end of the block and turn left on Main Street.
Continue three blocks to Crockett Street and turn left.

The first building on the right is the old Dixie Hotel.
This building enjoyed a "nationwide" reputation as a first-
rate house of prostitution from 1946 until the 1960s. Gambling and prostitution had been open concerns in Beaumont even before Spindletop, but vice raids in the 1960s
finally closed it all down. The Beaumont Historical Society purchased the hotel in an effort to preserve it, along
with the other buildings on this block. The façades on
these structures are all representative of the first thirty
years of the twentieth century when Beaumont flourished
as the new petroleum capital.

The historical society has instituted another program,
which has drawn recognition from all over the United
States. In an effort to help students become aware of their
built environment, the society has compiled an excellent
workbook, which has been adopted for use in the Beaumont Independent School District's eighth-grade classes.
In easily understood language, the book describes and
illustrates the various types of architecture. It points out
architectural features of Beaumont buildings and suggests
field trips to seek details that distinguish the different
forms. The program is designed to open the eyes of the
students, to encourage them to "look up" at the buildings,
and to appreciate what makes each structure unique.

Turn right at the second corner, Orleans Street.

The Kyle Building is in the second block on the right.
This structure has only recently been recognized as one of
the best examples of art-deco architecture in Texas. The
elaborate aluminum floral patterns over the entrances
and windows are definite features of the modern form.
Although completed in 1933 for office space and shops, the
building has never been totally occupied.

Turn right on the north side of the Kyle Building. Drive one
block and turn left on Pearl Street, then left again at the next
street, Calder Avenue, for a tour through "Old Town," which
begins in about seven blocks.

When Spindletop blew in, this area along Calder Avenue and the two streets on both sides already enjoyed tall trees, lovely gardens, and stately homes. Money from the lumber business had built the mansions. By the 1920s, however, nearby forests lay depleted and the early profit-takers had sold out or expanded into other areas. Many of the fine houses survived and are used for antique shops, art and gift emporiums, interior design shops, and excellent restaurants.

"Old Town" begins with the Mildred Building (southeast corner of Calder Avenue and Mariposa Street). The three-story portion on the east end houses eighteen apartments with terrazzo floors and marble columns. The adjoining portion of the 1929 structure served as Beaumont's first shopping center. Frank Yount, the oilman responsible for the second Spindletop boom, did not forget Beaumont during the Great Depression. Yount bought properties at prices far above the depression value and began building on them. The Mildred Building, named for Yount's eight-year-old daughter, became his first project. Local legend says Yount had several sets of the same furniture ordered so that, as pieces became worn, they could be replaced with identical items. The Mildred Building still offers apartment rental and the "shopping center" houses some exclusive antique shops.

Continue west on Calder Avenue to Third Street. Turn right one block to McFaddin Avenue and turn left.

On the right is the McFaddin mansion, which was built in 1906 on the original Mexican land grant to James McFaddin. This home with five floors is still occupied by a McFaddin descendant and is closed to the public. The structure sits within one hundred yards of the site of the original log cabin, built in 1833. The McFaddin family played important roles in the growth of Southeast Texas from the early cattle days to Spindletop. The McFaddins owned the Spindletop land and were partners in the company that sold the land to Arthur Stilwell for Port Arthur and Nederland.

Drive to the Green Beanery (southeast corner of McFaddin Avenue and Sixth Street).

This grand old home has been converted into a café serving crêpes, quiche, and soup for luncheon, a shop specializing in fine and commercial art, and other specialty stores. The café is open Monday through Saturday, 11:00 A.M. to 2:00 P.M.; closed Sunday; call 713/833-5913 for reservations.

Turn left on Sixth Street, drive one block to Calder Avenue, and turn right.

The left side of the street is lined with gift, antique, jewelry, and interior design shops, all creatively utilizing the homes that lumber fortunes had built. Johnson's Book Store, 2456 Calder Avenue, offers a wide variety of books. Texana buffs will enjoy browsing here.

Turn right at the next corner, Ninth Street, and drive six blocks to the Beaumont Art Museum. Cross Ashley Street and turn left into the driveway in the middle of the block.

J. Cook Wilson, one of the founders of Humble Oil Company, had this home built in 1935. The Wilson family presented the structure in 1969 to the Wilson Memorial Art Center of the Beaumont Art Museum. The facility enjoys a permanent collection of paintings, sculpture, and mixed media by Texas artists; however, the mainstay is the outstanding traveling exhibits, lecture series, and strong educational programs. The second floor accommodates a fine arts library and sales gallery. Metropolitan Museum calendars, address books, and other elegant items are on sale in the gallery.

The museum is open Tuesday through Friday, 10:00 A.M. to 5:00 P.M.; Saturday and Sunday, 2:00 P.M. to 5:00 P.M.; closed Monday. For a docent guide, call 713/832-3432. Donations appreciated. The second weekend in May, "Kaleidoscope," a creative arts and crafts festival, is held here on the grounds. Parking is available at the county fair grounds and a shuttle bus transports visitors to the museum.

Continue north on Ninth Street and turn right on U.S. Interstate 10. Take the Gulf Street exit. Turn left under the interstate and left on the access road. Enter the Babe Didrikson Zaharias Memorial driveway just before the facility's sign to find ample parking.

Port Arthur is the birthplace of Mildred Ella Didrikson Zaharias, but she moved with her family to Beaumont at age three. Her outstanding athletic ability and her tomboyish nature earned her the nickname "Babe," as she grew up during Babe Ruth's heyday.

In the 1932 Olympics in Los Angeles, Babe Didrikson won two gold medals and a silver one in three track and field events, set two world records, and tied another. She was on her way to world fame; she gained all-American status in basketball and became outstanding in tennis, baseball, bowling, and diving. She played professional women's basketball and baseball. In 1935 she began a golf career. After marrying George Zaharias, a wrestler, in 1938, she won every major golf title from 1940 to 1950, including the World Open and the National Open.

In 1953, she entered Hotel Dieu Hospital to undergo the first operation in her fight against cancer. Despite all odds, she returned to the pro circuit, won seven more tournaments, including the National Open, continued her work to benefit cancer research, and finally set up a national research fund. The Babe died at John Sealy Hospital in Galveston on September 27, 1956. Although voted by the Associated Press as the greatest woman athlete of the first half of the twentieth century and a charter member of the Ladies Professional Golf Association, Babe Zaharias did not live to realize her tremendous influence or the possibilities that she opened for women in sports.

This museum houses a myriad of trophies, awards, and scrapbooks filled with information about this outstanding athlete who is best remembered by her friends as a kind and gentle woman. The facility is open daily, 9:00 A.M. to 5:00 P.M. No admission charge.

Return to Houston via U.S. Interstate 10. If the arrival time in Houston corresponds with the afternoon traffic, some congestion can be avoided by taking U.S. Highway 90, College Street, before leaving Beaumont and traveling through Liberty on the way to Houston.

The industrial trail through the Golden Triangle of Southeast Texas is an adventure in bigness: cattle, lumber, shipping, oil, petrochemicals, and human achievement. Mixed thoroughly in this huge pot runs the continuing strand of concern for mankind. Giant oil magnates built pipelines, oil storage tanks, and apartment complexes to keep people employed during the Great Depression. The technology that propelled this part of the state into world competition has also developed a method of utilizing computers so that severely handicapped young people can speak for the first time.

3. Big Thicket Trail

This tour includes portions of present-day Big Thicket preserves, towns that have survived the ravages of lumber and oil booms, and towns that have not survived. Indians, trappers, settlers, lumbermen, oilmen, and tourists have all benefited from the riches in this region.

Travel northeast from Houston on U.S. Highway 90.

Liberty

One of the oldest settlements in the state, Liberty, because of its strategic location on the old Atascosito Road and the Trinity River, has played an important role in Texas history. That heritage is preserved in the impressive Sam Houston Regional Library and Research Center.

The Spanish used the Atascosito Road as a military highway to East Texas before 1756. By the following year, the settlement called Atascosito, about four miles north of present Liberty, held such importance as an outpost that it appeared on a Spanish map.

After Napoleon suffered defeat and later imprisonment on St. Helena, members of his palace guard and many ex-soldiers fled from France. In 1818, about four hundred men, women, and children of this group as well as some Spaniards, came up the Trinity River without permission from Spain and built a fort called Champ d'Asile near present Liberty. Instead of planting crops, they hunted and practiced military maneuvers. Many observers believed that they planned to overthrow the Spanish regime in Mexico, place Napoleon's brother Joseph on the Mexican throne, and free Napoleon from St. Helena. Within a few months, friendly Indians warned them of an advancing Spanish army. They quickly fled to Galveston where Laffite, not desiring attention brought to his privateering enterprises, gave them a ship on which they sailed to the United States.

Anglo-Americans who moved in here were also cut from different cloth than most of Texas' early settlers; they were loners and nonconformists. They did not join an organized group under an empresario, such as Stephen F. Austin, but took advantage individually of the liberal 1823 Mexican colonization law, which gave farmers at least a labor (about 177 acres), cattlemen a league (4,428.4 acres), and farmers who raised cattle a league and a labor of land. Settlers were exempted from taxes for six years and made only half-tax payments for another six years. Further, they could import merchandise and tools up to $2,000 free of duty. This law affected all colonists except Stephen F. Austin's original Old Three Hundred (Chap. 4), who fell under an 1821 law.

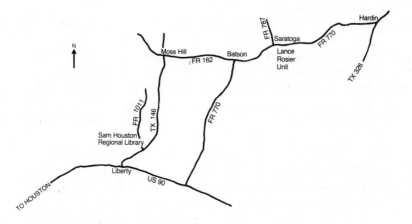

Enter Liberty on U.S. Highway 90, turn left on Milam Street, and drive two blocks to Sam Houston Street.

The Humphreys Cultural Center and Liberty Bell Tower are on this corner. This block is the result of individual, community, and national dedication. After the death of Geraldine Humphreys, a descendant of early Liberty settlers, the Humphreys Foundation and state grants made this combination museum, library, theater, and community meeting facility available. The museum, which employs rotating local exhibits as well as traveling collections, is housed on the second floor. The facility is open Monday through Friday, 10:00 A.M. to 6:00 P.M.; Saturday, 10:00 A.M. to noon and 1:00 P.M. to 4:00 P.M.; closed Sunday. No admission charge.

The bell in the tower at the rear of the museum has received national attention, for it is the first replica ever cast from the original 1752 mold of the Liberty Bell. It became a symbol of freedom from all afflictions when a local group decided to commemorate the work of the Liberty Muscular Dystrophy Research Foundation started here in 1950. Inspired by an older sister who later died of the disease, Sallie and Nadine (now deceased) Woods, themselves victims of the crippling malady, organized the first effort in the United States to support research in muscular dystrophy.

Although the bell was dedicated in 1960, this permanent tower was not completed until 1976, when Liberty served as a state and national Bicentennial City. When the bell is rung, symbolizing pride in the past and hope for the future, its rich tones are carried for four square miles.

Turn right on Sam Houston Street and drive to the second block, Main Street.

The site of Sam Houston's 1840 law office is on the southwest corner.

Drive one block farther on Sam Houston Street, turn left on Fannin Street, and drive one block to Trinity Street.

St. Stephen's Episcopal Church, on the northwest corner, was built in 1898 and is still used for worship.

Continue on Fannin to the T *intersection with Grand Street.*

The 1840s Abbott-Parker Home on the southeast corner served as a commissary during the Civil War. At that time Grand Street was the old Liberty-Nacogdoches Road.

Turn left on Grand and then right at the next corner, Main Street, or Texas 146. Drive about three miles to the intersection with Farm Road 1011.

The Texas historical marker for the original Atascosito settlement is on this corner. This old Spanish outpost, established by 1756 to prevent the French from trading with the Indians, was one of the earliest of the Spanish regime. Later, cattle being driven from South Texas to the New Orleans market used this route.

Turn left on Farm Road 1011 for a 0.7-mile drive to the Sam Houston Regional Library and Research Center.

Sam Houston Regional Library

Former Governor and Mrs. Price Daniel donated the 110 acres for this impressive center. Governor Daniel, whose family ranch adjoins this property, is a descendant of early settlers in this area, and his wife is a great-great-granddaughter of Sam Houston.

The library and research center houses collections from all ten counties represented in the Atascosito District. Some of the displays include the largest known

assemblage of pictures of Sam Houston; the desk that
Houston used at the Battle of San Jacinto; Jean Laffite's
journal, which had been saved by his great-grandson,
purchased by Governor and Mrs. Daniel, and given to
the library; a letter from Andrew Jackson to President Thomas Jefferson introducing Congressman Sam
Houston; and correspondence of General Sam Houston
and David G. Burnet. This fireproof depository offers a
gold mine for researchers and fascinating discoveries for
the casual visitor. The library is open Monday through
Saturday, 8:00 A.M. to 5:00 P.M.; closed Sunday and all
state holidays. No admission charge.

*Retrace the route on Farm Road 1011 to Texas 146 and turn
left for a drive that goes through areas of the Big Thicket. It
is about twelve miles north to Moss Hill and the intersection
with Farm Road 162. Turn right and continue east. At Batson, Farm Road 162 joins Farm Road 770 headed toward
Saratoga.*

Batson

Don't start looking for the Big Thicket around here. Although maps published as recently as the one in Campbell
and Lynn Loughmiller's 1977 *Big Thicket Legacy* show the
thicket beginning at Batson and spreading east for twenty
miles, it no longer covers such a large area. Forests are
only sprinkled through here. This trail will offer several
Big Thicket units, but not yet.

Batson sits on a salt dome, and after the Spindletop
boom in 1901 speculators began combing these dome sites
in Southeast Texas. In 1903 the third well in the area blew
in, producing fifteen thousand barrels a day. Overnight
the tiny post office community became an oil town of ten
thousand rowdy fortune-seekers and swindlers. Before the
townspeople built a jail, prisoners were kept chained to a
huge oak tree.

*Continue on Farm Road 770. Just beyond the intersection
with Farm Road 787 on the outskirts of Saratoga, watch for
a sign on the right pointing to Rosier Memorial Park.*

Lance Rosier Unit of the Big Thicket

A short trail winds through a portion of the Lance Rosier Unit of the Big Thicket. Palmettos grow in profusion through this hardwood forest, the largest unit in the preserve. Plans are underway by the National Park Service for hiking trails and an access road. Here, and in any other units, hikers should always use insect repellent, wear sturdy walking shoes that will survive mud, detour around all snakes, carry water, avoid drinking from the creeks, and stay on the trail. Look at and photograph the plants but do not collect specimens. Camera buffs will find most subjects in deep shade. For best results, use an adjustable camera, high speed film, and a tripod.

This route is a project of the Big Thicket Association in memory of the quiet little man who made a dramatic impact on all who knew him. Lance Rosier, or "Mr. Big Thicket," was born in Saratoga and began his love affair with the animals and plants at an early age. He learned every trail, the location of every baygall (shallow, stagnant water), and the name of every plant. Always available to anyone who wanted to see the thicket, Rosier guided the curious and the scientific. A self-taught naturalist, Rosier never went beyond high school. Yet, in the 1930s, when Cory and Parks did their research for *Biological Survey of the East Texas Big Thicket*, the authority on the area, Lance Rosier guided them through the forests, showing them the specimens they needed for their comprehensive work.

All his life, as he watched the thicket shrink, Rosier worked to educate people, to convince them of its value. When settlers began hacking their way into this area in the 1820s, or gave up and went around, it spread over 3 million acres. Today, twelve separate units compose the 85,000-acre Big Thicket National Preserve.

Immediately after entering town on Farm Road 770, look for a Big Thicket Museum sign pointing to the left.

Saratoga

The museum offers a slide presentation and exhibits that introduce the newcomer to the thicket, the biological crossroads of North America. Four of America's five kinds of carnivorous plants, more than forty varieties of orchids, and one thousand types of fern and fungi can be found in the thicket. Bears and panthers once roamed these forests along with deers, wolves, bobcats, beavers, raccoons, possums, foxes, and many other small mammals. Snakes abound, including five poisonous species.

The museum gift shop offers a large selection of wildlife books. The museum hours have undergone some changes and it is best to check ahead for correct times; call 713/274-2971. To arrange private tours, call 713/385-3230 or write to P.O. Box 198, Saratoga, TX 77585. Additional Big Thicket information is available from the National Park Service, P.O. Box 7408, Beaumont, TX 77706.

Return to Farm Road 770 and turn left through Saratoga.

About 1867, when an Alabama Indian told settlers of an oil spring near here, Fletcher Cotton remembered that his hogs returned from a certain area with a slick, glossy substance on them. Soon, he found a bubbling, stinking slough. He drove a pipe into the spring and oil came up through the pipe. Area residents built a bathhouse and named the spot Saratoga after the well-known New York spa. Patients suffering with ulcers and arthritis came here, but the "cures" did not "take" for long and the popularity slowly ebbed. By the turn of the century, the Big Thicket had about taken over Saratoga again.

After Spindletop, prospectors looking for salt domes, places where oil oozed from springs and from crawfish holes, combed the country. When the speculators came to Saratoga, they paid $85,000 for 160 acres, and a 790-foot gusher came in a few weeks later. Saratoga went through another boom with all the accompanying problems. The oil companies flared off escaping gases, which lit up the surrounding forest and scared off the game. Salt water

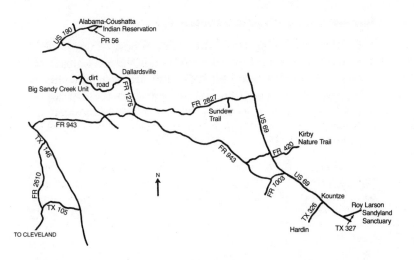

and black scum ran into pastures and ruined bayous. Local residents did not appreciate the intrusion and watch-
men had to be hired to guard the rigs. One crew found
their horses, their only means of transportation, smeared
with barn paint. The oil prosperity also passed, and Saratoga now sits on the fringe of the Lance Rosier Unit of
the Big Thicket, a sleepy shadow of a once-bustling
community.

*Drive to Hardin on Farm Road 770 and turn left on Texas
326 for the drive into Kountze.*

Several possibilities for exploring the Big Thicket are
available. The Roy Larson Sandyland Sanctuary offers the
best example of arid sandylands. The Kirby Nature Trail
goes through the heaviest concentration of plant variety
in the preserve. The Sundew Trail explores a wetland savannah (covered with low vegetation) in the Hickory
Creek Unit.

*Enter Kountze on Texas 326 and turn right on U.S. Highway
69. Drive 2.8 miles and turn left on Texas 327. In a little over
two miles, cross a creek, continue to the crest of the hill,
and turn left at the entrance to the Roy Larson Sandyland
Sanctuary.*

Roy Larson Sandyland Sanctuary

Six miles of walking trails through the best example of arid sandylands are offered here by the Nature Conservancy. A hiker can stand with one foot in a bog and the other on sand and cactus. The facility is open daily. No admission charge. If advance reservations are made, a naturalist will conduct group hikes. Write P.O. Box 909, Silsbee, TX 77565, or call 713/385-4135.

Upon leaving the sanctuary, turn right on Texas 327; turn right again on U.S. Highway 69 and return to Kountze. Continue north on U.S. Highway 69 about 7.7 miles. Turn right at the intersection with Farm Road 420. It is 2.5 miles to the

visitors' information center and the beginning of the Kirby Nature Trail, part of the Turkey Creek Unit.

Kirby Nature Trail

Trails here are 1.7 to 2.4 miles long. A large variety of plant life is visible, including species that grow as a result of flooding of nearby creeks. A booklet is available for identifying common plants. Do not disturb bee, wasp, or fire ant nests. A nine-mile trail with even more plant diversity is provided in the northern half of the Turkey Creek Unit. Ask at the information center for details. Ask for a listing of regularly scheduled, free ranger-guided tours via canoe and hiking trails. The visitor center is open spring through fall, daily, 10:00 A.M. to 4:30 P.M.; closed Tuesday and Wednesday in winter. Hiking is permitted even when the information center is closed.

This nature trail was named for John Henry Kirby, the lumber king who became a legend in his own time and earned the title of "Father of Industrial Texas." A lawyer, business executive, banker, and oil operator, Kirby employed about 16,500 in his various lumbering interests during the peak years of 1910–1920. As president of the National Lumber Manufacturers' Association, he had a part in the development of U.S. lumber standards. Skilled in maintaining good personnel relations, he avoided labor problems in the companies he headed.

Although logging mills started growing up in forest communities in 1870, poor transportation held the market to local use. Logs were floated down the Sabine and Neches rivers to shingle mills in Orange and Beaumont. With the coming of the railroads and roads, lumbering income increased by the turn of the century to $16 million annually, or four times what it had been in 1880.

This rapidly expanding industry, the largest in the state until oil took over in 1929, brought employment to the thicket, but it also brought strife and unhappiness. The forests were stripped bare, replantings were cut too soon, the wildlife disappeared, and by the late 1930s it began to look as if the lumber business had seen its day.

Conservation measures began with utilization of what had been considered waste material—tops and branches were used for newsprint—and careful replantings were begun. After years of untiring efforts of individuals, government and elected officials, and such organizations as the Big Thicket Association, the lumbering business has become a responsible industry that works alongside conservationists, who recognize the value of preserving natural resources. A later book, *Texas Auto Trails: The Northeast*, will include five of the fifteen woodland trails selected by the Texas Forestry Association for tourists who want to explore the natural beauty of the forest. The trails circle through land owned by individuals or companies who make their living from lumber.

Retrace the route on Farm Road 420 to U.S. Highway 69. Turn right and drive 0.6 mile to a road marked only by a T-intersection highway sign. Turn left for the trip directly to the Alabama-Coushatta Indian Reservation or drive about 6.5 miles to another Big Thicket trail by continuing north on U.S. Highway 69 for 4.9 miles to Farm Road 2827. Turn left 0.6 mile and left again for 0.4 mile on a dirt road to the entrance to the Sundew Trail.

Sundew Trail of the Hickory Creek Unit

Bluestem grass grows among the longleaf pines. Sundews and orchids, as well as dogwoods and yuccas, line this trail.

Return on the dirt road to Farm Road 2827, turn right, and then turn right again on U.S. Highway 69. Drive for 4.9 miles to the T intersection. Turn right. This road is paved, but rough. It is 3 miles to a stop sign at the intersection with Farm Road 943. Turn right. It is about 7.5 miles to an area called the Kaiser Burnout.

The Big Thicket always offered hiding places for fugitives. Many of the early settlers in this region came to Texas to escape bankruptcy, criminal charges, and a myriad of other problems. Indians found this almost impenetrable thicket a good safe harbor. During the Civil War, men in this area who did not want to get in the fight hid in the thicket and became known as Jayhawkers. They agreed with Sam Houston, who fought against secession and even resigned the governorship because he refused to "pull out of the Union."

According to Lance Rosier, many of the people around here were very poor and they did not want to fight for the blacks. Another person expressed it differently: it was "a rich man's war and a poor man's fight." Rosier said the Jayhawkers had plenty of game and fish. Their families hid ground corn wrapped in doeskins in the forks of trees beside a pond near the Jayhawkers' camp. That pond is still marked Doeskin Pond on county maps. Jayhawkers collected lots of honey and hid it for their families to pick up and sell in Beaumont for tobacco and coffee. So much honey was left at one site that it became known as Honey Island and is still a community south of here.

The Confederate government did not ignore the Jayhawkers. Believing that their presence in the thicket caused unrest among the soldiers, troops were sent in regularly to search out the draft dodgers, but without much luck. One account says that a Captain Kaiser received a large sum of money to get the Jayhawkers out of the thicket. Stories vary, but apparently Kaiser did set fire to the thicket in this area to drive out the hidden men. No one died and very few were caught, but the fire destroyed a very large portion of the woodland. Some of the tales say ominously that the trees never grew back.

Turn right on Farm Road 1276. Continue 13.5 miles to U.S. Highway 190.

Along this route, note the small blue signs marking the Alabama Trace, the route of an old Indian road used in pre-Republic days by white settlers. It ran from a village on the Trinity River through this area and north toward Nacogdoches where it connected with the old San Antonio Road. Markers noting the Liberty-Nacogdoches Road indicate the route used originally by the Spanish from the mouth of the Trinity, near present Anahuac, to

Nacogdoches. Later, Alabamas and Coushattas used this trace.

Turn right on U.S. Highway 190 and drive 4.8 miles to the Indian reservation entrance on the right, Park Road 56.

Alabama-Coushatta Indian Reservation

These 4,600 acres are a special part of Texas. Five hundred Alabama-Coushatta Indians, descendants of peace-loving tribes who quietly moved west before the advancing white settlers, call this site home. Despite the disappearance of other parts of the Big Thicket, this portion remains in its natural state because the Indians believe that, if they protect the forest, the forest will protect them.

The Alabama and Coushatta are separate tribes who have lived near each other for hundreds of years. Their languages, although never written down, are similar. Howard N. Martin, in *Myths and Folktales of the Alabama-Coushatta Indians of Texas*, reveals many of their tribal stories, which have been handed down through generations. The Indians tell that both tribes were made from the clay in a big cave where they lived. When they decided to go to the surface of the earth, they found a huge tree at the mouth of the cave. The Alabamas and Coushattas left the cave on opposite sides of a root of this big tree. This story intends to explain why they differ somewhat in speech but have remained close neighbors.

History first takes note of the Alabamas in 1541 when Hernando de Soto, a Spanish explorer, attacked an Alabama village in present northwest Mississippi. Later that year he visited a Coushatta village on the Tennessee River. By 1717, both tribes were on the upper Alabama River and had built the French Fort Toulouse near present Montgomery, Alabama. By the early 1800s, both tribes had migrated into East Texas and lived in small, scattered villages. Although the Alabama-Coushattas remained neutral during the Texas war for independence, settlers streaming east in the Runaway Scrape reported that members of the tribe fed them and offered assistance crossing the rain-swollen Trinity River.

In 1854 the state purchased 1,110 acres of this land for a permanent home for the Indians. Two years later, Governor Hardin Runnels asked the Alabama-Coushatta to move to the Brazos Reservation on the Brazos River in present Young County. After visiting the site, the Indians

insisted they did not wish to move. A series of incidents followed that shocked Governor Runnels into changing his mind. Caddo, Anadarko, Waco, and Tonkawa Indians lived on the reservation for protection from the warring Comanches. From fifty to one hundred reservation Indians served as scouts for the Rangers and this stirred anger among the wild Indians and the anti-Indian whites, who wanted the reservation land. Reservation Indians were blamed for various thefts. Finally, eighteen Indians were attacked as they slept and eight were found dead in their blankets. A few months later, as anger mounted, a group of whites came onto the reserve, killed a squaw, and scalped an old man. When the Indians retaliated, they lost their chief and killed two white men. Afterward, the reservation was disbanded and the Indians moved to Indian Territory (present Oklahoma) among the peaceable Wichita Indians. It was not long until a raiding party of Comanches swooped down on the village and almost wiped out both tribes. Governor Runnels experienced such horror at the treatment of the Indians that he decided not to ask the Alabama and Coushatta to give up their land and move into territory where he said they might "be indiscriminately slaughtered, for no other cause than that the Creator has made them Indians."

In 1928 the reservation was enlarged to its present size. Governor Price Daniel's administration allocated $40,000 for construction of the museum, restaurant, and arts and crafts shop. A few years later, the Alabama-Coushatta opened the reservation to the public. Their goal is self-determination, and funds from tourism are used for social services, such as medical assistance and educational loans.

Travelers will enjoy Indian-guided tours of the Big Thicket, either on a miniature train using a narrow-gauge railroad or on a bus with a plexiglass top. The "open" mode of travel enables the best view of the towering pines and other trees, which are so huge they have attained national championship ranking. Plants bloom in profusion. Redbuds and azaleas grow beneath towering magnolias. The guide skillfully maneuvers the bus along the one-way paved road while he points out the state champion water hickory, the iron wood tree from which Indians made their bows, the toothache (tickle tongue) tree, and the yellow-billed sap sucker. One tour guide has an alligator friend who reportedly lumbers from his watery den when he hears the bus horn.

The Indian Country Tour is a historical trip that includes a re-created Indian homesite. There are no tepees here. The Alabama-Coushatta adopted the ways of the whites, including European dress, log homes, and the use of guns, well before 1836.

A walking tour through the Living Indian Village in-

cludes work areas where reservation Indians are actually weaving baskets from the longleaf pine, making bead jewelry, grinding corn from which they make sofkee (a kind of corn soup), and preparing fry bread. Indians also weave moss blankets on hand looms and make arrowheads from pieces of flint.

Visitors sit in a four-sided dance arbor, similar to those used for generations by these tribes, and watch a variety of Indian dances. When the Alabama-Coushatta opened the reservation to the public, they had to travel to Oklahoma to renew their dancing skills because dancing had been stopped in earlier years by ardent missionaries.

The gift shop has a wide selection of Indian lore from this and other reservations. The longleaf pine baskets are the most elegant gifts. Some of the baskets have been woven around pine cones. The pottery made here and hand etched is individually signed and dated.

Beyond the Sundown, a drama by Kermit Hunter, portrays the Indians' involvement in the Texas war for independence. The Alabama-Coushatta have a long history of myths, folklore, and belief in animal deities that has been incorporated into the dances. This professional production includes a cast of fifty Indian, Hispanic, and Anglo performers recruited from all over the United States. The stage and auditorium present a permanent outdoor facility, one of the finest in the country. *Beyond the Sundown* is presented during the summer, 8:30 P.M., except Sunday. There is a separate charge for this production.

Spring and fall weekday admission fees are less than weekend charges. Prices include all facilities except the *Beyond the Sundown* production. Liberal group rates are available; call 713/563-4391, ext. 222. The reservation is open Monday through Saturday, 10:00 A.M. to 6:00 P.M., Sunday 12:30 P.M. to 6:00 P.M., June through August; during fall and spring, closes at 5:00 P.M. and closed Monday; closed to the public December through February. Campers will find excellent facilities here among 120-foot pines towering beside a 26-acre lake stocked with game fish. Complete recreational vehicle hookups are available as well as primitive sites for backpackers. Camping is offered here year-round; call 713/563-4391, ext. 222.

Visitors leave the reservation with a sense of appreciation for the Indians' heritage and their forest home.

From Park Road 56, turn left on U.S. Highway 190. Drive to Farm Road 1276 and turn left for about 9.6 miles to the northern edge of Dallardsville. Either continue south to Farm Road 943 and turn right for the drive to Cleveland or turn right here on an unpaved road for an 11-mile drive through an undeveloped portion of the Big Thicket.

Big Sandy Creek Unit

This preserve includes 14,300 acres of rolling hills and sandy soil. The varied animal and plant life includes beech and dogwood trees. Hiking paths, horseback riding trails, and backpack camping sites are planned for the future. Until the unit is opened, stay in the car and do not venture into the thicket.

After 3.5 miles continue straight at the T intersection.

Note the signs pointing out the Liberty-Nacogdoches Road and the Alabama Trace mentioned earlier. An actual road to the left still exists from this Alabama route.

At the four-way intersection, turn left.

This road is graded with room for meeting oncoming autos, but the sand may be loose and deceptively slippery. At the second Alabama Trace sign, stop and look to the right. The old trail is clearly visible where the vines have not grown back completely. These routes are seen more easily from the air.

The cattle guard marks the end of the preserve. Continue to the stop sign at Farm Road 943, turn right, and rejoin the trail. Drive 9.2 miles to Texas 146 and turn left. Travel 2.2 miles to Farm Road 2610 and turn right. This road will join Texas 105. Continue west.

Cleveland

Sitting on the fringe of Sam Houston National Forest with its 140-mile Lone Star Hiking Trail, Cleveland offers an area museum, the home base for an artist making a name for himself in Houston, and the internationally known Hilltop Herb Farm.

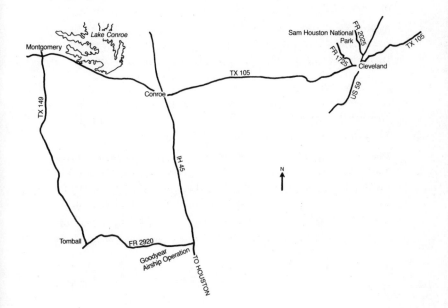

Enter Cleveland on Texas 105. At the intersection with Farm Road 321, do not turn right with the highway but continue straight on Bonham Street to the Austin Memorial Library in the second block.

This facility houses a small genealogy collection, census films, and a museum complete with area antiques and rotating collections. It is open Monday and Wednesday through Friday, 9:30 A.M. to 5:00 P.M.; Tuesday, noon to 8:00 P.M.; Saturday, 9:30 A.M. to 12:30 P.M.; closed Sunday. No admission charge.

Continue to the end of the block. Turn right on Dallas Street for three blocks to U.S. Highway 59, Washington Avenue. Turn left. It is 0.6 mile beyond the Cleveland city limits sign to the Ronny Wells Studio, just beyond the Biggs Mobile Home sign.

Wells displays original watercolors, limited-edition prints, and bronzes, with price ranges that bespeak an artist who is much in demand. His country farm scenes tug at the roots of folks with rural backgrounds. Open 9:00 A.M. to 3:00 P.M., Monday through Friday; closed Saturday and Sunday; call 713/592-4579.

For travelers who are interested, the entrance to the Lone Star Hiking Trail is seven miles north of Cleveland on Farm Road 2025, which is a left turn off U.S. Highway 59.

Several short trails loop off the longer one. For further information, write San Jacinto District Office, Sam Houston National Forest, P.O. Box 1818, Cleveland, TX 77327, or call 713/592-6462.

Return to Cleveland on U.S. Highway 59 and turn west on Texas 105 for the drive to the Hilltop Herb Farm. It is 0.9 mile to Farm Road 1725. Turn right and drive 10.4 miles through rolling country into the edge of the Sam Houston National Forest. Hilltop Herb Farm is on the left, at the top of a hill, of course. Drive through the gate and park at the rear of the property.

Hilltop Herb Farm

This is a wonderland for gardeners, plant enthusiasts, country store shoppers, herbalists, and lovers of fine food. In 1957 Jim and Madalene Hill retired to this quiet, unpolluted spot, planning to raise a few chickens and gladiolas for the market and herbs for their own pleasure. Things didn't work out somehow. Word spread about the herbs, and today they are shipped all over the United States and to many countries abroad. A renovated shed has been converted into a store where Madalene Hill's own creations of lime tarragon jelly, cucumber marmalade, and pickled mushrooms are on sale along with a vast array of other delicious things to eat and smell and select for special gifts. The chicken brooder, a huge thing, has been converted into a restaurant called the Garden Room that will seat two hundred. It looks like a giant greenhouse, filled with trees, vines, and a profusion of hanging baskets. The menus are specially prepared around the fruits and vegetables that are in season and include such delights as vermouth-flavored bean soup, diced artichoke hearts bathing in a creamy basil sauce, homemade bread always, and a tranquilitea made with eighteen herbs. Part of the luncheon fare includes Madalene Hill's informal discussion about the herbs she uses in the recipes and guided tours of the vegetable gardens. The gardens are laid out with herbs to test the theory that companion planting provides effective insect control. Guides are available to explain the lores and legends about the herbs in the English Garden, the Wheel of Thyme, the Grey Garden, and the Cutting Garden. And, it all smells so good.

Guests are welcome to bring a picnic and eat on the grounds. The meals served in the Garden Room are not for the harried traveler, eager to move on to the next stop. Reservations must be made three to six weeks in advance and a deposit is required. Dress is casual, but the meal is expensive. Plan to spend time here. The prices are set to encourage a leisurely stay and full enjoyment.

The farm is open year-round, Tuesday through Sat-

urday, 10:00 A.M. to 4:00 P.M.; Sunday, noon to 4:00
P.M.; closed Monday and most holidays. Meals are not
served from mid-July through August and mid-December
through February. Luncheon is served Tuesday, Wednesday, and Thursday at noon; dinner is served Saturday,
7:00 P.M. This is not really a public restaurant; diners are
guests here. No gratuities, please, and no smoking. Write
P.O. Box 1734, Cleveland, TX 77327; call 713/592-5859.
Sometimes space is available, so don't hesitate to enquire
on the spur of the moment.

*Turn right from the farm onto Farm Road 1725. Return to
Texas 105 and turn right.*

Conroe

This is a sprawling resort community, nestled beside towering pines, rolling hills, and the 22,000-acre Lake Conroe.
Sawmills dotted the landscape as early as the 1850s. Then
oil came in the 1930s, with a strike of such proportion that
the field became the third largest in the United States.
Still, the beauty has been retained and visitors will find a
variety of activities that take advantage of the natural
surroundings.

*Drive into town on Texas 105. After crossing the railroad
track, turn left immediately on North Pacific Street. Drive
three blocks to Collins Street and turn right. Turn right again
at the next corner, North Main Street.*

The Crighton Theater is on the right in the first block.
Built in 1934 at the end of the vaudeville days and the
beginning of Conroe's oil boom, the Crighton served for
years as a movie house. Restored, it is now the theater for
the performing arts in Conroe. The Little Theatre of Conroe, Inc., provides a full yearly schedule of performances.
Call 713/273-1810 for ticket and production information.

*Drive two blocks back to Texas 105, West Phillips Street, and
turn left. Follow Texas 105 through town. Before driving
under U.S. Interstate 45, stop at the Conroe Visitor and Convention Bureau on the right for details about camping, recre-*

ation, public boat launch and rental facilities, and fishing. Continue west on Texas 105 about twelve miles to the entrance to Walden on Lake Conroe.

This is a resort community of homes and condominiums that accept overnight guests. Walden visitors are entitled to all the privileges available to fulltime residents, including boat slips; fishing; sailing and ski boat rental, complete with driver, gas, and skis; a cruise on the fifty-five–foot party boat; bicycle rental for trips along the eight-and-a-half-mile Walden shoreline; and access to the championship golf course, the Walden tennis center, and either of two excellent restaurants. Meeting rooms that accommodate from twenty to one hundred, or a combined capacity of four hundred, are also available. The woods have a good jogging and hiking trail and the location is breathtaking. For information or reservations, call direct from Houston, 353-9737, or 713/582-6441.

Continue west on Texas 105 for 2.6 miles.

Montgomery

This tiny town served as the county seat and a thriving trade center in the mid-1800s. Many of the homes built in the days when cotton and lumber reigned are still here, maintained in excellent condition. The impressive home on the right, immediately after entering town, is Cathalorri, originally built in 1854. This is the birthplace of Gray I. Morriss, one of the American Legion's founders.

Turn right at the flashing light, Texas 149, Liberty Street.

The building on the right on the next corner is an old law office. In 1845, Nathaniel Hart Davis built this structure, which served as his living quarters until 1851 when he married and built the house next door. The logs that he used for the original portion of the home, nearest the law office, had been cut in 1831 and given to him as payment for legal services.

Continue to the next block.

The brick structure on the left, built in 1908, served as one of the first state banks in Texas. An antique shop occupies the building. The Country Store, across the street, is operated by the Historical Society and carries merchandise ranging from antiques to garage sale specialties. The proceeds are used in restoration projects. The store is open Friday, 1:00 P.M. to 5:00 P.M.; Saturday, 9:00 A.M. to 5:00 P.M.; closed Sunday through Thursday.

The Historical Society also sponsors the annual Montgomery Trek, a historical homes tour, the third Sunday in April unless that day is Easter, in which case the trek is held on the fourth Sunday. Many Montgomery homes are open, displaying large collections of antiques and pioneer artifacts.

Drive to the end of the next block and turn right on Clepper Street.

This is the old courthouse square, laid out in 1837 when the county was created and Montgomery was selected as the seat of government. After the county seat moved to Conroe in 1889, the old iron calaboose served as a drying-out place for drunks and a holding tank for prisoners awaiting a trip to the Conroe jail.

Turn right again at the end of the block on Maiden Street. Drive one block and turn left on Mason Street.

Homewood is the house that sits on this corner. Built in 1887, it has changed little except for the addition of a kitchen wing.

Turn right at the next corner, Prairie Street.

The house immediately on the left is Lazy Oaks, built in 1876 for the attorney Nathaniel Hart Davis, who constructed the log house a few blocks over. Apparently his law practice thrived in the thirty-one years after he erected and lived in that little office building.

Turn right at the next corner, Caroline Street, drive five blocks to Eugenia Street, and turn right.

The home on the left, Magnolia, was built in 1854. In 1868 a widower bought the property, complete with furnishings, as a home in which to raise his large brood of children.

Before turning right at the corner, College Street, note the rear of the home on the right.

It is obvious that this house was constructed in several sections. The back portion, erected between 1851 and 1854, was purchased by a Baptist preacher in 1854. He died during a revival meeting and his widow continued to live in the home.

Just around the corner, enclosed behind the picket fence that adjoins the Baptist preacher's home, is the Methodist parsonage, purchased by the congregation in 1886, but this is not the first parsonage in town. In 1842 the Methodists built the first Protestant parsonage in Texas near the present church site.

Turn right at the next corner, Pond Street, drive to the high-way, and turn right. It is less than 0.5 mile to Mrs. Winslow's Antiques.

This shop has a reputation for quality and quantity that has spread for miles. Open Saturday and Sunday or by appointment; call 713/597-4266.

Return to town on Texas 105; turn right on Texas 149.

Tomball

Like its giant neighbor to the south, Tomball is growing by leaps and bounds. However, the small-town atmosphere lingers and the pace here is slower.

Enter Tomball on Texas 149. Turn left on Farm Road 2920, Main Street, and drive to North Pine Street. Turn left for about four blocks to the Magdalene Charlton Memorial Museum.

This complex includes a home built about 1860 that now serves as a museum, housing the Charlton collection of antiques of the high Victorian period. Next door, the 1905 Trinity Lutheran Church retains the original furnishings. A huge barn houses farm implements and a one-horse cotton gin, which produced a bale of cotton each day when it operated one hundred years ago. An old doctor's office used for fifty years by a local physician retains early-day medical instruments and parts of a human skeleton. The facility is open March through September, Friday, Saturday, and Sunday. Hours may vary; call ahead, 713/255-2148 or 713/351-7222. No admission charge.

Return on Pine Street to Main Street, Farm Road 2920, turn left and drive to U.S. Interstate 45. Turn right on the access road for 1.2 miles to the Goodyear Airship Operation.

This "blimp" offers flights, by invitation only, as a public relations project for Goodyear customers. This is the same airship that is visible at night displaying signs and lights supporting various charities or simply advertising Goodyear. It is possible at certain times to either watch from the observation area or walk up to the airship. Mondays are usually nonflying days and visitors may approach the ship. Weekdays, 8:00 A.M. to 10:00 A.M., are usually good times for a close-up view. At other times visitors may watch from the observation area. From May 1 through November 1, the airship is usually gone, touring the country on different assignments, which include football games. There is no charge for viewing this lighter-than-air craft.

Take U.S. Interstate 45 into Houston.

This concludes the Big Thicket trail through an area of Texas blessed by natural resources and beauty—a paradox of remote wilderness from which economic giants have emerged.

4. Heritage Trail

This tour goes through the heart of Texas' early Anglo
settlement. Stephen F. Austin's Old Three Hundred staked
out this land. As the Mexican government required, Austin
brought pioneers who held high moral character and
intended to stay and improve the land, not drain it of
its resources and move on. It is evident as the traveler
crosses Austin's original territory, which sprawled over
200,000 acres from east of the Brazos to beyond the Colorado River, that the colonists and their descendants have
held true to the original intention.

A twist of fate, the death of Stephen F. Austin's father,
Moses, plunged the twenty-seven–year–old bachelor Stephen into settling three hundred families in the vast wilderness of Texas. It is fortunate for Texas that Stephen,
unlike his impetuous and often belligerent father, had the
disposition of a diplomat: deliberate, patient, and tactful.

Moses Austin had lost his wealth in a series of misfortunes, climaxed by the depression of 1818. He set his goals
on colonizing the Spanish province of Texas, traveled to
San Antonio, and finally secured permission to settle families in the new land. Before he could complete the arrangements, he died of pneumonia and his son rather
reluctantly took charge. The first families came to Texas,
which was part of the newly independent Mexico, under
the promise that each man would receive 640 acres for
himself, 320 for his wife, 160 for each child, and 80 for
each slave. Settlers began arriving immediately after Austin published his proposal in late 1821.

*Drive west from Houston's Loop 610 for thirty miles on U.S.
Interstate 10 to Brookshire. Take the Farm Road 359 exit.
Drive north into town to the traffic light at U.S. Highway 90
and turn left. Turn left again at the next traffic light, Cooper
Street.*

Brookshire

The Waller County Museum is on the next corner (Cooper and Fifth streets). The museum, lodged in an unusual house built by an Armenian doctor, won the 1980 Texas Heritage Council Award. The displays here depict the progress of the county from the earliest days of colonization.

Dr. Paul Donigan had the round-front home built about 1905. He wanted a cellar and did not let the problem of water seepage stand in his way. He had the home's first level built above the ground and enclosed with exterior walls of pressed tin. He used part of his "cellar" for his medical practice. The museum has enclosed the ground floor in glass and opened a gift shop there. The facility is open Monday through Friday, 9:00 A.M. to 3:00 P.M.; by appointment on Saturday and Sunday; call 713/934-2826.

Turn right on Fifth Street and drive three blocks to the end of the street.

The Cotton Gin Restaurant is just to the right. This is a restored gin, complete with a red tin roof. Gin stands separate the dining rooms, and the bar is where the gin press used to be. The restaurant is open Monday through

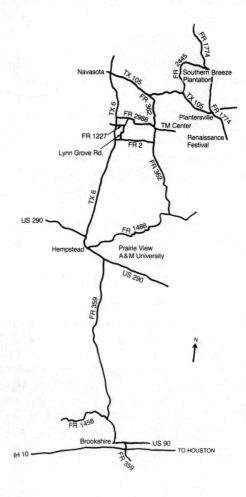

Thursday, 5:00 P.M. to 10:00 P.M.; Friday and Saturday,
5:00 P.M. to 11:00 P.M.; closed Sunday.

Turn left from the Cotton Gin parking lot, drive to the corner,
which is U.S. Highway 90. Cross the highway and continue
north on Farm Road 359.

This is plantation country, heart of the Old Three
Hundred settlement where landholders controlled vast
acreages and the slave labor to produce enormous cotton
crops. Before the outbreak of the Civil War, unrest grew
among local citizens over stories circulated about a slave
uprising. Since the black population in the area outnum-
bered the white, a group of white men formed a vigilance
committee in 1860. "Suspicious-acting" people were
brought in for questioning. If they could prove their inno-
cence, they were released. If not, they were held to "await
the judgement by the community."

Although the property is not open to the public, two
plantations with interesting histories lay west of Farm
Road 359, between here and the Brazos River. The Sunny-
side Plantation stretched west from Farm Road 359 and
Farm Road 529. In 1846, Norris Wright Cuney was born
there in slave quarters. He proved to be such a bright
young man that he was sent in 1859 to Wyle Street School
for Negroes in Pittsburgh, Pennsylvania. After the Civil
War, he returned to Texas, settled in Galveston, studied
law, and began a wharf contracting company.

An eloquent speaker, Cuney became active in the
Texas Union League, urging blacks to get involved in politics and to join the Republican Party. He organized the
Negro Longshoreman's Association in 1870 and stayed involved in local politics even while he worked nationally.
As chairman of the Texas delegation, he began attending
the Republican Party National Conventions in 1872. After
twenty-four years the Republican Party in Texas broke
Cuney's power in 1896, a move that effectively deprived
blacks of a place in Texas politics until the 1960s.

The site of Bernardo, one of five plantation homes
built by Jared E. Groce, a wealthy planter, lies west of

Farm Road 359 and Farm Road 1887. It is here that General Sam Houston camped for two weeks, training his little army before marching on toward San Jacinto. This is also the site of Groce's Ferry, an important early crossing on the Brazos River.

Groce's holdings in present Waller and Grimes counties amounted to baronial estates. It is said that when Groce came to Texas in early 1822, with ninety slaves and fifty wagons loaded with equipment, he also had men driving mules, sheep, cattle, and hogs. He received a land grant from the Mexican government totaling 8,856 acres, making him the largest landholder at the time. Groce and a few other planters started commercial cotton growing in these rich bottom lands along the Brazos River.

Bernardo Plantation became the social gathering place of the early years in Austin's Colony. Groce provided a bachelor hall in which guests were housed, separate buildings for the kitchens, a house for the doctor who cared for the slaves, and a nursery for the children of the field workers. He kept hounds for hunting, provided tutors for the children, and offered dinner, dancing, and chess for guests.

From the intersection of Farm Road 359 and U.S. Highway 290, it is about three miles east to Prairie View A&M University.

Prairie View A&M University

Texas' first state-supported institution of higher learning for black youth began in Kirby Hall, the palatial home on the 1,400-acre Alta Vista Plantation, which originally belonged to Colonel Jack Kirby. Four hundred slaves worked the surrounding fields. Kirby's son Jared inherited the plantation, and after his death in 1865 his widow, Helen Marr Kirby (later dean of women at the University of Texas), operated a girls' boarding school in the home. For the next seventy years after the college for black youths opened in 1876, the president of Texas A&M College in

Bryan supervised the head of the black school, who carried the title of "principal."

Drive west toward Hempstead on U.S. Highway 290.

The deep sand hills here enabled early farmers to turn the area into a watermelon paradise, and the need to get the fine crops to market prompted the establishment of Hempstead in 1857. The town lots were given to officials of the Houston and Texas Central Railroad as an inducement to get the line through here. As many as eighteen hundred carloads of watermelons were shipped out in one season. Farming is still good and the watermelons still entice people from all over the state. Fruit stands line the highways in season.

At this junction the traveler has alternative routes from which to choose. The twenty-one–mile route continues into Hempstead, turns right on Texas 6, and proceeds directly to Navasota. The other route, a forty-two–mile scenic jaunt, takes farm roads through bluebonnet country. There is an apiary not far off the road where local honey is available and another side trip to what local folk call the "Taj Mahal," being constructed way out in the country by proponents of Transcendental Meditation.

The scenic route begins on the eastern edge of Hempstead. Turn right on Farm Road 1488, which is three miles west of the intersection with Farm Road 359 (the route from Brookshire), or drive into Hempstead and return later to the scenic trail.

There are two very different and excellent eateries in Hempstead. One is a tearoom operating in a restored home with antiques for sale. The other is a barbeque stand, which earned a spot in *Texas Monthly* as one of the top ten barbeque places in the state.

After entering Hempstead, do not turn right with the highways at the traffic light. Continue on Austin Street three blocks to Farm Road 159, Thirteenth Street. Turn left.

Hempstead

The Ahrenbeck-Urban Home (1203 Thirteenth) is on land that originally belonged to Jared Groce, the wealthy planter and one of the Old Three Hundred. This structure was built about 1872 according to some penciled notations found on boards during the recent restoration.

Across the street and down one block, the Old House Restaurant and Tea Room (1346 Thirteenth) is well known locally for home cooking, baked goods, and antiques. Open Wednesday, Thursday, Friday, 11:00 A.M. to 1:30 P.M.; closed Saturday through Tuesday.

Return on Thirteenth Street to Austin Street, turn right, and drive to the traffic light at the intersection with U.S. Highway 290 and Texas 6, Tenth Street. Turn left and drive about four blocks to the Swan Country House Barbeque on the right.

The smoky scent of barbeque and the testimonials proclaiming the high quality of the food, which have been written on newsprint and are hung shoulder-to-shoulder from the rafters, create the ambience of an era long past. Orders are also available for take out. Open daily 9:00 A.M. to 9:00 P.M.

The short route to Navasota continues north on Texas 6. For the scenic trail, turn left on U.S. Highway 290 and head east of town to the intersection with Farm Road 1488, Second Street. Turn left.

The old Liendo Plantation, which is private property, begins in about 2.5 miles off to the right. In 1873, perhaps the most unusual and nonconforming couple in early Texas—Scotch philosopher and scientist Dr. Edmund Montgomery and his famous wife, German sculptor Elisabet Ney—bought the property. "Miss Ney," as she was called even after her marriage to Dr. Montgomery, had always been beautiful, talented, and self-willed. She shocked her family by going to Munich at the age of nineteen to study art. She soon made a name for herself as a sculptor, but she continued to scorn convention by her open affair with young Dr. Montgomery. She undertook many important commissions, even moving into a studio at the royal palace in Munich to execute a full-length statue of Ludwig II, the mad king who almost financially ruined Bavaria before he was assassinated.

After Miss Ney and Dr. Montgomery married, it is said that her relations with him and her political activities caused the couple to decide that the United States offered a better environment for them. After living about two years in a German colony in Georgia, they moved to Texas and bought Liendo the following year.

The nineteen years that they lived here became the only period in Miss Ney's life when she was artistically inactive. She devoted the time to rearing her children and trying to help the neighborhood blacks, but neither venture was very successful. The blacks ridiculed her, one child died, and the story is told that fear of spreading an epidemic prompted Miss Ney to cremate his body in the family fireplace. The other child separated himself from his mother because of her strict rules and the embarrassment he felt over the community talk generated by her life-style and behavior.

Miss Ney received a commission to execute the statues of Stephen F. Austin and Sam Houston for the Texas Exhibit at the 1893 World's Fair. (Both statues stand today in the state capitol in Austin.) She moved to Austin, built a studio, and lived there until her death in 1907. She continued to visit Dr. Montgomery periodically at Liendo, and she was buried here among the oak trees they had planted. Sometime after her death, friends organized the Texas Fine Arts Association, purchased her Austin studio, and developed it into a museum of her work. Dr. Montgomery became a leading local citizen, serving as a county commissioner and helping to found Prairie View College.

Continue on Farm Road 1488 until it joins Farm Road 362; when the roads separate again, turn left and follow Farm Road 362 north about 8.8 miles to Farm Road 2. Travelers wishing to detour via the apiary should turn left for 3.7 miles to Lynn Grove Road. Turn right and drive one mile to Weaver's Apiaries, Inc.

The business is on the right, but there is no sign. It's unnecessary for Weaver's to advertise, for it is one of the largest producers of queen bees in the world with offices in Hawaii and customers all over the world. This operation began in 1888 when Z. S. Weaver and his bride, Florence, received ten hives of honeybees as a wedding gift. Z. S. was a farmer and merchant, but he became so involved with his bees that they became his main source of income. One son joined him in 1916 and another son in 1925. They began producing Italian and Caucasian queen bees. In 1978 two grandsons and one great-grandson were operating the business.

The queen and her workers are carefully lifted by their wings and placed in tiny wooden boxes, which are then slipped into envelopes. Over one thousand a day are shipped out of here each April and May during the "queen bee season." Weaver's also packages bees for starting new hives and sells bees for artificial swarms. Bee hives are distributed along the back roads through the surrounding counties. When the honey begins coming in from June through August, a machine extracts the honey from the comb, a process that is handled here in these nondescript buildings. Visitors are welcome and will be shown the facilities if time permits. If travelers want a tour, it is best to call ahead to see if one of the Weavers is available; call 713/825-2312. Honey is available for sale in the office, usually open Monday through Friday, 8:00 A.M. to 5:00 P.M. No need to call ahead for that.

Continue north one mile on Lynn Grove Road.

Houston Capital of the Age of Enlightenment

This is another point where the tourist may choose to turn left on Farm Road 1227, go one mile to Texas 6, and continue into Navasota or turn right and follow the trail to the new academy building for the Houston Capital of the Age of Enlightenment. It will be easy to see why area residents refer to the gold-domed facility as the "Taj Mahal" or the "White House."

Turn right on Farm Road 2988 for 3.6 miles to a stop sign at the intersection with Farm Road 362. Jog to the right 0.2 mile and back to the left on Schroeder Road. (In 1980, plans were underway to blacktop this very rough country road. Watch for cattle that may be loose.) After driving 2.7 miles, turn left to the academy building.

This impressive structure, the "Lighthouse of Consciousness," has been constructed as a retreat facility for adherents of Transcendental Meditation who wish to do further study into the science of creative intelligence. Advanced studies are offered for TM teachers searching for more depth and understanding, and business people, doctors, and scientists who already practice meditation twice daily and find the technique beneficial come here for further study into the philosophy of TM.

The luxurious academy building offers 108 guest rooms, classrooms, and dining facilities. Course credits are transferable to the fully accredited four-year Maharish International University in Fairfield, Iowa. World Plan Executive Council, a nonprofit educational organization, operates many of these facilities all over the United States. It is funded by TM proponents, the national office, local fund raisers, and class fees. This beautiful wooded site is one of the highest points within forty-five miles of Houston—certainly a location removed from the harried pace of city and business pressures, an ideal focal point of consciousness. Guests are invited to examine the facility and to learn more about Transcendental Meditation. Open daily, 11:00 A.M. to 4:00 P.M. To arrange a tour, call 713/825-7926 (this number may now be changed; check with the Navasota operator).

Return to Farm Road 362 by Schroeder Road. Turn right and drive to Texas 105. From this point, it is five miles west to Navasota.

During weekends in October and November, an unusual event occurs nearby. The Renaissance Festival, a bawdy, brawling barrel of fun is staged in the middle of a huge field about fifteen miles from here. On the way, a plantation home, turned restaurant, offers homecooked meals in an atmosphere of country elegance.

Turn right on Texas 105, drive four miles to Farm Road 2445, and turn left for 3.8 miles to Southern Breeze Plantation.

This modern replica of a colonial home sits among moss-covered trees with a gazebo, cabanas, and a swimming pool—a lovely setting for outdoor family reunions and other large functions. The mansion is decorated in family antiques, heirloom needlework, and tapestries. Guests even use the family cutlery. The facilities here are set up to serve from eight to eighty at sit-down dinners. Three sisters operate the restaurant, preparing and serving their own menus. One sister specializes in Louisiana gumbo, another is a professional cake decorator, and all combine to offer a superb menu. Reservations and a 50 percent deposit are required four days in advance or two weeks in advance for a party of twenty or more. Entertainment ranging from violinists to belly dancers is available by reservation. No gratuities, please. Write Route 2, Box 3520, Navasota, TX 77868, or call 713/894-2435.

Return on Farm Road 2445 to the intersection with Texas 105 and turn left; it is 4.3 miles east to Plantersville. Turn right on Farm Road 1774 for 6.4 miles to the entrance of the Renaissance Festival.

Renaissance Festival

Artists and craftspersons from all over the country display their creations in a sixteenth-century atmosphere where one can find wood nymphs, beggars who splash around in the mud, strolling pipers and drummers, and chariot races. Happy Cockney wenches invite "me Lords and me Ladies" to sample the "king's brew" (from Lone Star kegs) or "queen's spirits" (milder liquids), while visitors munch on one-pound turkey legs and watch glassblowing, spinning, and blacksmithing. More-active participants can fence, try archery, or catapult water-filled balloons at giggling wenches. A taste of Shakespearean drama is pre-

sented on the Globe Theatre Stage. Henry VIII along with
Anne Boleyn and members of the royal court appear on
the Castle Stage. In this unique carnival atmosphere all
participants remain in their Renaissance roles throughout
the festival.

For more information, call 713/356-2178. The Renaissance Festival is held each weekend in October and the
first weekend in November, 9:00 A.M. to 7:00 P.M. Admission charge.

*Return on Farm Road 1774 to Texas 105, turn left, and con-
tinue into Navasota.*

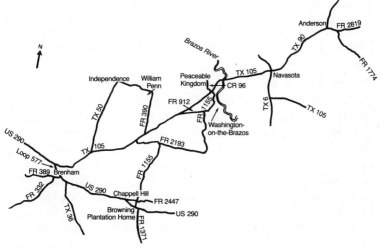

Navasota

This town owes its existence as a thriving Victorian community to cotton and the railroads. The present townsite
lay at the junction of two important roads: La Bahía,
which ran from present Goliad to Nacogdoches, and the
road to Boonville, a community east of present Bryan.
Cotton grew up and down the Brazos River bottoms, and
the unpredictable river served as the only route for transporting the valuable commodity to market. When it became clear that the plantation owners across the river
around Washington-on-the-Brazos did not intend to help
finance a rail line into that area, James Nolan, an early

settler, gave eighty acres to the Houston and Texas Central
Railroad for right-of-way, which became the town of
Navasota. Many of the streets in Navasota are lined with
outstanding Victorian mansions built during the 1870s,
Navasota's heyday.

Navasota is undergoing a downtown renewal as one
of the five Texas pilot towns chosen as models for the
Main Street Project sponsored by the National Trust for
Historic Preservation. The intention of this project is to
demonstrate how adaptive use of historic buildings can
revive new interest and economic activity in downtown
business districts.

At the T *intersection with Farm Road 508, South La Salle
Street, turn right. Drive about eleven blocks to Holland Street
and turn right.*

The First Presbyterian Church is on the first corner
(Holland and Nolan streets). Built in 1894, this stone
structure is Anglian in design. The congregation organized
in 1866, drawing its membership from the old community
of Washington-on-the-Brazos, which will be discussed
later. Although the building is generally open only for
11:00 A.M. worship on Sunday, it is open during the annual
Nostalgia Tour held the first weekend in May. Several historic churches and stately homes are open for the tour,
which is sponsored by the Grimes County Historical Commission. An antique show and sale as well as art and craft
exhibits are part of the festivities.

Continue east along Holland Street.

The Jesse Youens House at 708 Holland, built in 1871
to resemble the family home in Dartford, Kent, England,
has remained in the family all these years. Jesse Youens
and his brother, at the ages of ten and twelve, were sent to
America in 1858 to "seek the family fortune." After serving
in the Confederate army at Galveston, Jesse settled in
Washington-on-the-Brazos and entered a lumberyard
partnership. When it became clear that Navasota would
get the railroad and develop into the business center,
Youens moved his business here. He and his partner built

one of the first planing mills and lathe shops in Texas.
They produced much of the gingerbread trim seen on
homes in this area.

*Drive past some of the Victorian homes by continuing on
Holland to Ketchum Street. Turn left on Ketchum and left
again on McAlpine Street. Go to La Salle Street and turn
right toward the business district. Turn left at the next corner, Washington Avenue, and drive two blocks through
downtown. Stop at the railroad tracks.*

Like some other Texas towns, Navasota had serious problems during the "break up" at the end of the Civil War. Confederate soldiers who had endured the hopeless fighting, ill-equipped and often providing their own food and clothing, were more than ready to give up in April 1865, when word came of Lee's surrender. Although Texas had not suffered from Union invasions, only a thin shell of defense protected the coastline and no amount of "reasoning" on the part of the military leaders could keep the soldiers from leaving in huge numbers. The army had been paid in worthless paper (which the Confederate government had even refused in payment of taxes), and there were reports of enormous mismanagement and embezzlements in the commissary and supply department. As these exhausted and angry soldiers headed home, they broke into government stores and "divided" the goods. In some places, they broke into private businesses and carried off what they wanted. Entire towns rallied in self-defense and made great efforts to feed the returning men.

According to an article published in 1876 by Dr. A. R. Kilpatrick, early-day physician and historian, disgruntled Confederate soldiers went on a rampage in May 1865 that spelled disaster for Navasota. They set fire to a warehouse across the railroad tracks south of Washington Avenue. The building, containing gunpowder, bayonets, swords, and cotton, exploded and fire destroyed structures along that side of the street. Swords were later found embedded in the street, bales of cotton were blown across town, several people were killed, and others were injured.

A determined population had recovered from the fire when the yellow fever epidemic of 1867 broke out. Between August and November, 176 victims died. Of the 3,000 population, only about 1,200 to 1,300 remained in the city. Dr. Kilpatrick claimed that the epidemic "completely revolutionized the city and prostrated it more than the four years [of] war had done."

Notice the patched brick on the wall of the building at the northwest corner of Washington Avenue and Railroad Street. About 1889 a train wrecked at this corner and the engine crashed through the wall. The War Horse Antique Shop, specializing in English pieces, occupies the first floor. The shop is open Wednesday through Saturday, 4:00 P.M. to 10:00 P.M.; Sunday, 1:00 P.M. to 10:00 P.M.; for an appointment on Monday or Tuesday, call 713/825-3223.

Return east on Washington Avenue to the traffic light (only one in town) and turn left on La Salle Street.

The H. Schumacher Oil Works is the large building on the left beyond the creek. In 1873, Henry Schumacher, a German immigrant, began a cottonseed oil mill, one of the first four or five in the United States. Schumacher discovered that he could mix cotton seed hulls, which he had been giving away, with cotton seed meal and produce feed on which livestock thrived. The facility is used now as a warehouse during cotton harvest each fall, when bales of cotton line the street beside the building.

Turn left on Chase Street beside the warehouse and drive to the end of the block.

La Bahía Antiques and Imports is housed on the right in the old Schumacher home, built in 1873, and is operated by his great-granddaughters. They have chosen the name La Bahía for the famous old road that ran along here. The shop is usually open daily, 1:30 P.M. to 5:00 P.M. Watch for the one-eyed Shetland pony who grazes near La Bahía Antiques. He is often found drinking from the bird bath.

Return to La Salle Street and turn right. Turn left at the traffic light on Washington Avenue.

The La Salle statue is just ahead at the beginning of the esplanade. René Robert Cavelier, Sieur de la Salle, the French explorer, met death at the hands of his own men near Navasota (some scholars disagree on the site) in March 1687. As an envoy of King Louis XIV, La Salle had discovered the mouth of the Mississippi River and had returned with an expedition, intending to colonize that area. However, La Salle accidentally bypassed the Mississippi and came inland on the Texas coast at Matagorda Bay (see Chap. 6, Indianola section).

Three ships that accompanied La Salle's expedition were lost and the fourth went back to France, leaving La Salle and a handful of men and women stranded at Matagorda Bay. Finally, La Salle and seventeen men made an attempt to return to an old fort that La Salle had built earlier on the Illinois River. They traveled only to this area before the men killed La Salle's nephew and then ambushed their leader.

La Salle's brief stint in this region caused Spain to become apprehensive about French intrusion. The Spanish had established the first mission in Texas intending to Christianize the Indians, who would then serve as a buffer against French intrusion. Colonization became Spain's next step to halt French and, later, United States encroachment.

Continue east on Washington Avenue.

The Sangster Home at 1113 East Washington is on the left. There is a story that Buck Sangster worked as a shoe clerk in a downtown store. One day, in the midst of fitting a pair of shoes, he got word that he had won the English lottery. He threw the shoes down, left the store, and never returned. He built this magnificent home in 1901–02, bought land, and enjoyed his new wealth.

The 1882 Horlock House Museum at 1215 East Washington Avenue is being developed as the new museum for Grimes County. Plans call for each community in the county to place an exhibit here. Several beautiful homes along this street attest to the prosperity of this area when cotton reigned as king. The land now serves the cattle and dairy industries, with row crops used entirely for forage.

The next portion of the trail includes a nine-mile side trip through bluebonnet country to Anderson, a much older and more primitive settlement than Navasota. Travelers may choose to leave Navasota on Texas 105 and travel west directly to Washington-on-the-Brazos.

Continue east on Washington Avenue, Texas 90, and travel northeast to Anderson.

Anderson

In 1833 Henry Fanthorp built his home at the intersection
of two major stage lines, the Houston to Old Springfield
route and the Nacogdoches to Austin road. (The Fanthorp
Inn will be discussed later in this section.) The community that grew up around this stage line intersection became known as the Rome of Texas. Like Rome, present
Anderson is situated on seven hills, and in its heyday it
became the fourth-largest town in Texas.

Residents in 1857 insisted that they did not want the
Houston and Texas Central Railroad "running through
here, for they would scare our mules and our Negroes. Put
the railroad off ten miles to one side." The railroad went
to Navasota and Anderson's prosperity soon disappeared.

*Upon entering Anderson, turn right on Appolonia Street,
Farm Road 1774.*

The 1860 log cabin on the right was moved to this site
several years ago.

Turn left in two blocks on Main Street.

This entire town is designated as a National Historic
District. Looking up Main Street toward the Grimes
County Courthouse gives only a glimpse of what lies
ahead. This tiny town opens for visitors during the Texas
Trek, the first weekend in April. The homes are open, and
arts, crafts, and baked goods are available. On Saturday
night, everyone is invited to a street dance in front of the
courthouse.

Marie's Antique Shop is in the first block on the right.
Merchandise here ranges from antiques, such as a Civil
War bed and dresser, to collectibles, such as cream pitch-
ers, from all over the world. Note the rings in the cement
in front of the store. Visitors arriving on horseback can
still tie up right here at the curb. This shop is open Monday and Wednesday through Saturday, 10:00 A.M. to 5:00
P.M.; Sunday, 1:00 P.M. to 6:00 P.M.; closed Tuesday.

Oberkampf Drug Store is on the right, across from the
courthouse. This is the other spot in town where horses

can still be hitched to the original rings. Oberkampf's was built in 1910 and still maintains the Gay Nineties look. Ice cream and cold drinks are available seven days a week on a loose schedule from about 9:00 A.M. until around 5:00 P.M. Monday through Saturday; Sunday, afternoons only.

The Grimes County Courthouse, built in 1894, is one of the most appealing in the state with its tiers of outside steps ascending in an arch across the front of the building. There is a story that the selection of the Grimes county seat in 1846 was made by having the competing towns serve a dinner. Anderson won the vote with the best meal and has held the position all these years despite attempts at removal.

Turn right beside the courthouse on Buffington Avenue. Continue one block to Fanthorp Street and turn right.

This narrow lane became known as New York Row because of the hotels along here where drummers sold their merchandise. The old Preston Hotel is on the left at the end of the block, facing Appolonia Street. This was the largest hotel in town, one of the favorite stops for drummers. It is now a residence.

The Becker-Lyons Home, built in 1848, is in the next block on the left. This structure served as courthouse, and a murder trial took place here sometime before 1850.

The Baptist Church is at the end of the next block on the right. George Washington Baines, great-grandfather of President Lyndon B. Johnson, served as pastor here from 1852 to 1861. In 1855, he began publishing the first Baptist newspaper in the state, the *Texas Baptist*, which was read by many outside the church. Slaves helped to construct the church in 1855. As the congregation prepared the one hundredth anniversary celebration in 1955, a fire completely gutted the structure, leaving only the stone walls. The church was rebuilt and is still used for worship services.

Turn right beside the church on Johnson Avenue and left again at the next corner, Main Street.

The Fanthorp Inn, original hub of the town, is just down this road in a grove of trees on the left. When Henry Fanthorp first settled here in 1833, he built a structure that served as a corn crib and a dwelling. Then, with plans to marry Rachel Kennard the next spring, he had a large home built on the site. Since no Catholic priest was around to perform the ceremony, as required by Mexican law, the couple married "by bond," which means that they agreed to have a priest perform the rites at a later time. That formality out of the way, the wedding proceeded in true Protestant fashion.

Because of the location on the two major stage routes, the Fanthorps were practically forced into the hotel business. Fanthorp enlarged the building into an inn, operated a post office, and opened a store nearby. Such prominent people as Sam Houston, Zachary Taylor, Jefferson Davis, Robert E. Lee, and U. S. Grant were all guests at the Fanthorp Inn. During the yellow fever epidemic of 1867, Anderson, like the rest of Texas, was beseiged. Henry and Rachel Fanthorp contracted the disease and died within three days of each other.

The Parks and Wildlife Service purchased this historic site in 1977 and has long-range plans for restoring the property and eventually opening the facility to the public.

This road dead-ends. Turn around and drive back up Main Street. Turn left on Appolonia Street and return to Texas 90. Turn left and return to Navasota. Texas 90, Washington Avenue, becomes Texas 105 in downtown Navasota. Continue west on Texas 105.

Washington-on-the-Brazos

This once-thriving port on the Brazos River has become a state park. It boasts a fine museum, a replica of the hall where the Texas Declaration of Independence was signed, and the home of Dr. Anson Jones, the last president of the Republic of Texas. This site is significant to Texas and the United States because it is here that Texans declared their independence from Mexico, drafted a constitution for the new republic, and organized the new government. It is also here that Texans gave up their republic, became citizens of the United States, and drafted the new state constitution.

Turn left off Texas 105 on Farm Road 1155. It is one mile from here to Washington.

Reba's Country Cupboard is in Washington on the right just before the T intersection. Reba offers soups, sandwiches, and plates of chicken salad, ham, turkey, sausage, and cheeses. The shop is filled with attractive crafts that make fine gifts or take-home remembrances, such as homemade jelly. Reba holds a Christmas Open House, at which customers may sample Christmas treats and baked goods. The shop is filled at this time with home decorator items, jewelry, and other gift selections. This special event occurs the first Tuesday in December, 2:00 P.M. to 9:00 P.M. Reba's regular hours are Wednesday, Thursday, and Friday, 11:00 A.M. to 3:00 P.M.; Saturday 11:00 A.M. to 5:00 P.M.; Sunday 11:00 A.M. to 9:00 P.M.; closed Monday, Tuesday, July 4, and December 25 through the first week in January.

Turn right at the T *intersection and continue 0.2 mile to the park entrance, Park Road 12. Drive first to the Star of the Republic of Texas Museum.*

The exhibits here are not limited to Washington-on-the-Brazos or Washington County, but take a broad view of the events that occurred here. A twenty-five–minute slide presentation introduces Washington and the republic and places the history in perspective. The exhibits change regularly, each portraying some special segment of Texas' heritage. The museum also offers a fine rare book collection and library. An observation deck provides a view of the surrounding area.

A replica of Independence Hall stands on the far side of the parking lot. This is where sixty-one delegates met to draw up the Declaration of Independence from Mexico, write a new constitution, form the ad interim government, and elect officers of that government: David G. Burnet, president; Lorenzo de Zavala, vice-president; and Sam Houston, commander-in-chief of the army. The conditions were miserable: it was March, the temperatures hovered near freezing, this unfinished building had cotton cloth stretched across the windows to keep out the cold. In seventeen days the representatives completed an amazing amount of work. During that time, word came of the advance into Texas of Santa Anna's and Urrea's armies. Then came William Travis' request for aid at the Alamo. On March 15, news of the fall of the Alamo reached the delegation.

North of the museum is Barrington, the plantation home of Dr. Anson Jones. The home has been moved to this site and furnished in much the same way as when the Jones family lived there during the days of the republic. Anson Jones: a frontier physician, veteran of the Battle of San Jacinto, one of the organizers of the first Masonic

lodge in Texas, congressman, senator, and the last president of the Republic of Texas. The holder of any of these
positions would leave his mark as an early leader, but an
individual with such an impressive list was bound to be a
major mover and shaker of early Texas history. However,
Anson Jones carried personal problems with him throughout his career. Before becoming a successful doctor in
Brazoria, he had been a financial failure in several under-
takings, including medicine. He came to Texas in 1833 and
found himself allied politically with Sam Houston, whose
private indulgences Jones disapproved. While Jones
served as secretary of state under Houston, Jones' and
Houston's relations became strained over annexation and
other political matters. And Jones may have been jealous
of Houston's popularity. When Jones became president of
the republic, he held out on accepting the offer of annexation to the United States because he believed that Texas'
best interests lay, not in rushing headlong to join the
Union, but in using the new power to negotiate for the
best terms. Texans, eager to become United States citizens, did not understand Jones, burned him in effigy, and
brought about an abrupt end to his political career. After
annexation, Jones and his family moved onto their 1,172-
acre plantation near here. Jones prospered significantly,
yet he brooded over his misfortunes. Finally, under the
guise of moving his family to Galveston for a new start,
Jones traveled ahead, stopped in Houston, and there on
January 9, 1858, he killed himself.

*Follow the road beyond Jones' plantation home to the picnic
area overlooking the Brazos River.*

These steep banks confronted travelers in 1822 when
Andrew Robinson first began operating a nearby ferry below the junction with the Navasota River.

The buildings in the park are open March through
August, daily, 10:00 A.M. to 5:00 P.M.; September through
February, Wednesday through Sunday only, 10:00 A.M. to
5:00 P.M.; closed Thanksgiving and Christmas through
New Year's Day. No admission charge. The park is open
daily, 8:00 A.M. to sundown.

At the park entrance, turn right on Farm Road 1155 and drive back through the present community of Washington.

In 1842–1845 the capital of the republic operated here. With the moving of the county seat to Brenham in 1844 and the capital to Austin the following year, prospects for the town dwindled until the arrival of river steamers. Businessmen and planters formed the Brazos Steam Association to buy and operate steamboats on the river and to clear the channel for future navigation. Until this organization began operation, the river was too shallow for navigation past Columbia. This opportunity to ship cotton to the Gulf kept Washington's economy alive and well.

By 1860 Washington had a population of four thousand, but the residents here, as in Anderson, did not want to give up valuable cotton plantation land to railroad right-of-way. Much talk transpired about the importance of building a tap line across the river, but many plantation owners, who had invested in steamships, refused to support the venture. Great changes loomed on the horizon. The 1860 United States census showed that Washington County's slave population had reached 52 percent, but emancipation brought an end to that labor force. Financial failures came during the Civil War and subsequent Reconstruction. All these changes could not be overcome without the commerce that the railroad would have brought. Residents began moving en masse to Brenham and the new railroad town of Navasota across the river. Anglo-American landholders sold their property to Germans, and many of their descendants still own the land.

The Washington Civic Club sponsors an annual Octoberfest. There are booths of food, arts, crafts, and games, as well as German folk dances, a street dance, antique car exhibit, and craft and blacksmithing demonstrations. The Octoberfest is held the first weekend in October: Saturday 10:00 A.M. to 11:30 P.M.; Sunday, 10:00 A.M. to 6:00 P.M. No admission charge.

At this point, another route selection is possible. Either drive directly to Independence or travel about 3 miles to Peaceable Kingdom, a foundation for the arts, where classes in pottery, weaving, woodworking, and blacksmithing are offered and travelers can visit a solar greenhouse, herb garden, and general store.

To take the road to Independence, retrace the route past the park entrance on Farm Road 1155. Continue straight on Farm Road 912 when Farm Road 1155 turns left.

Watch out for the ducks strolling in the middle of the road. In 1853, slave labor built the red brick plantation home on the right.

Turn left at the intersection with Texas 105. Drive 4.5 miles to Farm Road 390 and turn right. Continue traveling on Farm Road 390 into Independence. Or, for the drive to Peaceable Kingdom, travel north from Washington back toward Navasota on Farm Road 1155 to the intersection with Texas 105. Turn left and then jog back to the right, following the arrow for the Old River Road, County Road 96. Drive 0.6 mile and take the right fork for 1.1 miles to the entrance to Peaceable Kingdom.

Peaceable Kingdom

"Peaceable" is the appropriate description of this little domain, a collection of artists and craftspersons who practice their trade in various barns scattered about the rolling 152 acres. Out back, a lush herb garden flourishes and an impressive solar greenhouse is filled with plants and early starts for the garden.

The school began in 1971 and is a nonprofit foundation, supported by private donations, without state or federal aid. Classes that range from yoga to organic gardening, from solar energy to home-brewed beer are usually offered over the weekend or for one-week sessions. Rustic cabins are available for overnight occupancy. The artists here are in demand at surrounding universities, and they teach classes to 4-H and women's clubs. For information, call 713/878-2353. Peaceable Kingdom and the General Store and Trading Post are open Wednesday through Sunday, 10:00 A.M. to 4:00 P.M.; closed Monday and Tuesday.

Return by the Old River Road, County Road 96, to Texas 105 and turn right for nine miles to Farm Road 390. Turn right and continue toward Independence.

In about five miles, Farm Road 390 passes through the community of William Penn, founded in the 1840s, one of the few Quaker settlements in Texas.

Independence

John P. and Mary Eleanor Coles came to Texas as part of Stephen F. Austin's Old Three Hundred. In 1824 they moved to this area, built a cedar log house, which is still standing, and planted the first corn in present Washington County. It is said that Coles went to Mexico for the corn seed. Upon his return, he was stranded by river flooding and had to eat the corn. It took a second trip to Mexico to get the seeds for planting. He built a public house, a combination store and saloon, and colonists began moving into what they called Coles Settlement.

An unusually large number of educated colonists, interested in establishing permanent homes with educational, religious, and social opportunities for them and their children, settled in Washington County. By 1834 the Coles had five daughters and one son, which is probably why they encouraged Judith Somes Trask to open a girls' boarding school at Coles Settlement.

On the right, just inside Independence, are the ruins of the Blanton Hotel and Store. This hotel housed many important Texans who traveled the La Bahía Road, which ran along the route of present Farm Road 390. The night after the signing of the Texas Declaration of Independence in Washington, some of the representatives stayed at this hotel. It is said that the name Coles Settlement was changed to Independence that night in commemoration of what had taken place that day in Washington.

The home on the left before the intersection with Texas 50 is where Margaret Lea Houston, Sam Houston's widow, moved to after the death of her husband. Mrs. Houston came here in July 1863 to be near her mother and to educate her eight children at Baylor University, which was in Independence at the time. The home, built in the 1830s, is privately owned and is not open to the public at any time.

Margaret Lea Houston, daughter of a Baptist preacher, was a devout Christian, as was her strong-willed mother, Nancy Lea. The Houston-Lea Family Cemetery is on the corner of Farm Road 390 and Texas 50. This is part of Nancy Lea's homestead lot. She built her home next to the site in 1850, and family records indicate that "Grandma" had this vault constructed. She also bought a metallic coffin with a glass cover several years before her death. She stored her coffee and sugar in the coffin, knowing that the slaves feared the coffin so much they would never take what was stored in it. After her death in February 1864, her body could be seen through the glass cover of the casket, a handkerchief covering her face. Several years later, the vault and the glass coffin lid cracked and the body decomposed. Her body was removed to a plot beside her daughter, Margaret Lea Houston, who had been a victim of the yellow fever epidemic in 1867.

The Independence Baptist Church (across Texas 50), founded in 1839, is one of the earliest in Texas. This building was erected in 1872 after a fire destroyed the first structure. The church is best known for the admission of General Sam Houston after his baptism in a creek south of here. In 1856, Nancy Lea gave a 502-pound copper-and-tin bell to the church. It hung in the bell tower until it fell in 1969. Since then it has been restored and is displayed in the church museum and Baptist shrine. The museum, which features relics from this area, is open Wednesday through Saturday, 10:00 A.M. to 4:00 P.M.; Sunday, 1:00 P.M. to 5:00 P.M.; closed Monday and Tuesday.

Continue west on Farm Road 390 to the fork. Take Spur 390 to the right.

The log house sitting in the Y is the restored J. P. Cole home mentioned earlier.

Continue toward the stone columns in the distance, ruins of the old Baylor Female College.

Independence became known as the "Athens of Texas" because of the gathering here in the early and mid-nineteenth century of the shapers of Texas' cultural, intellectual, religious, and social standards.

In 1865 Baylor Female College was organized from the women's department of Baylor University, which had been chartered in 1845. The students referred to the creek that divided the extensive facilities for men and women as the "River Jordan." The college for women was moved to Belton and is now called Mary Hardin-Baylor College. Baylor University was moved to Waco in 1886. The loss of the two outstanding institutions started the slow decline of Independence.

The Reverend George Washington Baines, great-grandfather of Lyndon B. Johnson, served as pastor at the Independence Baptist Church in 1851 and became president of Baylor University in 1861.

Return to Texas 50 for the drive to Brenham and turn right.

The old Baylor University site is to the left of the highway beyond the second intersection, but nothing remains of the school.

It is 8.5 miles to the intersection with Texas 105. Turn right.

The bridge just beyond this corner crosses New Year's Creek. When the first contingent of the Old Three Hundred traveled to Texas in December 1821, eighteen settlers came on the *Lively*, a ship from New Orleans (see Chap. 6). Another group came overland. On the night of December 31, 1821, several of the Old Three Hundred camped along this creek, and the next morning they named it "New Year's Creek."

Brenham

In the spring of 1844 the Republic of Texas declared Brenham the county seat of Washington County. The town was platted and lots were laid out. The community began as a center for cotton planters and it remains an agricultural hub.

Continue into town on Texas 105. Turn right at the Phillips 66 Service Station on Independence Street. Drive one block and turn left on Crockett Street.

The Giddings-Wilkin House at 805 Crockett is on the right. About a year before Brenham was laid out, Jabez Deming Giddings built this Greek revival structure for his bride. The home boasted a rooftop reservoir for holding 9,275 gallons of rainwater and is believed to be the oldest surviving house in Brenham.

Giddings came to Texas to claim the league of land due his brother Giles, who had died from injuries suffered in the Battle of San Jacinto. After Giddings settled here, he became a leader in the Methodist church, banking, and the railroad. Yes, the town of Giddings is named for this fellow; as a railroad stockholder, Giddings played a key role in getting the rail line through that part of Lee County.

In 1972, when a group of concerned citizens discovered plans for moving the Giddings-Wilkin House to
Washington, they organized the Heritage Society of Washington County, purchased the home, and restored it. The
society operates it as a museum with Giddings family and
other period furnishings. Listed on the National Register
of Historic Places, the home can be seen by appointment.
Call the chamber of commerce, 713/836-3695, or the library, 713/836-2313.

The restored village west of the Giddings-Wilkin
House contains Washington County structures from the
1840s to the turn of the century. By 1980 the village consisted of a log house that had been a doctor's office in the
nearby Wesley community and an 1880 Victorian cottage
now used as a country store with merchandise for sale to
visitors. Two more houses are planned for this village, and
dreams call for completion in late 1982. The huge crape
myrtles were planted here in the 1870s and continue to
shade the lawn.

Each spring this facility and several of Brenham's fine
Victorian mansions are open for the Washington County
Historical Tour. Proceeds from these tours are used for
further restoration.

*Drive to the next corner and turn left on Gayhill Street. Turn
right at the next corner, Academy Street, and drive about
eight blocks to North Park Street, or Austin Parkway. Turn
left and stay in the left lane. In the next block the street forks
and the right fork becomes Austin. Continue straight on
Park, not Austin, by crossing the esplanade.*

B'Nai Abraham Synagogue is on the left at 304 North
Park Street. Organized in 1885, this was one of the first
orthodox Jewish congregations in Texas. Its members followed the old Jewish law, which segregated men and
women during worship, used no instrumental music, and
observed strict dietary laws. Today the congregation is
served by traveling rabbis. This 1893 synagogue, like
many of the fine structures in town, is open each spring
for the Washington County Historical Tour.

Continue south one block to Vulcan Street and turn left in front of the city hall building.

The Silsby steam pumper displayed in the glass case was first used here in 1879. Although the pumper was designed to be drawn by hand or by horses, the fire company pulled it by hand because horses were hard to keep.

Brenham's fire department didn't have ordinary beginnings. After the Civil War, hostilities arose between townspeople and several drunk soldiers in a Union infantry company stationed in Brenham. A store was set afire and the soldiers stood guard to keep the fire from being put out. Three houses and five stores were destroyed.

The following month, the Freedman's Bureau, a federally organized group authorized to help the freed slaves become established in the communities, tried to organize a tax-supported school for blacks in Brenham. The editor of the *Brenham Banner-Press* spoke against the bureau several times, and a fire, set to destroy the newspaper office, destroyed the entire block of businesses on the west side of the square.

Under the guise of establishing a fire department, some of Brenham's most influential residents organized a military unit to halt the lawlessness of the Union troops. From that first effort to protect the lives and property of local citizens, a volunteer fire department emerged.

Turn right at the corner on North Baylor Street and right again on Main Street. Drive three blocks and turn left on Austin Street. Continue about six blocks and turn right on College Street. It is five blocks to Blinn College.

German Methodists began this school in 1883 for the purpose of training ministers. Called Mission Institute, the college opened with three male students. Usually, the men received free tuition but were obligated to return the money if they did not enter the ministry.

Old Main, the red brick building on the right, was constructed in 1907–08 at a cost of $28,000. Andrew Carnegie, the steel millionaire and philanthropist, donated $13,000 toward the cost. Carnegie, a poor Scottish immigrant, became one of the richest men in the world, and before his death in 1919 he had given an estimated $350 million to support education, advance the world peace movement, and build public libraries. In 1937, Blinn became the first countywide junior college in the state.

Return to South Austin Street and turn right. After four blocks, when the highway jogs to the right, continue straight on South Austin. In six blocks, turn left on Stone Street. Drive four blocks to Heritage Drive and turn right. Go right again at the next street, Century Circle, and follow the circle around to the Giddings-Stone Mansion at the top of the hill.

This is another J. D. Giddings home and it's evident that he prospered considerably before he built this Greek revival house in 1869. Concerned about the terrible yellow fever epidemic of 1867, Giddings decided that this high location outside town would be more healthful than the family home in Brenham. This house has twelve rooms, five baths, and eight fireplaces. The Giddings and then the Stone families occupied the structure until 1975, when the Stone estate presented the house to the Heritage Society. Placed on the National Register of Historic Places, the house is now being restored. Completion is projected for the late 1980s.

Circle past the mansion back to the corner of Heritage Drive and Stone Street. Turn right and proceed to Loop 577. Turn left and watch for the Blue Bell Creamery on the right.

This operation began in 1912 with an old tub filled with crushed ice. The company has moved from making a whopping two gallons of ice cream a day to millions of gallons a year. A twenty-minute tour includes the 40,000-gallon milk and 6,000-gallon cream storage tanks, the 2,000-gallon "mixing bowls," the pasteurizing and homogenizing machines, and the flavoring room. Drop-in tours are available each Tuesday and Thursday at 10:00 A.M. For groups of ten or more, advance reservations are required and special tours are offered Monday through Friday, 9:00 A.M. to 10:30 A.M. and 1:00 P.M. to 2:00 P.M. No admission

charge. Call Houston, 713/463-8622, or Brenham, 713/
836-7977.

*Turn left from the creamery on Loop 577; drive south to U.S.
Highway 290. Turn left and continue east for five miles to
Farm Road 2447. Leave U.S. Highway 290 and veer left to
Chappell Hill.*

Chappell Hill

"Old South" is the best description of Chappell Hill, ten
miles east of Brenham. It's off the beaten path but very
much alive as a preserved mid-nineteenth-century educational, religious, and travel center. Few communities have
retained that nineteenth-century charm as well. On weekends the pace picks up because city folk arrive, looking for
a spot to slow down.

There were probably families living in this area for
some time before the town was laid out in 1847. Chappell
Hill is perhaps the only place in Texas bought and laid out
by a woman. In February 1847, while her husband, Jacob,
was away buying merchandise for his trading post, Mary
Hargrove Haller bought this one-hundred-acre site, had
the tract divided into lots, and named her husband the
first postmaster.

In 1850, the Hallers built the Stagecoach Inn, which is
part of the first complex of buildings on the left just inside
Chappell Hill. The following year, the Hallers sold the inn
to Mary's mother, Charlotte Hargrove, who operated the
Hargrove House for travelers on the stagecoach route
from Houston to Austin and for travelers from Austin
making connection with the Houston and Texas Central
Railroad at Hempstead.

Stop at the sign for Hackberry Tree Antiques on the left.

This beautifully landscaped group of buildings, which
includes the Stagecoach Inn on the corner, is owned by
Harvin C. and Elizabeth Moore. Harvin Moore, a Fellow
in the American Institute of Architects, is nationally
known for his work in historic preservation.

First, visit the Stagecoach Inn, which is the Moores'
retirement home. This fine example of early Greek Revival
architecture has been restored, placed on the National
Register of Historic Places, and recorded in the Historic
American Buildings Survey in the Library of Congress.
The craftsmanship is outstanding in the home. Note the
Greek key frieze on the cornice (under the eaves). Even the
downspout heads are dated with the year of their addition
to the structure, 1851.

Since this is a private residence, visitors have an
opportunity to see how actual living arrangements in a
restored home can be more than comfortable—in fact,
elegant. The furnishings are locally made pieces as well as
family heirlooms. The Stagecoach Inn is open for guided
tours, Monday through Saturday, 10:00 A.M. to 4:00 P.M.,
Sunday, by appointment. Call Chappell Hill, 713/836-9515,
or Houston, 713/961-3937. There is a tour fee.

Hackberry Tree Antiques occupies the 1866 Weems
Home to the rear of the complex. The shop specializes in
Texas pieces, quilts, and pottery—select items chosen by
the owners with an eye to quality.

Turn right at the corner, Main Street.

The downtown area covers two blocks, much as it did when this community served the surrounding plantations. Planters from the Old South came here and established huge landholdings. It has been said that with one stroke of his pen Lincoln changed the agricultural system in the South from slave to free contract labor. The effects were not as severe here as in other regions of the Deep South because many of the freedmen stayed on and worked for wages, homes, food, and medical care. They were not allowed, however, to leave or to entertain visitors on the plantations even though they were "free." Slowly, with urgings from the Freedman's Bureau, the ex-slaves began to visualize life without hard labor. By the 1870s, planters, unable to obtain a sufficient labor force, organized the Washington County Emigration Society. Agents traveled to Germany and found 250 farmers willing to emigrate to Texas as laborers. These thrifty and industrious men did not last long in the Chappell Hill area when it became clear that they could not buy land of their own. Soon they purchased small tracts in other sections of the county, and many of their descendants still own the land today.

Watch for the old bell from the Chappell Hill Male and Female Institute, which is displayed on the right about the middle of the first block on Main Street.

This bell, cast in 1873, is all that remains of the Methodist college that began here in 1850 and finally closed in 1912. This school and Soule University for men, 1856–1888, made Chappell Hill an important educational center.

The Farmers State Bank is next door. The bank, which still serves the community, looks much the way it did when it was chartered in 1907. The doorknobs are about knee-high to modern folk, the screenline on the teller's cage is polished, and the original vault opens into the lobby, which is cooled by ceiling fans. Even the original ledger, which shows an 83¢ overdraft from the first week of operation, is on display. Although the atmosphere is still small town and friendly, the services are up to date.

The Old Rock Store is on the right at the next corner.

Built in 1869, this structure has been a mercantile store and a post office. It is owned by the Chappell Hill Historical Society. Women of Chappell Hill have created two folk-art panels of stitchery depicting the history of the town. The hangings are 30' × 6' and 27' × 6' and adorn opposite walls in this old store. Tours of the building are available; inquire at the Stagecoach Inn.

Each weekend in October, the Chappell Hill Historical Society hosts the "Scarecrow Festival." Townspeople display unique scarecrows on their porches, arts and crafts are available at the Old Rock Store, and an antique auction at the museum adds to the fun.

Turn left at the next corner, Poplar Street, and drive to the end of the street.

The Chappell Hill Historical Society Community Center and Museum is housed in this old school building, which was built on the site of the Chappell Hill Male and Female Institute. The museum contains five rooms of exhibits, which include pioneer and Victorian furnishings, farm implements, a Confederate room, and local history records and photographs. Open Sunday, 1:30 P.M. to 5:00 P.M., or by appointment; call 713/836-5894.

Turn left on Church Street.

The Methodist Church, on the right, was founded before the town was laid out in 1847. Chappell Hill became known as a Methodist center and hosted several annual conferences. The first building was destroyed in the 1900 storm and this one was completed the next year.

Drive to the end of the street, Farm Road 2447; jog right, then left, and then right again.

Waverly, a Greek revival antebellum home, is on the left. A local doctor built this structure in 1850 and Colonel William Sledge bought the plantation four years later. Sledge mortgaged half of his cotton crop in 1856 to finance the construction of a railroad bridge across the Brazos River.

Wealthy planters had depended on ox trains and the undependable Brazos River for transporting their cotton to markets. When it became clear that Washington-on-the-Brazos residents were not going to build the railroad through their land, local planters knew they must construct a line that would cross the Brazos and connect at Hempstead. A work crew of about twenty-nine slaves completed the task by 1859. Colonel Sledge financed the bridge and Brenham financiers J. D. and D. C. Giddings acquired a loan from county school funds to buy two locomotives and cars. The line reached Brenham the following year.

Waverly has been designated a Texas Historic Landmark and is decorated in mid-1800 pieces, including some family heirlooms and items from the Chappell Hill area. The detached kitchen and dining room have been converted into a guesthouse and furnished in German and Texas primitive pieces. The area east of the structures includes a Lone Star Garden. The home is open for tours,

Monday through Saturday, 10:00 A.M. to 4:00 P.M. Admission charge.

Retrace the route on Farm Road 2447 to Church Street; turn left to Cedar Street and turn right.

On the right is the Chappell Hill Circulating Library, which was organized in 1893 and is operated by the Historical Society under a rather unusual arrangement: each member is furnished a key to the building and is responsible for checking books out and returning them promptly to the library.

Continue to Main Street, turn left, and drive to the intersection with U.S. Highway 290.

The site on the right is the former location of Soule [Soul] University, the Methodist school for men, which opened in 1856 with ninety-five students. The young men from the Chappell Hill Male and Female Institute were absorbed into Soule. The future looked bright until the Civil War began. From then on, the university served as a Confederate military hospital. After the war, operations resumed, but the 1867 yellow fever epidemic spelled the beginning of the end for Chappell Hill and its fine institutions of higher learning. The epidemic took not only lives but also population; families who were able to left this area and many never returned. Southwestern University in Georgetown later became the new Methodist institution of higher learning in the state.

Cross U.S. Highway 290, take Farm Road 1371 left, then jog to the right on the narrow lane. It is about 0.7 mile to the W. W. Browning Plantation Home.

This lane served the young men in the community as a field for games of chivalry before the Civil War. After generous helpings of Sir Walter Scott's Waverly Novels, the fellows dressed in brilliantly colored knight costumes for the games. At a banquet following the events, the "Victor Knight" named the "Queen of the Day." These occasions lasted several days and huge crowds came from all the surrounding counties.

This home, part of that noble era, was built in 1857 by W. W. Browning and served as the hub of his vast plantation empire. The 1860 census lists sixty-two slaves for Browning. He was also one of the planters who invested in the railroad line from Hempstead across the Brazos River. In 1981 restoration began on this impressive structure listed on the National Register of Historic Places. The original trim is being maintained on all the windows and the separate kitchen building is being restored. The log cabin, in which the Brownings lived while the big house was being constructed, is also intact. Although restoration is still underway, plans call for the home to be open to the public in the spring of 1982. For hours and tour fee information, inquire at the Stagecoach Inn.

Return to U.S. Highway 290 and turn left.

Before the Civil War, a medical doctor, George Bickley, organized a secret group called "Knights of the Golden Circle." Members dreamed of a slavery empire that would extend from the southern states through Central and South America. Everyone would be rich, never work again, and own all the slaves necessary to meet those ends. This utopia would control the world's supply of tobacco, cotton, sugar, rice, and coffee. Thousands joined this society, earnestly seeking a fine cultured life for their families. There were thirty-one known "castles," local groups, in Texas, with two in Washington County. The Knights of the Golden Circle Castle in Chappell Hill had seventeen members. This organization is credited with a major role in the secession movement in Texas. Dr. Bickley is reported to have said after the Civil War that he helped start the bloodiest war in history.

Some say that Chappell Hill is old-fashioned, out of step with the modern high-speed technology of the 1980s, yet they come here seeking something not quite definable. Perhaps it is a calmness and a wisp of the unhurried past.

From the intersection of U.S. Highway 290 and Texas 36, it is thirty-four miles south to Sealy. However, an alternate, seventy-three–mile route goes through rolling countryside, where travelers can visit a Czech-Moravian

Brethren Church with an interior painted in unusual religious symbols, a country store where eggs are still examined under a light, the oldest German settlement in Texas, and a restaurant in a former funeral parlor.

Continue west on U.S. Highway 290 to Farm Road 389, Blinn College exit. Turn left over U.S. Highway 290 and drive one mile to Farm Road 332. Turn left and continue 7.7 miles into Wesley. Drive past the junction with Farm Road 2502 and turn left at the next road. There is a sign for the Wesley Brethren Church and a weathered dance hall on this corner, but both are easily overlooked. The church is 0.4 mile down this road.

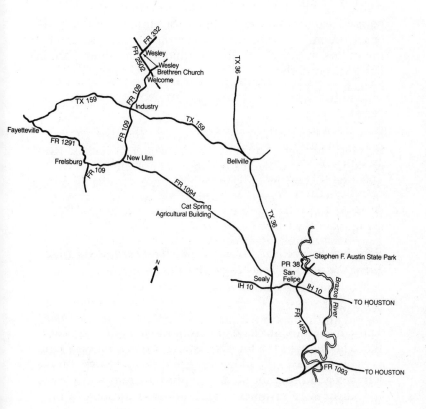

Wesley

Czech immigrants began arriving in Texas in the 1850s.
Although most of them were Roman Catholics, 10 to 15
percent were Protestant and most of those were United
Brethren. This community was first called Veseli, and
then the name was Anglicized to Wesley. Church services
were held in homes from 1864 until the congregation built
this structure in 1866; they enlarged it and added the steeple in 1883. For many years the building served as the
local school with the minister acting as teacher. In 1888
the Reverend B. E. Lacjac began decorating the interior of
the building with unusual drawings. He died in 1891 in a
hunting accident without ever explaining his strange and
inspiring work. Local tradition has said that the bricks
painted around the walls suggest the strength of the walls
of Jerusalem, the white pillars and their shadows depict
the pillars in Solomon's Temple, and the continuous chain
design around the edge of the ceiling denotes the un-
broken chain of brotherhood.

In 1964 the congregation moved into the new sanctuary next door, but the old structure has been preserved as
a memorial to the heritage of this area. The strange drawings have brought visitors who also wonder what the Reverend Lacjac intended as he labored here. He is buried
along with other pastors and early settlers in the adjoining cemetery. The church building has been placed on
the National Register of Historic Places. Open daily; no
set hours.

Return to Farm Road 332 and turn left on Farm Road 2502.
Travel 3.2 miles to Farm Road 109 and turn right.

Welcome

This community got its name from an early German settler who thought the forests, flowers, and meadows in the
area "welcomed" the pioneers. The Welcome Store, on the
left, is a good stop for picnic supplies (there is a nice park
in Industry), refreshments, and spotless restrooms. This
is where a light is used to examine every egg before it is

sold. The proprietor said, "We don't want to sell a bad egg or buy one either."

Continue on Farm Road 109 toward Industry.

If mountain peaks towered in the distance, this area, with its rolling meadows and fat cattle, would look like the pastures below the Bavarian Alps. It is easy to understand why Germans flocked to this region.

Industry

Improved manufacturing processes during the Industrial Revolution in Germany deprived farmers of the income they had been receiving for their sideline crafts. Added to the burden came periods of crop failures, which made Texas lands sound even more inviting to the immigrants.

Watch for the Friedrich Ernst Memorial Park sign and turn right before entering Industry.

This is land originally acquired by Friedrich Ernst, a German immigrant who settled here in 1831. Ernst wrote a letter to a friend in Germany praising the rich land he had found. The letter, eventually published in a newspaper and a book on Texas travel, prompted many families to emigrate. In 1838, after families had settled here, Ernst laid out the town of Industry, the first permanent German settlement in Texas. Ernst had been making cigars with tobacco from his garden, and he named the town for this "industry." Cotton also became an important crop. The Germans competed comfortably with the giant plantations closer to the Brazos River.

This park road is on the old route between Houston, San Felipe, and Austin. The first house on the right before the picnic area is the office of the last doctor in Industry, and his tools are on display here. In order to get the building opened for a tour, call 713/357-2100 or stop at the Gulf Service Station on the corner of Farm Road 109 and Texas 159.

A picnic in this park may offer some surprises. Cows graze just beyond the fence and the presence of strangers

seems to make them moo a lot. The brick structure beyond the picnic area is claimed to be the second post
office in the state, built in 1838. Note the holes around
back, they are not there as rifle slits but for the scaffolding
used during construction. The black persimmon tree behind the post office produces a fruit as black as olives that
makes good eating in the fall. It is said that Ernst brought
this plant with him from Germany. The home was moved
here from New Ulm. One of the rooms still has the stenciling around the top of the walls that was so stylish in
many German homes.

*Return to Farm Road 109, turn right, and drive to the traffic
light at the intersection with Farm Road 159.*

New Ulm (ŏŏl · ĕm) is about six miles south on Farm
Road 109. However, a twenty-seven–mile detour through
Fayetteville is beautiful, even in winter. Fayetteville is
nearly untouched, much like it appeared a hundred years

ago. And the residents, mostly Czech, German, and a few
Houston transplants, still love dancing, beer-drinking,
and church socials.

*Turn right on Texas 159 and drive thirteen miles to
Fayetteville.*

Fayetteville

The original settlers around here belonged to Stephen F.
Austin's Old Three Hundred. Germans began arriving in
the 1840s. By the 1870s, Czech immigrants, impressed
with the rich soil, began buying up the land. Lush gardens
today attest to the fertility of this earth and the industry
of the populace.

*After entering town, drive to the square and park on the
corner of Texas 159 and Live Oak Street. Walking is the best
way to get a close-up view of all the buildings.*

The Red & White Store (in the blue building) on the
corner advertises as a "family saloon." Constructed about
1855, this is said to be the oldest building on the square. It
has served as an opera house, a hat shop, and a furniture
store. Today beer, wine, ice cream, and chess are the bill
of fare.

The Fayetteville Courthouse, Justice Court Precinct
No. 2, occupies the square. This two-story frame structure, built in 1880, is one of the few precinct courthouses
erected during that early period. Justice of the peace
court, which handled petty crimes and civil cases, was
held here as early as 1850. Local residents raised $600 to
construct the building. Wooden cells were later added upstairs, and the leg irons are still attached to the floor. In
1934, after ten years of fund-raising, ladies in the Do Your
Duty Club donated the four-sided Seth Thomas clock.
Robert Ripley's *Believe It or Not* claims that Fayetteville is
the smallest town in the United States with a town clock
in its courthouse tower.

Continue around the square on Washington Street.

The building that houses the Emporium Gift and
Drug Store was built in 1888 as a general store. The back
portion, which is now an art gallery, served as a
warehouse.

*Follow the red brick path beside the Emporium to the work-
shop in the rear.*

Visitors will find wooden hand-carved columns from
Mexico, pottery, screen printing, stained glass, and newly
hand-carved doors. Often the artists are working in the
studios.

Continue to the next corner, Washington and Fayette streets.

The 1900 two-story red brick building houses the
offices of architect Clovis Heimsath, a Houston transplant.
His firm has been involved in many restoration projects,
including pianist James Dick's Festival Hill at Round Top.

For a time this building served as a mercantile store
and a hospital. During Prohibition, a bar operated in the
basement. The Country Place Hotel is open on the second
floor, the Country Place Restaurant is located at the rear
of the building, and an antique shop is nestled in a tiny
room in the middle of the complex.

While dining at the Country Place Restaurant, note
the "elevator" near the entrance. This apparatus consists
of a base hoisted by ropes tied at each of the four corners.
During the mercantile store days, feed and other supplies
could be lowered to the basement by this device. In the
hospital days, patients could be lifted to the floor above.

The restaurant serves California-style Mexican food
on Friday and a European cuisine on Saturday, 7:00 P.M.
to 11:00 P.M.; a Sunday brunch, 11:00 A.M. to 2:00 P.M.,
features blintzes and crepes, closed Monday through
Thursday. Reservations are required; call 713/387-2712 or
713/378-2380.

The hotel upstairs is for travelers who want something different from the usual motel atmosphere. The
men's room and the ladies' room have claw-foot bathtubs.
Air conditioning comes from fully operational windows
and ceiling fans, as well as handmade quilts in winter.

Lodging is not expensive and is made-to-order for those seeking a quiet evening away from the rush of city life. Accommodations must be paid in advance. The architectural firm will answer the phone since one number serves all: dial 713/387-2712.

The antique shop is open when the architectural firm is open. The hours, along with those of other businesses in town, are at the owners' discretion. Generally, Monday is not a good day for finding most businesses open here. A walking tour of Fayetteville is available, which gives more detail about ownership and construction dates. Ask for a free copy at Heimsath's office.

Turn right on Fayette Street and continue down the west side of the square.

There are several buildings along this block that have pressed tin façades. Note the rugged, individual design in some of the old doors along this block.

Cross the next street, Live Oak, and walk to the Lickskillet Inn in the middle of the block.

This is thought to be the oldest house in town. Built in 1853, it originally had an open dog run down the middle. The inn's name is taken from one of the names the town used in the early days. Residents loved a feast as much then as they do today. On at least one occasion, food, which was always served free, ran short, and the latecomers were told to "lick the skillet." For a time, the community was called Lickskillet. The lower floor of this home has been converted into a boarding house. The rooms are furnished with antiques, and a Continental breakfast is included in the room rate. Evening meals are available featuring home-grown vegetables in season. For reservations, call 713/378-2846.

Lickskillet Day is still an annual event the third Sunday in October. The Baca Band, which began as a family affair in Fayetteville in 1892, provides the music each year. The Baca Band has performed at such events as Richard Nixon's inaugural ball and the American Folklife Festival in Washington, D.C. Other events of the day include a parade, beard-growing contest, dancing, and plenty of food. No one will have to lick the skillet.

Return to the square and conclude the walking tour along Live Oak Street. Retrace the route on Texas 159 for two blocks to Farm Road 1291. Turn right toward New Ulm.

Drive carefully over the railroad track at the edge of Fayetteville, for it is very steep and extremely rough. Watch for goats and a bull that are kept in a small pasture just beyond the red barn on the right. It is possible, on occasions, to see the bull and a goat snuggled contentedly together.

Continue on Farm Road 1291 into Frelsburg. At the one intersection in town, continue straight on Farm Road 109.

New Ulm

This is a prosperous German farming community that began as a village in 1850.

After crossing the railroad track in town, turn right on Front Street and drive four blocks to the Parlour Restaurant.

Yes, "parlour" as in funeral, because that is what originally occupied this building. The façade of several structures and the Parlour are all that remain on this block from the early days. Originally, this street made up the heart of the town when the railroad came through here. This block boasted a dance hall, saloon, grocery, feed and hardware store, and this combination funeral parlour and furniture store.

It is believed the parlour was constructed before the 1900 storm because six holes are drilled in the floor. All the buildings in this area that survived the flooding of that storm have similar holes, bored to keep the structures from floating off their piers. Painters achieved the marbleized effect on the ceiling by holding a smoking coal oil lamp up to the wet paint. German sweet rice and boiled cabbage as well as fried shrimp and steaks are the specialties here. Open Tuesday through Thursday, 4:00

P.M. to 10:00 P.M.; Friday through Sunday, 11:00 A.M. to
10:00 P.M.; closed Monday.

*Continue to the third block, turn left, and drive two blocks to
the stop sign. Turn right on Farm Road 1094 and drive 10.5
miles to the Cat Spring Agricultural Building.*

This structure houses one of the first agricultural societies formed in Texas (1856) to help Germans improve
their farming methods, the Landwirthschaftlicher Verein.
By the 1880s Germans had organized many of these societies all over the state. Anglo-Americans did not join,
probably because German was spoken at the meetings.
The German settlers formed every imaginable kind of
club—singing, shooting, gymnastics, literary, and mutual
help societies—but few survived after the turn of the century. This one became a nucleus for social gatherings.

*Continue along Farm Road 1094. Turn right on Texas 36 and
drive into Sealy.*

Sealy

This railroad town was founded in 1873 when Galvestonians, angry because Houston laid a quarantine on Galveston every time yellow fever broke out, decided to build a railroad that would reach the interior of the state without going through Houston. The line extended only to Richmond before it ran out of money and John Sealy, a Galveston banker and financier, bought out the company and reorganized it. When the railroad reached here, the company bought 11,635 acres at fifty cents an acre from the San Felipe Town tract and laid out the town named for John Sealy.

R. H. Haynes' Sealy Mattress Company helped put the town on the map when Haynes invented machines and the process for manufacturing a felted cotton, non-tufted mattress in 1885. The business continued to operate here until 1975.

Follow Texas 36 through Sealy to North Wye and turn left on U.S. Highway 90. Join U.S. Interstate 10. Drive east to the San Felipe exit, Farm Road 1458. Drive north 2.1 miles to the Stephen F. Austin Memorial Park on the Brazos River; enter on Park Road 38.

San Felipe

San Felipe de Austin is one of the most important towns in Texas' history. (Many Austin Countians say "San Phillip," the Anglicized pronunciation that became popular among the colonists.) As the first Anglo-American settlement, founded in 1823, it served as the social and economic capital of the Austin Colony. Many of Texas' important early leaders either lived here or came to transact business. Laid out on the Mexican plan, San Felipe had four plazas. Boats landed at the dock on the river and the ferry crossed at the Atascosito Road. The cut made by wagon ruts down the steep bank of the Brazos, although overgrown in brush, is still visible. It lies just to the left of the present bridge.

From here, Stephen F. Austin and his secretary, Samuel May Williams (Chap. 1, Galveston section), conducted most of the business of the colony, which eventually stretched from the Gulf of Mexico to the old San Antonio Road and from the Lavaca River to the San Jacinto. Colonists held conventions here in 1832 and again in 1833, asking for reforms in the Mexican government. At the 1833 convention, Texans requested separate statehood and Stephen F. Austin went to Mexico to present the petition. He ended up in jail and did not return to Texas until August 1835. The following November, delegates at the Consultation here voted to remain within Mexico as a separate state and named San Felipe as the capital.

A replica of Austin's log cabin is displayed in the park. One room served as his private quarters, and colonial business transactions took place in the other room. Austin's desk, at which he spent hours writing colonial business, in the required Spanish, is displayed here. The J. J. Josey Store, built about 1847, is now a museum featuring items that would have been for sale during the late 1840s, as well as newspapers, ledgers, and other historical material. Open Saturday and Sunday and most holidays, March through November, 9:00 A.M. to 5:00 P.M.; December through February, 1:00 P.M. to 5:00 P.M.; closed during Christmas holidays. Admission charge.

The old town of San Felipe de Austin did not survive the Texas Revolution. When Sam Houston and his army came through here after receiving news of the fall of the Alamo, they camped north of town at Groce's Crossing, the ferry site mentioned earlier. During this time, residents of San Felipe and the entire countryside began fleeing from Santa Anna's approaching army in the Runaway Scrape. The provisional government fled to Harrisburg, and San Felipe was burned to keep the Mexican army from taking over the town. After a skirmish with Texans stationed across the river, the Mexican army moved south and crossed the Brazos at Richmond.

San Felipe rebuilt after independence and served as the county seat until the government was removed to Bellville in 1848. Part of the original San Felipe tract was sold to the railroad in 1875 for the present town of Sealy.

The Stephen F. Austin Memorial Park, established in 1928, is about all that is left to remind the world of the significance of this site. If it had not been for the reasonable judgment exercised here, the careful planning and exact record-keeping, Texas might never have become the giant land of opportunity that it is even today.

Return south on Farm Road 1458. Turn right on Park Road 38 to an eighteen-hole golf course, swimming pool, interpretive center, and hiking trails along the Brazos River. At the intersection with U.S. Interstate 10 turn left back to Houston to end the trail or continue over the interstate south on Farm Road 1458 past an indoor, air-conditioned rodeo arena and a take-home barbeque house.

Many historians believe that Sam Houston's retreating tactics were unsuccessful efforts to draw Santa Anna into a trap. Catching the enemy at a river crossing would have been an ideal set up, but when the Mexicans reached San Felipe, they stopped nibbling at the bait and marched back south along this route, taking the farmers' corn and butchering their cattle as they moved. That April in 1836, constant rains and the accompanying mud dealt misery to both armies. This route proved to be the high road between the Brazos River on the left and the Bernard River on the right.

At the intersection with Farm Road 1093, turn left. It is 3.9 miles to the Roundup.

The enormous building on the left houses an air-conditioned, indoor rodeo arena. Rodeos are held here every Saturday night, year round. On the first weekend of each month, such national recording stars as Darrell McCall, Moe Bandy, Reba McEntire, and Johnny Duncan appear here. On the other Saturdays, the entertainment is just as lively with cowboys coming from all over the country. The steakhouse, which serves barbeque plates and sandwiches, opens at 5:00 P.M., Thursday, Friday, and Saturday; closed Sunday through Wednesday. The music begins at 7:45 P.M., and a good foot-stomping country-western dance follows each rodeo performance.

This is where many dignitaries, society cowboys, and just plain folks come for special events, especially convention planners who want to show non-Texans what a rodeo is really like. To "hire a rodeo" for a private function, call 713/346-1534.

Continue east on Farm Road 1093. The intersection at Fulshear requires a dogleg to the left and back to the right for the trip on into Houston, where Farm Road 1093 becomes Westheimer Road. To make a stop at Dozier's Barbeque, drive straight on Farm Road 359 instead of turning right on Farm Road 1093.

Dozier's is on the left in a small grocery store. This good barbeque makes a nice treat for weary travelers to take home. Open Tuesday, Wednesday, and Thursday, 8:00 A.M. to 6:30 P.M.; Friday, Saturday, and Sunday, 8:00 A.M. to 7:00 P.M.; closed Monday.

Return to Farm Road 1093 and turn left to Houston.

This heartland of the original Austin colony is rich in history and offers an appeal that is hard to resist both for descendants of the Old Three Hundred, who still hug the land, and for the weekender yearning for relief from the hectic urban pace.

5. Cattlemen's Trail

This tour weaves through the country that the early cattlemen knew, lingers for a time in the locales where they grazed vast herds, relates stories of their adventures, and points out some of the opulent structures built with cattle money.

Leave Houston on U.S. Highway 59, the Southwest Freeway; just beyond Stafford, exit on U.S. Highway 90A to Sugar Land.

Sugar Land

The Imperial Sugar Company, the only pure cane sugar refinery in Texas and one of the largest sugar refineries in the United States, dominates the landscape, but pioneers who shaped early Texas history left their mark on this land. In 1828, Samuel May Williams, Stephen F. Austin's secretary, whose home is included in the Galveston section of Chapter 1, received the league of land that now constitutes Sugar Land in payment for his services to the colonists. As noted earlier, Williams played an important role as a financier of the Texas Revolution, early banker, and investor. After the revolution Williams was in such heavy debt that he began selling his landholdings. His brothers Nathaniel and Matthew bought this plantation, planted the first sugarcane in 1840, and built a crude powered sugar mill in 1843.

After W. J. Kyle and B. F. Terry got rich in the 1849 California Gold Rush, they came back to Texas, bought the Williams plantation, and named it Sugar Land. B. F. Terry is the "Terry" of Terry's Texas Rangers. This unit, the 8th Texas Cavalry, C.S.A., mustered at Houston on Sep-

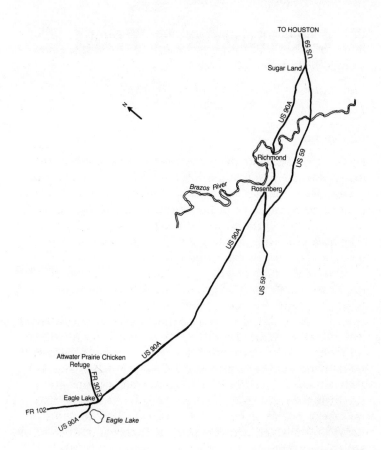

tember 9, 1861. Known as the "white-gloved gentry of Texas," the one hundred men who made up this unit provided their own horses, saddles, uniforms, guns, and ammunition. It is said that they "rode like Arabs, shot like marksmen, and fought like devils."

In the 1890s Edward E. Cunningham built the first sugar refinery here; Sugar Land remained a company-owned town until it was incorporated in 1959. It is possible to visit the sugar refinery for a one-hour tour, which includes the entire refining operation from the raw state to the packaged product. Tours are offered Monday through Friday only, 10:00 A.M. and 2:00 P.M. For a group of ten or more, call for reservations: 713/491-9181, extension 268. No admission charge.

Continue into Richmond on U.S. Highway 90A.

Richmond

Richmond is the site of an early settlement of Stephen F. Austin's Old Three Hundred. Such famous Texans as Mirabeau B. Lamar and Jane Long, the "Mother of Texas," lived here. Many turn-of-the-century homes have been preserved, sites around which the Jaybird-Woodpecker War took place are pointed out, and stories abound of pioneer courage, bravery, and a little bullheadedness.

When the first contingent of Austin's Old Three Hundred came to Texas, one group traveled overland (see Chap. 4, Brenham section) and another group of eighteen came by ship, the *Lively*, to the mouth of the Brazos River. After landing in late December, they waited for Austin to meet them. When he did not come (they were supposed to have landed at the mouth of the Colorado River and Austin went there [see Chap. 6]), most of them returned to the United States. Two or three moved up the river and may have been the group that settled in 1822 on "the bend" in the river, which is present Richmond. They built a one-room log house, which became known as "the fort" or Fort Settlement. Since it sat just below the bend in the river, Fort Bend eventually became the name.

While crossing the Brazos River bridge, look to the left some two hundred yards. This is the area thought to be the original site of the fort. Turn left on Fifth Street, drive two blocks to Houston Street, and turn right beside the Fort Bend County Museum.

Walking and driving tour maps are available here as well as displays representing the first one hundred years in Richmond. The museum is open Tuesday through Friday, 10:00 A.M. to 4:00 P.M.; Saturday and Sunday, 1:00 P.M. to 5:00 P.M.; closed Monday. No admission charge.

The Moore Home is the mansion on the grounds with the museum. This impressive structure was built in 1883 by John M. Moore and then enlarged to its present size in 1905. One of Moore's daughters planted the magnolia tree on the front lawn during the 1890s. Moore was a U.S. congressman, cattle breeder, and land developer. His son Judge John M. Moore, Jr., gave the home to the Fort Bend County Museum Association upon his death in 1975. The facility serves as a house museum, furnished to depict the gracious style of living in the early 1900s. The mansion is open for tours Sunday only, 1:00 P.M. to 5:00 P.M. The last tour begins at 4:15 P.M. Admission charge.

This home and others in the city are open by appointment for groups of ten or more, Tuesday through Friday, 9:30 A.M. to 4:00 P.M. Luncheons may be arranged. Make inquiries through the Museum Association, 500 Houston Street, Richmond, TX 77469, 713/342-6478.

Turn right on Sixth Street, drive two blocks back to Jackson Street, and turn right. Turn left on Fifth Street.

The McFarlane House, built in 1889, and the area behind the house, played an important role in the Battle of Richmond, the culmination of the Jaybird-Woodpecker War, 1888–1890. After the Civil War, blacks gained control of the political arena in Fort Bend County, much to the chagrin of about 90 percent of the white population. The Jaybirds represented the white faction made up of the wealthy citizens who had controlled the Democratic county. The Woodpeckers numbered about forty officials and ex-officials elected by the black-dominated Republican vote during Reconstruction. The community divided as a result of the bitter contentions for power. After one Jaybird was killed and another wounded, the Jaybirds sent out a warning for certain blacks to leave the county within ten hours. Both factions armed themselves and the Texas Rangers came in to ensure order on polling day in 1888. The Democratic Jaybirds lost the election and the killings continued the next year. On August 16, 1889, shots rang out between the McFarlane House and the courthouse, which stood one block behind this home. When the firing started, a young man, Earle McFarlane, began shooting from the second-floor rear window of the house at men who were visible in the courthouse door. Three other young men joined McFarlane, and at least one man in the courthouse was shot from this vantage.

The Woodpeckers retreated and the Jaybirds took control. The twenty-minute battle left five men dead. At a meeting of the Jaybird Democratic Organization in October 1889, 441 men signed a membership roll, accepting a constitution that gave county control to white people of Fort Bend County. The McFarlane House has been restored and serves as a visitor's reception center for travelers to Fort Bend County and the Texas Gulf Coast.

Continue north past the site where the old courthouse stood. Note the horse-watering trough on the corner. Turn right on Morton Street.

The Jaybird Monument next to the present city hall is in commemoration of the lives lost during the Jaybird-Woodpecker War and perhaps it serves as a reminder of who won that conflict.

The old National Hotel, from which some of the shots were fired, stood catercorner from the present monument. The hotel belonged to David and Carry Nation, the same lady who later carried her hatchet into saloons throughout Kansas and is credited with starting the movement that resulted in national prohibition.

David Nation was a correspondent for the *Houston Post* and wrote articles reporting on the meetings of the Jaybirds. After the battle, several young Jaybirds physically assaulted Nation because of his articles. Afterward, the Nations moved on to Kansas where Carry began her relentless crusade against tobacco and alcohol, saloons in particular.

Carry Nation had first married Dr. Charles Gloyd, a drunkard, who soon died. She and David Nation, a lawyer and minister, married and in 1881 opened the National Hotel in Richmond. When a terrible fire threatened the hotel in 1885, she prayed "loudly and fervently" for the hotel to be spared. After the wind shifted and the structure survived, she believed that she had divine protection. She also believed that her name, Carry A. Nation, had been preordained and she claimed to receive visions.

After a Kansas law banning liquor sales went unheeded, Carry Nation began praying outside saloons. She progressed to smashing the establishments with stones and, later, with her hatchet. She closed the saloons where she lived and then moved on to neighboring villages. Although arrested for disturbing the peace when she entered states where liquor sales were legal, the nearly six-foot-tall Carry continued her crusade, her eloquent speech often inspiring others. David Nation divorced her in 1901 for desertion.

Turn left on Fourth Street.

The site of Jane Long's boarding house is on the right in the middle of the block. Jane Long's story begins in

Chapter 1 as she followed her husband, James Long, to
Texas on his ill-fated expedition in 1819–1821 to free Texas
from Spanish rule. After Long's death, Jane lived in San
Felipe and Brazoria before opening a boarding house
here. Many men were taken with her beauty and charm
and were entertained here, including Ben Milam, Sam
Houston, and Mirabeau B. Lamar, in whose papers ap-
pears an account of her life. Jane never remarried and ran
this boarding house until her plantation was completed
just outside town. She left her slave, Kian, in charge of
the boarding house and moved to the plantation where
she lived until her death at age eighty-two.

Turn left at the next corner on Calhoun Street.

The Confederate Museum is in the middle of the block
between Sixth and Seventh streets. This structure has
served as a tin shop, blacksmith shop, and saloon. It is
open by appointment. Contact the Museum Association,
713/342-6478.

Return to Sixth Street and turn left.

Decker Park encompasses the next block and includes
a replica of the 1822 cabin constructed as the fort on the
bend in the river and the 1850s house that belonged to
Carry Nation's daughter and her husband in 1883. The
depot that was erected in 1901 also occupies this site. At
times these buildings house craft and antique shops.

At the end of this block, the 1896 county jail is being
restored, with plans for opening it as a museum. Details
and/or admission information can be secured at the Fort
Bend County Museum.

*Turn right on Preston Street, drive two blocks to Fourth
Street, and turn right two blocks to Morton Street. Turn left
on Morton.*

The Barker House Restaurant is on the northeast corner of Third and Morton streets. Built before the 1880s,
the McCloy-Dillard Drug Store occupied this structure
during the Jaybird-Woodpecker trouble. The Jaybirds used

the building as a hiding place for their guns and
ammunition.

The Barker House Restaurant is known for "country
dining in the atmosphere of Old Richmond." The sandwiches for lunch are delicious and the antiques and hanging plants add to the gracious surroundings. Abigail's Attic,
a cluster of three shops, occupies the loft. Gifts, antiques,
and restored wicker make this a delightful stop. Open
Monday through Thursday, 11:00 A.M. to 9:00 P.M.; Friday
and Saturday, 11:00 A.M. to 10:00 P.M.; closed Sunday.

*Drive to Second Street and turn right one block to Jackson
Street, U.S. Highway 90A, near the Brazos River bridge.*

The Brazos River makes a pronounced hairpin curve
north of town. This portion of the river is on private property and is where Santa Anna crossed with his men on
April 14, 1836. The "Napoleon of the West" felt such confi-
dence in his ability to capture the "land thieves," as he
called President Burnet's ad interim government, that he
took fewer than six hundred men with him (others joined
later) to Harrisburg, leaving the bulk of his force here to
await his return in three days. When the Mexican general
arrived in Harrisburg, he discovered that the government
had fled to Galveston Island. The rest of the story is related in Chapter 1.

This "bend" is also where the sidewheeler *Yellow
Stone* ran the Mexican gauntlet. When Sam Houston's
army needed to cross the rain-swollen Brazos River, north
of San Felipe, to reach Groce's Plantation near present
Hempstead, Houston impressed the *Yellow Stone* to ferry
the army across. The load of cotton bales remained on
board as protection from possible enemy fire. With the
mission completed, the *Yellow Stone's* captain headed
down river knowing that Santa Anna's army waited at the
bend. The ship approached the bend with a full head
of steam, but as it rounded the curve the captain maneuvered the course, bumped the side, and turned completely around in midstream. It is said that a passenger
became so frightened he tried to jump overboard, appar-

ently believing it was safer with the Mexicans. The Mexicans, who had never seen a steamboat, stared in awe and then began firing their muskets. When no response came from behind the cotton bales, some adventurous souls tried to lasso the smokestacks. The vessel ran the course safely and, with loud blasts of the whistle, steamed on down to Quintana.

The *Yellow Stone* continued in service to Texas upon arriving in Galveston. The craft transported President Burnet and his cabinet to the scene of the Battle of San Jacinto and picked up other officials, as well as Santa Anna, whom it carried back to Velasco for the signing of the peace treaty. The following December the *Yellow Stone* performed one last task for the new republic. The ship transported the body of Stephen F. Austin, the empresario and Father of Texas, in a solemn trip from Columbia down the Brazos to the Peach Point Plantation Cemetery (Chap. 6).

Drive southwest through Richmond on U.S. Highway 90A. The underpass is the city limits demarcation.

Rosenberg

Rosenberg is a railroad town. As discussed earlier, great rivalry grew up between Houston and Galveston and when Houston virtually stopped all business out of Galveston each year by imposing a yellow fever quarantine, investors decided to construct a railroad around Houston that would go to the interior of the state.

The law required that railroads go within a mile of each county courthouse. When the Gulf, Colorado, and Santa Fe came into Fort Bend County, the developers asked Richmond for the customary cash bonus and right-of-way into town. The citizens refused since they already had a railroad. The line, accustomed to "going around" towns, came to within a mile of the courthouse (as prescribed by law) and built Rosenberg Junction depot in 1880 at a site where it crossed the Galveston, Harrisburg, and San Antonio Railroad. The site was named for the same Henry Rosenberg discussed in Chapter 1. Among Rosenberg's many business endeavors, he served as president of the Gulf, Colorado, and Santa Fe Railroad.

Rosenberg remained simply a junction for the next year, until Count Joseph Telfener opened his headquarters and began laying a railroad from here to Victoria. Telfener brought in twelve hundred Italian laborers and the track became known as the "Macaroni Line." This will be discussed later in this chapter. Business began coming into the area. The railroad laid out the town in 1883, and thrifty Germans from nearby counties bought railroad land; then Czech, Polish, and Mexican families poured in, turning the community into the melting pot of the county.

Today, the annual Fort Bend Czech Fest is a family affair. Such Czech foods as *kolaches* (delicious pastries), *bramborove placky* (potato pancakes), *klobase* (sausage), *klobasniky* (foot-long sausage in *kolache* dough), and *pivo* (beer) are served. Activities include dances on Friday and Saturday nights, a domino tournament, and displays of Czech crafts and antiques. Fairy tales are enacted with plays, skits, and pantomimes for the children. The Czech Fest is held the first weekend in May at the Fair Grounds.

Between Thanksgiving and Christmas, take a side trip. Turn left on Lawrence Street, across from the Fort Bend County Fairgrounds. Drive two long blocks to Avenue J and turn right one block to Royl's Toys (1201 Tobola Street).

The toys at Royl's are hand carved and range from folk games to tree ornaments and stick horses. Roy Hauger started carving as a hobby, and during the year he continues the fun. Then, partly to clear out the collection, and to share with others, he opens his garage shop for one month between Thanksgiving and Christmas, Monday through Saturday, 10:00 A.M. to 5:00 P.M.; closed Sunday.

Return on Avenue J to Lawrence Street, turn left to U.S. Highway 90A, and turn left again. At the edge of town, take the right fork at the first Y. At the second Y, take the left fork and continue west on U.S. Highway 90A. Turn right on Farm Road 3013 just after entering Eagle Lake. Drive six miles to the entrance to the park.

Attwater Prairie Chicken National Wildlife Refuge

This is a photographer's and bird watcher's delight. Contact park headquarters for information on road conditions. During rainy seasons, the trails through this area are often impassable. No camping, picnicking, hunting, or fishing is allowed. Write P.O. Box 845, Eagle Lake, TX 77434, or call 713/234-3021.

Return to Eagle Lake.

Eagle Lake

A post office opened here in 1849, and ten years later the Buffalo Bayou, Brazos, and Colorado Railroad, the first railroad in Texas, reached Eagle Lake. The town served as the center of sugar cane plantations until 1898 when rice farming was added to the economy. In addition, three railroads came through here, with the accompanying number of drummers and travelers.

Enter Eagle Lake on U.S. Highway 90A, Main Street; turn right beyond the city hall on McCarty Street. Cross the railroad track to the Farris 1912 Hotel.

A hotel has occupied this site since the 1850s, accommodating the large number of travelers that came through. The present structure, built in 1912 during Eagle Lake's golden era, underwent restoration and was reopened in 1977 by new owners, who named the facility Farris 1912.

Today's travelers are hunters from all over the world who fly or drive to Eagle Lake, the "Goose Hunting Capital of the World." Bill and Helyn Farris, proprietors of Farris 1912, operate a flower, antique, and gift shop on the first floor as well as a delightful restaurant, which serves by reservation only. Hotel guests enjoy the open, plant-filled public rooms enlivened with Victorian and turn-of-the-century antiques. The sixteen rooms upstairs boast pieces saved from the early hotel days and are all decorated in rich, warm hues. Each room opens onto the charming mezzanine, which is brightened by an enor-

mous skylight and affords a quiet, relaxed atmosphere.

This hotel, built about the same time as the sumptuous Galvez in Galveston, also charged an exorbitant $2 a night. Often newlyweds, on their way to Galveston, stopped here for one night before proceeding to the Galvez for their honeymoon. Today, during goose hunting season (November, December, and January), the Farris 1912 offers only the American Plan for overnight guests. This includes three "country gourmet" meals (all you can eat) each day. Hors d'oeuvres before dinner, snacks, and setups are all part of the package. Believe it or not, this also includes filling each guest's coffee or hot chocolate ther-

mos, dry shoes waiting in the mud shed, and pickup service at the airport. Several hunt clubs operate around
Eagle Lake and some guides come to the hotel to meet
their parties.

Guests from February through October are served under the European Plan, which includes a Continental
breakfast. During March, April, and May the hotel opens
on weekends only for guests. In February and June
through October, only large groups can be accommodated.
Advance reservations are required at all times and a 50
percent deposit is necessary for confirmation.

Lunch in the Drummers Room is available by reservation on Thursday, Friday, and Saturday, 11:45 A.M. to
1:45 P.M. During hunting season, meals are available three
times a day for nonregistered guests by reservation only.
Groups touring the area will find this an ideal stop for
lunch or dinner. In 1980 the Farris 1912 opened an adjoining building, which offers guest rooms the year round. For
reservations, call 713/234-2546 or write 201 North Mc-
Carty at Post Office Street, Eagle Lake, TX 77434. The
food and facilities are not oriented for children under
twelve. No gratuities please.

*For the trip to Columbus, take Farm Road 102, which runs
beside the Farris 1912.*

In about twelve miles, watch for the Texas historical
marker on the right, which tells the story of Alleyton, one
of the most important cities in Texas during the Civil War.

The Buffalo Bayou, Brazos, and Colorado Railroad
had moved on from Eagle Lake to Alleyton by 1860 and
did not go farther west until after the Civil War. Cotton
came into Alleyton on the railroad and was ferried across
the Colorado River three miles to Columbus where it was
loaded onto big-bedded wagons and high-wheeled Mexican carts pulled by horses, oxen, or mules. The valuable
cotton was transported from Columbus via Goliad, San
Patricio, the King Ranch, and on to Brownsville, marking
the trail with white cotton fluff. Across the border, at the
neutral port of Matamoros, the cotton was loaded onto
blockade runners, which sneaked past the Union gunboats

and finally reached European markets. The carts and wagons brought back ammunition, clothing, and medicine for the Confederate army. With the fall of Vicksburg in 1863, the Mississippi River was sealed off and the Confederacy was divided. This Texas-Mexico trade route served as the South's major supply line.

Continue to U.S. Interstate 10, cross on the overpass, and drive into Columbus on U.S. Highway 90, the first exit off U.S. Interstate 10.

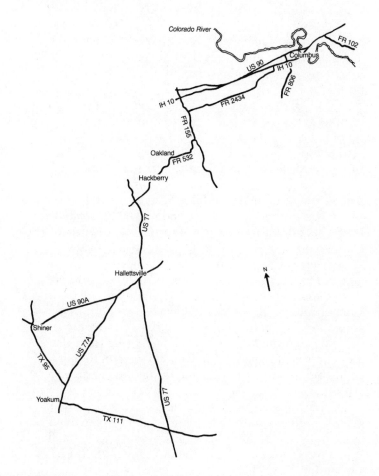

Columbus

It is appropriate for the city of magnolias and beautiful homes built from the 1850s through the early 1900s to choose "Magnolia Homes Tour" as the title of its annual bash, which exquisitely shows off the heritage of this community during the third weekend in May. Restoration is not new in Columbus; it began in an organized fashion in 1961, before it became the stylish thing to do. The Colorado County Courthouse District begins one block beyond the Colorado River bridge. This twelve-block area has been placed on the National Register of Historic Places because of the concentration of nineteenth-century Victorian commercial and residential structures, which set this area apart from the surrounding, more modern buildings.

In 1823, Stephen F. Austin had the site of present Columbus surveyed with the intention of making it the capital of his colony. However, with most of the colonists settled along the Brazos and the problems of frequent Indian raids here, San Felipe de Austin became the best choice. None of the structures here survived that early period because, in March 1836, Sam Houston had the village of Columbus burned. He had moved his army here from Gonzales after hearing of the fall of the Alamo. They camped on the east side of the river for five or six days, while General Santa Anna's army camped on the west side of the river. If Houston had seen any way that his little band could stand up to that mighty force, the Texas war for independence would have been fought on this soil. Houston knew better, however, and, after burning the town to keep the Mexicans from benefiting from the stores, the Texan general moved his men on to San Felipe in his bid for time to build a fighting unit capable of winning.

After independence, the colonists returned and slowly rebuilt their town. In 1838 plans to erect a courthouse had to be halted. Pine lumber cut at Bastrop was being floated down the Colorado, but, as the building material reached Columbus, a strong current suddenly caught the raft and

floated it on downstream. The present courthouse, built
on the square in 1890–91, replaced the 1850s structure.
During a restoration project in 1980, the building's original stained-glass dome, which had been in storage, was
replaced in the ceiling of the district courtroom on the
second floor. This elegant work can be viewed 8:00 A.M. to
5:00 P.M., Monday through Friday, except when district
court is in session. Stand in the middle of the courtroom,
centered under the dome, and listen to the echo.

The building catercorner from the square (northwest
corner of Walnut and Milam streets), built between 1850
and 1854, originally housed a grocery. Close examination
of the side of the building facing Walnut Street documents
a social phenomenon of most small towns. The brick is
worn away about eighteen inches up the wall where men
have stood with one foot braced against the wall watching
the "action" on the square. Inside, the wooden floor is
worn away in an area where clerks stood behind the
counter. This fine old building houses The First Edition, a
bookstore with a large Texana collection as well as gift
items and china. The 1883 tower on the southwest corner
of the square (Milam and Spring streets) housed Columbus' first water supply system. Today the United Daughters of the Confederacy operate a Confederate Museum
here. It is open during the Magnolia Homes Tour.

Fans of Nicholas J. Clayton, the brilliant architect
whose structures dominate the Galveston landscape
(Chap. 1), probably have already noticed the Stafford Opera House, one of Clayton's designs (south side of the
square). R. E. (Bob) Stafford became a millionaire by
rounding up the unbranded cattle that roamed the open
prairies after the Civil War. He had this structure built in
1886 to house his bank and a department store. The one-
thousand-seat opera house occupied the second floor. The
building cost $50,000, plus another $10,000 for stage
equipment and curtains hand painted in oils. Stafford
also erected the Victorian mansion next door. It is said
that he had his home built so that he could watch the
productions on the opera house stage from his bedroom
window.

Bob Stafford and his brother John came to Texas when all men carried guns and citizens had little regard for the law. Fighting became the accepted way of settling disputes and the Staffords adapted readily. They made enemies right off with the Townsend boys, sons of an old, aristocratic family in the area; cattle provided the reason. In the midst of killings, and threats of more killings, a Townsend became sheriff. On July 7, 1890, the day the courthouse cornerstone was laid, Larkin and Marian Hope, nephews of Sheriff Townsend, shot and killed Bob and John Stafford in front of a saloon across the street from the opera house. Descendants of the Townsend-Stafford feud still live in the area but are good friends.

After Bob Stafford's death, the opera house continued to host such notables as Lillian Russell, the Great Houdini, and the young Al Jolson until it was sold in 1916 to the Ford agency. The fabulous curtains are gone because one of the Ford agency owners, in a fit of rage because someone had poisoned his prize bird dog, ripped the curtains down, ran out, and threw them over his hog pen. After years of neglect, the building was purchased by Magnolia Homes Tour, Inc. The first floor has been restored and is used as office space and the second floor, with partial restoration, serves the community's local theater group. Walking-tour maps and information on the annual Magnolia Homes Tour are available from the chamber of commerce office here. Open Monday through Friday, 9:00 A.M. to noon and 1:00 P.M. to 4:00 P.M.; closed Saturday and Sunday.

Drive east on Spring Street to the second block, Front Street, and turn left to the Koliba Home Museum Complex in the middle of the block (1124 Front).

This is a stop for collectors. Stephen Townsend, the first Colorado County sheriff (1837–38), occupied the early part of the home. Today, Mrs. Homer Koliba, a Townsend descendant, and her husband, a former state representative, own the home. The eighteen rooms of displays include an early history of Columbus, items used in homes during the colonial period, as well as Mr. Koliba's legislative room with photographs and citations from his years of public service. A swept backyard contains endless stands of bottle trees, blacksmith tools, and a large collection of hand irons. The museum is open daily, 10:00 A.M. to 6:00 P.M. Admission charge.

Go back on Front Street to Spring Street, turn right, and then turn left on Milam Street.

In four blocks look for the masonry fence, the only one left in town. In the 1850s many fences as well as buildings were fashioned with this lime, sand, and gravel mixture. (Gravel is still being mined outside town.)

Continue one more block to Wallace Street and turn right.

The Tait Town House is on the right (526 Wallace). Dr. Charles W. Tait began this town home in 1856 in order to get his family to drier land away from his plantation on the Colorado River where five children had died in infancy. Interrupted by the Civil War, Dr. Tait did not complete the structure until he returned from serving in the Confederate army. A story is told that Dr. Tait had to move hurriedly to Texas from Alabama because of his part in a duel. The overseer on Tait's plantation had "presumed" to seek the hand of Tait's sister Lucy. As the older brother, Tait was "obligated" to put the man in his place with the challenge of a duel. Tait fatally wounded the overseer and promptly set his sights for Texas.

Turn right at the next corner, Bowie Street. During school hours, this block is cordoned off for a playground. If necessary, drive one more block and circle back to Bowie. Continue four blocks to the corner of Bowie and Washington streets.

The Dilue Rose Harris House is on the northwest corner. Built in 1860, this is the oldest home still standing in Columbus. It is made of tabby construction: a mixture of lime, sand, and gravel poured to form the walls. The concrete-like surface is then scored to look like stone. Mrs. Dilue Rose Harris became well acquainted with the leaders of the Texas Revolution and the republic, and her reminiscences have been a primary source of early Texas history. They were published in the *Quarterly of the Texas Historical Association* (1900–1904).

The antique shop next door (604 Washington) specializes in late-eighteenth-century and early-nineteenth-century pieces. The hours vary. The Alley Log Cabin, behind the Dilue Rose Harris home, was built in 1836 about eight miles south of town just after the Runaway Scrape. Its owner was a brother of the man for whom Alleyton was named. In 1976, Alley descendants gave the cabin, its present site, and restoration monies to Magnolia Homes Tour, Inc. This is another structure that is open during the spring home tour.

Turn left on Walnut Street.

The Tate-Senftenberg-Brandon House (616 Walnut) is on the right. Originally a four-room structure when built in the 1860s, the house was enlarged to this impressive size in the 1880s. Owned by Magnolia Homes Tour, Inc., it is a museum of small-town, nineteenth-century life. This is the headquarters for the homes tour the third weekend in May. In addition to home tours, an art show sponsored by the Live Oak Art Club is held under the magnolias on

the square, buggy and surrey rides are available, and continuous entertainment is provided. The only event held away from the square is the antique show and sale at the Veterans Hall just beyond the old cemetery on U.S. Highway 90 west.

Besides sponsoring the May event, Magnolia Homes Tour, Inc., offers a tour package of three homes and a luncheon to groups of thirty or more. This service is provided from September 1 through April 15 and reservations are required thirty days in advance. Write Magnolia Homes Tour, Inc., P.O. Box 817, Columbus, TX 78934.

Continue west on Walnut Street.

The old city cemetery is on the left, three blocks beyond the Texas 71 intersection. Among the gravestones is one of an avowed infidel. He wrote his own epitaph and ended his life with self-administered chloroform. It is said that while he served as deputy sheriff in Colorado County he was responsible for black restrooms being constructed. This effort could be construed two ways: before the lavatories were designated, black people had no access at all to public facilities. This is the wording on the headstone:

Here Rests
Ike Towell
An infidel who had
No hope of heaven
Nor fear of hell
Was free of superstition
To do right and love
Justice was his religion. .

Continue west on Walnut Street, U.S. Highway 90. About four blocks beyond the golf course, turn left on Farm Road 806. Turn right on U.S. Interstate 10 and drive 1.8 miles to the Farm Road 2434 exit. It is 11.8 miles on Farm Road 2434 to Farm Road 155. Turn left for 3.4 miles to Farm Road 532 and turn right.

This rolling land is especially beautiful in the spring. Cattle dot the hillsides and wild flowers grow in profusion. The cotton route, over which teamsters transported cotton to Mexico during the Civil War, came through here from Columbus to Hallettsville. The rich grassland made good grazing for the mules and oxen.

The land that is present Oakland was originally granted to James Bowie, land speculator and slave trader of later Alamo fame. Hugo Neuhaus built the two-story rock store at Hackberry. It is said that the stagecoach stopped here on the route from Columbus to Gonzales.

Turn left at the intersection with U.S. Highway 77.

Hallettsville

After John Hallet died in 1836, his widow left their home in Goliad and moved into a cabin her husband had built in 1833 on his league of land on the east bank of the Lavaca River. Margaret Hallet stocked the cabin with merchandise and planted corn. Soon others began settling nearby, and Hallettsville became the county seat in 1852. The beautiful 1897 courthouse still dominates the square.

Soon after entering Hallettsville, just beyond the city park and golf course, turn right on Crockett Street.

At the intersection with La Grange Street, note the entrance to the Hallettsville Garden and Cultural Center. The trees lining this entranceway are said to be the ones that the Hallets planted to line the lane to their cabin. In addition to picnic facilities, this park offers electrical hookups. On the fourth Sunday in January, the State Championship Domino Tourney is held right around the corner at the American Legion Hall.

Turn left on La Grange Street. Drive three blocks to Brewster Street and turn right. Turn left at the next corner, North Main Street.

The 1886 jail is on the right just across Lieberknecht Branch. For ten years after Hallettsville became the county seat, Lavaca County prisoners were held in homes and barns. Eventually a walled-in cellar with strong cages was constructed. The cages were moved into this structure when it opened.

Continue south on Main Street to the courthouse square.

Listed on the National Register of Historic Places, this courthouse design was strongly influenced by the Allegheny County Courthouse in Pittsburgh. During World War II, Hallettsville became known to flyers as the Christmas Tree Town because they could mark the site by the

star atop the courthouse. Today, Christmas lights are strung from the clock tower to form a giant Christmas tree, which is beautiful for miles as travelers approach the city.

Drive one block to Fourth Street, U.S. Highway 90A, and turn right. Cross the Lavaca River, pass the drive-in grocery on the left, and watch for the Lay-Bozka House.

This home, built in 1878–1882 and listed on the National Register of Historic Places, is appropriately called "the wedding cake house." It does look like a fancy cake.

Lavaca County residents have never been conformers. The phrase "free state of Lavaca" was coined in reference to the independent behavior of county citizens. Never was this more evident than during the Civil War. When the call for volunteers went out Lavaca County men responded immediately. By 1862, however, more men were needed to hold off the Union strength. The conscript law called for the draft of all men eighteen to thirty-five for a period of three years and eventually extended the ages from seventeen to fifty. To enforce the law, Home Guards searched for draft dodgers and deserters. Bohemians and Germans in Lavaca County had little concern for the plight of the big planters and they had little faith in the principle of state sovereignty. While most of them served in the Confederacy, some made their way to Mexico, but others stayed on their farms and dressed as women while they worked in the fields or hid in Somer's Thicket along the Lavaca River in the southern part of the county.

As months passed with no pay, poor rations, insufficient clothing, and families suffering in the absence of the men, desertions increased. The weary soldiers saw the conflict as a "rich man's war, poor man's fight." The government tax on cotton increased from one-fifth to one-half and other goods were impressed as needed. The owners were given worthless certificates of indebtedness, which the Confederacy would not accept in payment of taxes. Lavaca Countians were not alone in their independence, however. The entire state suffered and grew weary of the conflict.

Independence reared up again in the early twentieth century when Hallettsville became a hot bed of socialism. Small farmers who resented large landholders and wanted labor conditions improved and government ownership of transportation, communication, and exchange facilities joined the growing Socialist Party. From 1911 to 1917, the *Rebel*, the state's largest socialist newspaper, was published here in the office of the local paper. The circulation rose to 25,000, and the Socialist Party in Texas took 25,000 votes in the 1912 presidential election. In an effort to stop any movement that stirred discontent against the government during World War I, the 1917 Sedition Act was passed. This law effectively shut down papers like the *Rebel* because it halted the newspaper's use of the mails.

Continue west on U.S. Highway 90A to Shiner.

Shiner

A Czech and German town, Shiner has maintained its 1890s downtown, its own brewery, and a wire works that started from scrap wire and has grown to international status. Claims of the "cleanest little city in Texas" are well deserved.

The steeple that is visible for miles before reaching Shiner is on the Sts. Cyril and Methodios Catholic Church. The building, reminiscent of cathedrals in the Bavarian Alps, is to the left, less than a block off the highway. Built in 1921 at a cost of $130,000, this grand Gothic structure is worth a stop. It is open every day.

Turn right on Texas 95, Fifth Street, at the four-way flashing stop light.

Kaspar Wire Works is on the right, less than a mile out Texas 95. When barbed wire began being used in this area, smooth wire lost value and August Kaspar, son of a Swiss Lutheran missionary, worked some wire scraps with a pair of pliers to make a corn shuck basket. A neighbor bought the first basket and soon Kaspar was selling them as rapidly as he could make them. In 1898 he began making baskets and horse muzzles full-time, using a rented wagon for his showroom.

A son took over the operation in 1924 and a grandson joined the organization in 1949. Today, the assembly-line business manufactures display racks, gym suit baskets, cold drink racks, deep fry baskets—most anything that is made of wire is probably fashioned right here. The products are shipped all over the world. Tours of the wire works are welcome from 8:00 A.M. to 5:00 P.M., Monday through Friday only. No admission charge. For groups of more than five, please make advance arrangements with Mr. Little at 512/594-3327.

Retrace the route on Texas 95 approximately 0.2 mile to Helweg Street and turn right.

Spoetzl Brewery is at the end of the block. A local stock company built this business in 1909 and sold it to Kosmas Spoetzl in 1915. During Prohibition, they manufactured "near beer" and ice. Near beer is made by boiling the original product until the alcohol content is diminished to the accepted federal level of less than 5 percent by weight. It is said that the boiling process spread a very unpleasant odor over the entire area.

Some say that Lavaca Countians, members of the "free state of Lavaca," ignored the restrictions imposed during Prohibition and that county officials made no real effort to enforce the law. Unsubstantiated claims say mysterious "night production" continued. In 1922 the owners' daughter joined the staff and in 1950 she became the only woman in the United States to be sole owner of a brewery. Tours of the brewery and cold beer in the hospitality room are available 10:00 A.M. to noon and 1:00 P.M. to 5:00 P.M., Monday through Friday only. No admission charge.

Each year on the Sunday before Labor Day, Sts. Cyril and Methodios Catholic Church sponsors a "Church Feast." A huge chicken dinner is served at Legion Park and Shiner beer is the featured beverage.

For the drive into downtown, proceed across the bridge if it has been rebuilt. A flood in 1981 destroyed the old one-lane bridge and, at the time this was written, no date had been set for the new crossing. If the bridge is still out, return to State Highway 95, turn right, and cross Boggy Creek. Turn right at the second intersection, Avenue C, and continue across the tracks into downtown Shiner. After crossing the railroad tracks, turn left immediately on Seventh Street.

Shiner was laid out when the railroad came through in 1887. Soon it became a trade center for German and Czech farmers. This downtown area has retained the original simplicity and Old World charm so representative of German and Czech heritage. Note the Opera House in the first block. When the structure was built in 1895, a saloon and other businesses occupied the first floor. The second floor served as an opera house with theatrical productions and social gatherings until the 1920s. Today the Gaslight Theater, an area drama group, provides regular performances. Check times at the office on the first floor.

At the end of the second block, Avenue E, turn left two blocks. At the flashing stop light, Texas 95, Fifth Street, turn right. Follow Texas 95 to U.S. Highway 77A and turn right. It is 1.5 miles to Business U.S. Highway 77A. Turn left.

Yoakum

Tanneries and leather factories, wild flowers in the spring, and the Tom Tom Rodeo (that is tom as in tomato) provide some of the reasons to travel through this community. In the years after the Civil War, before Yoakum was even laid out, trail riders gathered here with their herds of Longhorns for the trip up the Chisholm Trail to market in Kansas. Finally, with the coming of the railroad in 1877, the town developed. There are many leather factories here, but Tex Tan is on the route.

Continue into town on Business U.S. Highway 77A, West Gonzales Street.

Tex Tan Welhausen Company (107 West Gonzales Street) offers free tours. Visitors see saddles, belts, billfolds, and even saddletrees being manufactured. Please make reservations two days in advance; call 512/293-2311.

Continue on Business U.S. Highway 77A through town. Watch for the right turn the route takes on Irvine Street. It is about six blocks to West Morris Street, Texas 111. Turn left, drive about thirteen miles to U.S. Highway 77, and turn right.

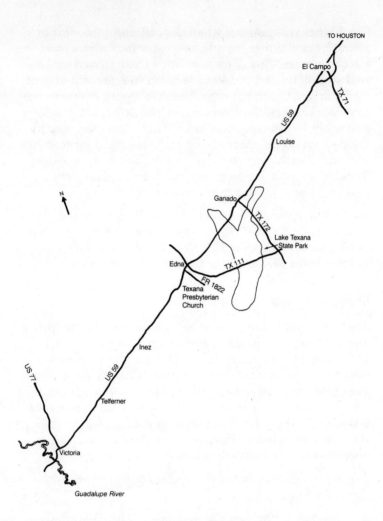

Victoria

After the traveler enters the city limits, it becomes increasingly evident that Victoria is a rapidly expanding city cleverly maintaining its small-town appreciation of its unique history.

Drive several miles into town on U.S. Highway 77. At the
intersection with Rio Grande Street, turn right. It is four
blocks to Main Street. Turn left. The huge sign marking La
Calle de los Diez Amigos (the Street of Ten Friends) is dis-
played prominently in five blocks on the corner of Main
Street and Goodwin Avenue.

Main Street originally carried this title because
Martín de León, the Mexican empresario who settled Victoria in 1824, established ten of his friends in homes along
this street. These men served as the financial and political
leaders of the new Mexican colony.

Don Martín de León, born in 1765 into a wealthy Mexican family, chose the adventures of the frontier rather
than the European education his family sought for him.
After establishing ranches near present San Patricio, he
acquired permission to settle forty-one families on the
Guadalupe River. The community prospered, its primary
source of income being the sale of the vast herds of cattle
and horses that roamed the open range in this area. Not
all the families were Mexican but both Mexicans and Anglos sided with the Texans in anger over mistreatment
from the constantly changing Mexican government. They
were especially opposed to the tyrant Santa Anna.

De Leon Plaza begins in the next block.

The ornate lampposts lining the square bear bronze
plaques with the name, birth, and death dates of prominent Victoria citizens. Bianchi Pharmacy is on the southeast corner of the square, in the location where a drugstore has operated since 1847.

Continue south two blocks on Main Street.

Fossati's, claimed as the oldest delicatessen in Texas,
is on the southeast corner of Main and Juan Linn streets.
Frank Fossati came from Italy in 1883 and worked for a
time carving tombstones before going into the saloon and
delicatessen business. His son continued to operate the
delicatessen for fifty years. Today, Fossati's is still open for
business. Note the worn wooden steps at the front door.

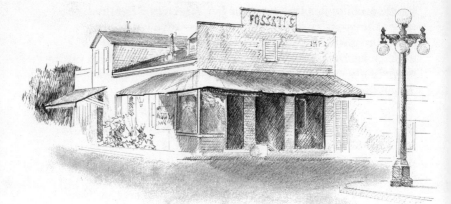

The old bar and shelves lined with canned goods are still here. In the evenings a piano player romps through good beer-drinking songs for enthusiastic crowds.

Before 1836 one of Martín de León's sons-in-law built a "Round Top House" on the site where Fossati's is located. The structure served as his home and as a fortress where residents gathered during Indian raids. Families gathered here in August 1840, during the Great Comanche Raid, as approximately five hundred warriors encircled the town. This encounter had been precipitated the previous March when sixty-five Comanches, headed by twelve chiefs, met at the Council House in San Antonio for peace treaty negotiations. The whites believed that thirteen Indian-held captives were to be part of the dealings. When the Indians brought only one white girl and she confirmed that others remained behind, the Indians were informed that they would be held hostage until all the captives were released. A fierce battle ensued with all twelve chiefs, three Indian women, and two of their children being killed. Seven Texans died.

The Comanches gathered their wounded and retreated to the hills to grieve and to plot their revenge. The following August the vast horde, which included women and children, swept down across Central Texas. Whereas their attacks in the past had consisted mainly of stealing

cattle and horses, this time they embarked on deadly war-
fare. They took captives, killed anyone who got in their
way, and gathered horses as they traveled. Perhaps Victoria survived because a large drove of horses (reports say
from 500 to 1,500) had been brought into the area by
Mexican traders and the Comanches found satisfaction in
gathering up this booty. At any rate, they skirted Victoria
and moved on down to Linnville, a seaport near present
Port Lavaca. They continued to kill, took captives, plundered the warehouses, and finally burned the town while
residents, who had escaped into the bay, watched in horror from aboard boats.

As the Indians began their trip back across the country, angry Texans gathered to cut off their retreat at Plum
Creek near present Lockhart. Part of the Texan force of
two hundred included thirteen Tonkawa Indians, who
wore white arm rags to distinguish them from the enemy.
As the Comanches approached, witnesses said, they
spread out across the horizon; singing, gyrating, and
wearing the prizes from Linnville. Ribbons waved from
the horses' tails, Indians carried umbrellas, and yards of
brightly colored cloth draped both the Indians and their
mounts. One chief wore a silk top hat and a morning coat
turned backward, the shiny brass buttons glistening down
his back. The Texans surprised the Comanches in a boggy
branch. Over eighty warriors and chiefs died in the battle.
When it ended, the Comanches had lost their strength on
the Central and South Texas frontiers.

Turn right at the next corner, Church Street.

Martín de León founded St. Mary's Catholic Church
(Main and Church streets) soon after he arrived. The pres-
ent structure, a design of the famed Galveston architect
Nicholas Clayton, was erected in 1905.

*Continue around the present city hall square to the south-
west corner of Bridge and Juan Linn streets.*

John Joseph Linn built a frame home on this site
in 1831. The story of Juan Linn, as the Mexicans affec-
tionately called him, presents the opportunity to tell of

the transition of Victoria from a Mexican community to an Anglo community.

At the age of two John Joseph Linn emigrated with his father to New York from Ireland. As a young man, he operated a mercantile business in New Orleans. Upon returning from a trip to Mexico, he became interested in Texas and the Victoria area, settling here in 1829. He immediately became a leader in the community and, although his mercantile business caused him to travel to Mexico, he sided with the Texans, as did most of the Mexicans living in Victoria. He was elected to represent the municipality at the Consultation in 1835 and at the convention in Washington-on-the-Brazos (see Chap. 4), which adopted Texas' Declaration of Independence. He served as the last *alcalde* (mayor/judge) of Victoria before independence. He sent supplies to Fannin's men at Goliad, and the women met at the Linn home to mold bullets for Fannin's men before they were massacred by the Mexicans. After Juan Linn led his family to safety, he found it too late to reach Sam Houston in time for the battle of San Jacinto. Instead, he provided the first shipment of supplies to reach the victorious Texans after the fight.

Upon his return to Victoria, Juan Linn found his home plundered by the Mexican army and learned that the army had mistreated the city's inhabitants who had remained behind instead of joining the Runaway Scrape. The irony is that, as Texans began returning to their homes and as opportunists from the United States arrived, the hate that Santa Anna's army had generated became centered on the Mexican Texans who had remained loyal to the cause for freedom and had supported it with their supplies and with their lives. Some of the accusations against the Mexican locals also stemmed from the greed of Anglos who wanted the vast lands and cattle of the wealthy Mexican citizens.

Martín de León had died in 1833 in the cholera epidemic and at that time his property in and around Victoria was valued at one million dollars. It is further estimated that the other De León family members owned property worth at least half that amount. None of the

Mexican families suffered more ill-treatment at the hands of the Texans than the De León family; they were arrested, falsely accused, and stripped of most of their land. Finally, late in 1836, the family took a ship to New Orleans, leaving their vast holdings behind. One son, Don Fernándo, returned in later years, found his lands and cattle gone, and lived until 1853, fighting one law suit after another to recover the property.

Meanwhile, Juan Linn, the friend of Mexicans and Texans, remained the only line of communication between the warring factions. He served as the first mayor of Victoria and then as a member of the House of Representatives. He had established the seaport of Linnville in 1831 and built warehouses and a wharf on which to receive goods shipped from New Orleans. This is the town the Comanches destroyed in 1840 and Linn never rebuilt it. At the age of eighty-seven, two years before his death in 1883, Juan Linn wrote *Reminiscences of Fifty Years in Texas*, a valuable source of information about early days.

Continue north on Bridge Street to Constitution Street.

After Texas independence, Victorians for a time were so anti-Mexican that they renamed De Leon Plaza "Constitution Square." The 1891 courthouse across the street is on the National Register of Historic Places. Note the openness of the building, designed especially to provide ventilation during the hot summers.

Turn right on the north side of De Leon Plaza, Forrest Street. Drive one block to the Open Door (northeast corner Forrest and Main streets).

This is an excellent example of adaptive reuse of a historic structure. The O'Connor-Proctor Building, built in 1895, has housed law and medical offices, a bank, and shops and even served as an apartment house during World War II. The Kathryn Stoner O'Connor Foundation donated the building in 1974 to the Victoria Junior Service League. After extensive restoration, the Open Door Creativity Center began offering classes to all Victorians. Courses range from creative play for kindergartners to

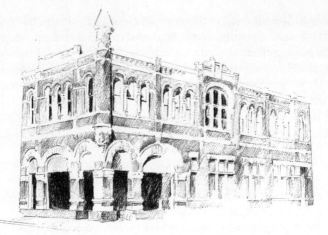

advanced stained glass, sex education, and introduction to photography. Prominent authorities are invited for workshops and lectures. The center is open Monday through Friday, 8:00 A.M. to 4:30 P.M.; closed Saturday and Sunday.

The Open Door Store, located on the first floor, sells finely crafted items created by local and statewide artists. This shop provides fascinating browsing and outstanding gift ideas. Open Monday through Friday, 10:00 A.M. to 4:00 P.M.; closed Saturday and Sunday.

Drive east one block to Hauschild's (Forrest and Liberty streets).

This 1893 structure served until 1980 as Hauschild's Music Store. For many years, the upper floor held Victoria's leading theater.

Turn left on North Liberty Street.

The two-story brick structure at the rear of Hauschild's was built in 1914 as the George H. Hauschild Cigar Factory.

Turn right at the next corner, Goodwin Avenue, and drive four blocks to Ruggle's Restaurant (corner Goodwin Avenue and Navarro streets).

This house was erected in 1885 by W. J. Craig, who
served as Victoria's mayor, 1910–1912. Today, Ruggle's,
which also operates two restaurants in Houston, serves a
fine Continental menu, Sunday brunch, and beef steaks
for Texans. Open 11:30 A.M. to 2:30 P.M. and 6:00 P.M. to
10:30 P.M., Monday through Friday; open until 11:00 P.M.
on Saturday and Sunday.

*Retrace the route on Goodwin Avenue two blocks to De Leon
Street and turn right for one block to Memorial Square.*

Originally this site served as the city cemetery, although it was never very popular because families pre-
ferred home burials. In 1846, soon after Texas entered the
Union, the Mexican War broke out and every available
wagon became necessary for the army. On the coast at
Carlshafen (present Indianola, Chap. 6), four thousand
German immigrants waited, expecting to be moved inland to establish homes. With no transportation, the families remained stranded on the crowded beach. Sickness
began sweeping through their tents: "bilious fever," dysen-
tery, cholera, and petechial fever (spinal meningitis).
These desperate folk tried to escape the plagues. Those
who could, walked; some even crawled. Then it began
raining and the trip extended to eleven days in the mud.
As the immigrants arrived in Victoria, they brought the
sickness with them. They died so rapidly that coffins could
not be built fast enough. They were wrapped in the blankets on which they died and buried here in the public
cemetery.

It is said that after Fannin's men were massacred at
Goliad in 1836 ten of the bodies were brought here and
buried about where the old locomotive stands today. Victorians say that during Reconstruction a group of black
Union soldiers went on a rampage and desecrated the
headstones in this cemetery. Residents were so appalled
that they closed the burial ground and designated the site
as a memorial.

One of Victoria's prides is the 1870 wind-powered
grist mill in Memorial Park. The top of the mill, which
holds the blades, can be turned to face the prevailing

wind. The main shaft of the sturdy structure is made from
a twenty-foot tree, fifteen inches in diameter. The grinding
stones came from Norway into the port of Indianola and
then inland by oxcart. They are nine inches thick and four
feet across and are said to be the oldest still in existence
in the United States.

Henry Ford made a bid to buy the rare old mill, but
descendants of the original owners, wanting to keep the
relic close to home, deeded the structure to the Morning
Study Club in 1935 and it was moved to this site.

*Turn left on Commercial Street for two blocks to North Lib-
erty Street. Turn right and drive to the McNamara House
(502 North Liberty).*

Built by cattle and hide dealer W. J. McNamara, the
home remained in the family until it was donated in
1959 for a museum. Furnishings from fine homes of the
mid-1800s are on display in this house museum, as well as
documents and artifacts related to the history of this area.
The rear gallery presents changing historical exhibits. On
the north side of the house, huge blocks of concrete,
carved with the names of early residents, form a "Memory
Walk" to the rear gallery. Open only on Wednesday, 10:00
A.M. to noon and 3:00 P.M. to 5:00 P.M., and Sunday, 3:00
P.M. to 5:00 P.M. Admission charge.

*Drive to North Street and turn left for four blocks to an inter-
section formed by North, Moody, and Rio Grande streets.
Continue one block on North Street to Vine Street and turn
right. In two blocks, turn right on West Guadalupe Street.*

The Callender House at 404 West Guadalupe, built
originally as a hunting lodge on Green Lake, was torn
down, the boards were numbered, and the house was rebuilt here in 1854. It is considered one of the oldest surviving homes in town and is recorded in the Library of
Congress as an excellent example of pioneer architecture.

Return to Vine Street, turn right, and continue north.

Evergreen Cemetery, which opened after 1849 with a
donation of twenty-seven acres, lines both sides of the

street and contains over nine thousand graves, including those of many area pioneers.

Continue several blocks past undeveloped land to Magnolia Avenue. Turn left into Riverside Park, which hugs the meandering Guadalupe River.

Just past the Little League baseball diamonds is a Texas historical marker noting the site of Tonkawa Bank. This is the old Indian river crossing where missionaries from Mission Espíritu Santo, at present Goliad, set up a campsite so they could "visit" the Indians around here. After their conversion, the Indians served as the mission's cowboys, herding the cattle that eventually spread across South Texas. The steep drive down to the boat ramp offers a better view of the river, which is banked with pecan trees.

By 1854 cargo and passengers that came into Indianola were transferred to a riverboat and brought up the Guadalupe River to Victoria, hampered only by low water or rises so great that logs and debris blocked the channel. During the Civil War, the Confederates stopped all traffic by either sinking the boats or putting them into use elsewhere. After the war, traffic resumed until steamship owner Charles Morgan (discussed in Chap. 1) completed the Gulf, West Texas, and Pacific Railroad from Indianola to Cuero. A channel, the Victoria Barge Canal connecting with the Intracoastal Waterway, has been completed to just south of the city limits. Vast amounts of cargo are moved on modern barges to the businesses and industries that line this channel.

Return to the park road.

The Victoria Rose Garden adds to the beauty of the park and serves as a reminder of the day when Victoria carried the title of "City of Roses."

Follow the park road, which becomes McCright Drive, to the Y. Take the left fork on Memorial Drive.

The Texas Zoo provides exhibits of Texas animals, which range from the javelina to the coatimundi (a raccoon relative from South Texas). The zoo is accessible to

the handicapped. To arrange group tours or special programs, call 512/573-7681.

Continue along Memorial Drive.

The triangular area near the stadium is where the
Starlight Concert series is held on Thursday nights during
the summer. Families bring picnics and blankets and enjoy the music under the pecan trees. For time and information, call 512/576-1317. No admission charge.

*After leaving the park, follow Stayton Avenue for three blocks
to Craig Street and turn left.*

Victoria is a city of many mansions and a short drive
around a few blocks will offer a sampling of what is here.
The Judge A. H. Phillips Home, built in 1851, is at 705
North Craig. Slaves built this home of bricks fired in a
kiln near the Guadalupe River. Sam Houston visited here
in 1857.

*Turn right on West Nueces Street and right again on Victoria
Street. Drive to Goodwin Avenue and turn left.*

The cattle business built many of these fine homes. As
mentioned earlier, the Spanish missionaries brought the
cattle to this area, and by 1770 the two missions near
present Goliad claimed fifty thousand head. As cattle
ranches increased after the Civil War, cattle that had
roamed unbranded for four years were rounded up and
the huge cattle drives began. It is estimated that for the
next thirty years ten million Longhorns made the trip up
the famed Chisholm and other trails to Kansas markets.

Oil and gas did not come in until during the Great
Depression, the worst possible time because the price of
oil had reached its lowest level. Victoria had no booms, no
gushers, just the steady growth that eventually became a
great industry and added to the wealth of this area. At one
time the city claimed more millionaires per capita than
any town in the United States.

Drive to the corner of Goodwin Avenue and Moody Street.

The Nave Museum on the northeast corner offers changing exhibitions of paintings, sculpture, and historical artifacts. The structure opened in 1933 to house the Bronte Club Library and the paintings of Royston Nave, an artist who came to Victoria in the 1920s after a distinguished career in New York. When the new Victoria Public Library opened in 1975, Nave's family gave the building to the city for a fine arts museum. Open Tuesday through Sunday, 1:00 P.M. to 5:00 P.M.; closed Monday. No admission charge.

Turn left on Moody Street, U.S. Highway 59, and follow the route out of Victoria.

Victoria has been referred to as the "City of Rawhide and Roses," where cattle- and oilmen came to enjoy the refinements that all their wealth could provide.

The Victoria County Airport is on the left just beyond the city limits. This is the site of old Foster Field, an installation that, as much as anything, moved Victoria from a small, agricultural-based community to a sprawling city with a diversified economy. At the time of Pearl Harbor, the first class of air cadets were only five days short of graduation. Aerial gunnery classes were held here with actual practice conducted on Matagorda Island and Matagorda Peninsula on the coast. After Foster Field closed in 1945, the young men who had been stationed here carried the memory of the friendly community with them. Today, as they reach retirement age, many of them are returning to the town where they felt so at home.

Note the highway sign to Telferner. The name, although misspelled, comes from Count Telfener, the Italian discussed earlier, who built the New York, Texas, and Mexican Railway from Rosenberg to Victoria in the early 1880s. Several stops along the way bear names of Telfener kin, but accounts vary as to how each one was related to Telfener.

Count Telfener had two partners in his venture: John W. Mackay, who became a silver king in the Comstock Lode at Virginia City, Nevada, and Mackay's father-in-law, a former barber turned adventurer, Colonel Daniel E. Hungerford. Hungerford had two daughters, according to one account: Mary Louise, who married John W. Mackay, and Edna (or Ada), who married Count Telfener. According to another source, Inez, the next community along U.S. Highway 59, received its name from one of Telfener's daughters.

Edna

Originally, the community that grew up here as Telfener's railroad came through served as a commissary for the Italian laborers brought in to work on the line. It came to be known as Macaroni Station. In fact, the entire ninety-two–mile railroad continues to be called the Macaroni Line. (Many old Victoria and surrounding-area families are descendants of those Italian laborers who liked Texas and never left.) Later, the town became Edna for Telfener's wife (some accounts say daughter). One of the biggest celebrations in Jackson County occurred on July 2, 1882, when the first trains arrived. They met here: one from Rosenberg and the other from Victoria.

Take the business exit into Edna. Watch for Farm Road 1822. Turn right and drive 0.5 mile to the restored Texana Presbyterian Church.

This structure, erected in 1858 at nearby Texana (a ghost town to be discussed later), was built by a congregation originally founded by John Adams Brackenridge. This gentleman was the man who loaned law books to Abraham Lincoln for his self-taught studies and was the father of the well-known San Antonio Brackenridge family.

Return to Business U.S. Highway 59 and turn right into Edna. Drive to the courthouse square and turn left on Texas 111, North Wells Street. It is two blocks to the Texana Museum on the left at the corner of West Cypress Street.

This Jackson County historical museum offers books on local cemeteries and local murders, an authentic country store, and traveling exhibits from such notable sources

as the Institute of Texan Cultures. The facility is open
Tuesday through Friday, 1:00 P.M. to 5:00 P.M.; Saturday,
8:00 A.M. to noon; closed Sunday and Monday.

A choice may be made at this point. It is about ten
miles on U.S. Highway 59 into Ganado. Or, a trip of about
eighteen miles will travel across the new Lake Texana,
past a private marina and picnic, camping, and boating
facilities, and through the land frequented by the Wildman of the Navidad.

*Retrace the route on Texas 111 to U.S. Highway 59. Turn left
for the trip directly to Ganado. Continue straight on Texas
111 for the Lake Texana route.*

Lake Texana, completed in 1980, has inundated the
important old Texas port city of Texana, a ghost town
that some say fell victim to the Allen brothers' (Houston
founders) curse. Texana began in 1832 at the head of navigation on the Navidad River. At first, settlers called the
town Santa Anna, in an effort to gain favor with the
Mexican dictator. Then, as relations with Mexico grew
strained, the name of Texana seemed more appropriate.
During the Texas Revolution, the port served as a major
supply route for military posts in the area.

Tradition claims that the Allen brothers, John K. and
Augustus C., capitalists from New York who had become
Texas land speculators, searched the Texas coast for an
inland port. They found the wide, sixteen-foot-deep
Navidad the most ideal river. They offered Dr. F. F. Wells,
one of the town founders, $100,000 in gold for a league of
land for their dream port. Dr. Wells countered with a request for $200,000. It is said that the Allen brothers be-
came so angry that one of them climbed on a stump and
said, "Never will this town amount to anything, I curse it.
You people listening within the sound of my voice will live
to see rabbits and other animals inhabiting its streets."
The Allen brothers left, made a second offer (which received a rejection) on Harrisburg, and then bought their
third choice, the site on the Buffalo Bayou that developed
into Houston.

Texana continued as an important port city with fifteen to twenty vessels landing here each week. Then, in 1881, officials of Count Telfener's railroad asked the city businessmen to put up a $30,000 bonus for the road to come through Texana. After deliberating for a time, the men decided to reject the proposition. After all, they reasoned, as did other Texas riverport towns, the port facility provided sufficient commerce and $30,000 represented a very large outlay.

The railroad thus bypassed Texana and established present Edna, and Texana began a rapid decline. After voters moved the county seat to Edna in 1883, a mass exodus took place. Homes and businesses were placed atop log rollers and pulled by ox teams the seven miles to Edna. Sure enough, rabbits and other animals soon played in the streets. And, by the time Lake Texana began filling, the streets were no longer discernible.

Lake Texana State Park

The 600-acre park provides camping, picnicking, swimming, and boating. The lake is stocked with Florida bass, walleye, catfish, and threadfin shad. The private marina provides a motel and restaurant, boat storage slips, and over one hundred nearby campsites. This complex hugs the live oak–covered shoreline.

Continue across the lake on Texas 111. It is then 2.1 miles to Texas 172. Turn left for the drive into Ganado.

This area along the river is where the Wildman of the Navidad roamed from about 1836 until 1851. Residents in this bottomland began missing a few sweet potatoes and some ears of corn from their fields and gardens. Each time something disappeared, they noticed at least one set of large tracks and another set of small ones, but no one could ever catch the pair of thieves. Finally, only the small prints came. Even with guards posted in the fields, "it" remained elusive. On bright, moonlit nights, settlers reported seeing a tiny dark creature with long black hair, but no one ever got close enough to catch "the thing that comes," as the slaves called it. J. Frank Dobie, in *Tales of*

Old-Time Texas, called it "Wild Woman of the Navidad," because area residents believed the small footprints belonged to a woman.

Tools also disappeared; some reports say they were returned polished to a high sheen. Camps were found, but the creature always eluded the most extensive search parties. Then, food began disappearing from inside cabins: the creature had actually entered, stepped over sleeping dogs, taken only small portions, and left without being detected.

In 1850 or 1851, dogs trained in hunting down runaway slaves found him: a black man who wore no clothes and spoke no English. About six months later a sailor who knew a little of the captive's dialect came into port at Texana. He discovered that, although the black man's father was chief of a tribe, he had sold his son into slavery for a knife and some tobacco. The son and a slave companion had escaped after reaching Texas. The companion died after a few years, and the small one continued to forage alone, afraid to contact anyone for fear of being recaptured. After recounting this tragic tale, the black son of an African chief was sold back into slavery, but he never stopped seeking his freedom. He ran away from his Refugio County master and later his Victoria County master until freedom came at the end of the Civil War. "Old Jimbo," as he became known, lived until 1884.

Ganado

Ranchers had lived in this area for years before the railroad came through. A railroad official, observing the large herds of wild cattle on the plains, called the site "Ganado," which is Spanish for herd.

Turn right on Business U.S. Highway 59 to the junction with U.S. Highway 59.

El Campo

When the railroad came through in 1881, the siding and shipping point that grew up here, which railroad con-

struction gangs used for a station, was called Prairie
Switch. After rounding up their herds, cattlemen camped
here. The Mexican cowboys called the site "El Campo"
(the camp), and that name became official in 1890.

Early settlers were quoted as saying, "Mosquitoes
were so thick you could make a strike through the air and
the streak was easily visible." Stock suffered so much
from mosquitoes and greenhead flies and black horseflies
that horses had to be covered while they worked in the
hay meadows. At night, smoke from huge fires helped to
keep the mosquitoes at bay. Longhorn cattle, as well as
wolves, bobcats, coyotes, geese, and ducks, were found on
the rich prairie land. Today, El Campo boasts a fine museum filled with animals, the big-game variety.

*Stay on U.S. Highway 59 as it circles El Campo to the south
and east. Exit on Texas 71, South Mechanic Street, and continue north into downtown.*

The block between East First Street and Railroad Avenue offers some interesting shops housed in El Campo's
early buildings. The Downtown Delicatessen utilizes the
oldest building in town, erected in the 1890s after a devastating fire took most of the business houses. This tidy deli
specializes in sandwiches, wine, gifts, and gourmet cook-
ware. Open 9:30 A.M. to 5:30 P.M., Monday through Friday;
9:30 A.M. to 3:00 P.M., Saturday; closed Sunday.

The Doll House, on the corner, occupies an old bank
building constructed about 1908. Clothing, quilts, cover-
lets, and accessories for the well-dressed preschooler are
featured here. Open Monday through Saturday, 9:00 A.M.
to 5:30 P.M.; closed Sunday.

*Turn right on Railroad Avenue, drive one block, and turn left
on North Washington Street. Turn right at the second corner,
East Jackson Street, Business U.S. Highway 59.*

The El Campo Museum of Art–History–Natural Science is housed with the chamber of commerce in the
building on this corner. This outstanding big-game trophy
museum contains some animals in the world-record class
from the Arctic, Asia, Africa, and the Americas. The white

rhinoceros is one of the few full mounts in a museum in the United States. The collection also claims a "grand slam in rams," which contains one of every kind. These exhibits are arranged against huge murals painted by very talented local artists. The displays are changed seasonally. During the Christmas season, local artists prepare a different setting in which to portray the animals, such as an "Ice Castle Palace" or an "Enchanted Forest," complete with live characters. The professional quality of these exhibits attracts student and adult groups from a wide area.

The trophies and the building were deeded to the city by Dr. and Mrs. E. A. Weinheimer. Dr. Weinheimer, a local surgeon, is classified as a world-game professional hunter. The museum is open Monday through Friday, 9:00 A.M. to noon and 1:00 P.M. to 5:00 P.M.; Saturday and Sunday, 1:00 P.M. to 5:00 P.M. For group appointments, call 713/543-2713. No admission charge.

Continue east on Business U.S. Highway 59 for 0.6 mile to the Apparel Mart on the right.

This is the outlet for Isaacson-Carrico Double Seat panties. Mothers have been dressing their little girls in Double Seat panties since Irene Isaacson and Esther Carrico began the business in a home here in El Campo in 1948. Double Seat panties are sold all over the United States and in many foreign countries. This store also carries sleepwear and slips, which are also made locally. Open Monday through Saturday, 9:00 A.M. to 5:30 P.M.; closed Sunday.

Continue east and rejoin U.S. Highway 59.

Pierce

In 1881, when the railroad came through, Abel Head (Shanghai) Pierce owned the land around here (his holdings in South Texas totaled about 250,000 acres). Chris Emmett, in his delightful book, *Shanghai Pierce, a Fair Likeness*, said that Pierce dreamed of his town becoming the county seat. As the painter put the name of the town on the end of the railroad depot, Shanghai, who had been watching from a pile of lumber, jumped up and shouted, "Hold on there, by God, sir. Put the apostrophe s on it. I own it, don't I? I paid for it?" The painter then stenciled "Pierce's Station."

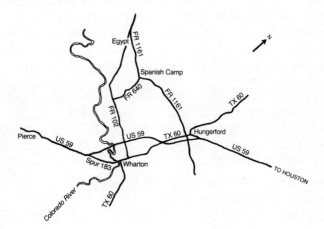

Enter present-day Pierce by continuing straight into town as the main highway circles to the left.

The white frame church building on the left, next to the highway, has been moved to this site. It is said to be the church building that Chris Emmett mentions in his book. After Shanghai had donated half a calf to a barbeque held to pay for a lot and church parsonage, he wrote to the railroad asking that two big cars of lumber be deadheaded at Pierce because "I am pioneering in another matter. I am trying to introduce religion in the community." He then proceeded to order pews and a pulpit. After the facility was completed, Shanghai proudly showed it to all visitors. One gentleman asked, "Colonel Pierce, do you belong to that church?" "Hell, no!" Pierce shouted. "The church belongs to me."

When the six-foot-four Abel Head Pierce arrived at the docks in Port Lavaca in December 1854, the nineteen-year-old "loud mouthed Yankee with the nasal twang and too short pants" had stowed away on a ship from New York. He had not made himself known until the vessel reached the high seas.

Soon after landing at Port Lavaca, Pierce announced to William Bradford Grimes, the cattleman who hired him, that he planned to go into the cattle business. In fact, he requested to be paid that first year in cows and calves. Grimes paid Pierce with cows that were ten to twenty years old. The following year, Pierce rounded up mavericks and branded them for Grimes at $1 a head. Pierce is reported to have told a fellow cowboy at the end of the year, "I'm d—— glad he [Grimes] didn't ask me whose branding iron I used this year." That spelled the beginning of Pierce's cattle acquisitions. After the Civil War, when the only profit from beef lay in hides and tallow (the carcasses were fed to the hogs or thrown away), he went into the slaughtering business. Finally, when the Chisholm Trail opened to Abilene, Kansas, Shanghai Pierce became one of the first to drive a herd to that market.

Shanghai believed that ticks caused fever in cattle and, after touring Europe, he decided that Brahman cattle would be immune because he had observed that the "'Bremmers' sweated and the ticks fell off, and the cattle got fat thereafter." After his death in 1900, his estate and another Victoria rancher, Thomas O'Connor, undertook the importation of Brahmans, the beginning of a new cattle industry for this part of the country.

While Shanghai visited Europe he became quite impressed with the statuary that he saw. Upon his return, he commissioned a German sculptor to create a life-size work that would cause people who passed to say, "There stands old Pierce." Today, the statue stands atop a ten-foot Palladian pilaster mounted on a ten-foot section of highly polished granite in the cemetery outside Blessing (Chap. 6).

This man who had no qualms about taking along a farmer's only milk cow as his herds moved across the country had another side: after losing over $1.25 million in the 1900 storm and other business failures, he canceled debts owed to him by people who had also suffered losses during the storm. His name still brings strong response from descendants of the folks who knew him; there are those who love and those who despise Shanghai Pierce. Word is that those folks will never change their opinions.

The Pierce Ranch headquarters occupies the land across the railroad track from the town. The ranch is still a big operation and the addition of oil and gas discoveries makes it one of the largest taxpayers in Wharton County. The ranch house is on private property and is not open to the public.

Continue through town on Business U.S. Highway 59 and rejoin U.S. Highway 59.

Wharton

Take the first exit, Business U.S. Highway 59, into town. While crossing the Colorado River bridge, watch for Pier 59 Restaurant on the right river bank. Turn right at the first traffic light on Burleson Street and then right again for one block to Pier 59's driveway.

Both the deck and the dining room of the restaurant afford good views of the river. House specialties are prime rib and lobster, as well as a salad bar and a lighter luncheon menu. Lunch is served Monday, Thursday, and Friday, 11:00 A.M. to 2:00 P.M.; dinner is served Sunday through Thursday, 5:00 P.M. to 10:00 P.M. and until 11:00 P.M. on Friday and Saturday.

Return to Burleson Street, turn right, and drive one block to the courthouse square. At the southeast corner, turn right on Fulton Street.

This is the area where a widow from Mississippi, Lucinda Flowers, settled in 1843 with her one hundred slaves. Three years later, with the establishment of the county, the city of Wharton was laid out. Other planters began arriving with their slaves, and by 1847 the total black population in the county reached 1,315, compared to 413 whites. The early Mexican immigration laws had encouraged slavery by offering settlers eighty acres for each slave. Then, although a new law forbade importing slaves, it did not free those already in Texas, and it did allow planters to bring in indentured servants.

Because of the lopsided population, blacks held political power during the Reconstruction. The White Man's Union Association organized in 1889, about the time Fort Bend County went through the Jaybird-Woodpecker War (see Richmond section). This group pulled off a "bloodless coup" and regained white supremacy in county politics.

The Wharton County Museum, housed in the building behind the jail, opened in 1980 after county residents compiled a graphic record of their history. The facility offers changing exhibits featuring the history of county medicine, religion, farming, and floods. The museum is open Friday, Saturday, and Sunday, 2:00 P.M. to 5:00 P.M.; closed Monday through Thursday. No admission charge.

Return to the square.

On the east side is the Apple Barrel Deli, a combination antique shop and delicatessen serving hot sandwiches, homemade meals, pies, and ice cream. The salad bar is laid out in a footed bathtub. Open Monday through Saturday, 11:00 A.M. to 2:00 P.M.; closed Sunday.

Turn left on Milam Street.

Before leaving the square, note the façades on the buildings. Wharton merchants have maintained pride in their structures, allowing them to retain their original beauty, which gives this town its special quality, not duplicated anywhere.

Return to Business U.S. Highway 59 and turn right. After crossing the railroad track, turn left at the next corner on Farm Road 102, and continue for eleven miles to Egypt.

Egypt

Egypt consists of a post office, store, family burial ground, and a beautiful plantation home, but it hasn't always been a quiet, out-of-the-way place. When Stephen F. Austin's settlers first arrived, they suffered under a severe drought; however, this area remained as lush as Egypt's fertile Nile River valley. Families came here for corn, and soon the site took on the name "Egypt" in reference to the biblical stories of the Hebrews going down to Egypt during times of drought to get grain.

William Jones Elliot Heard settled here in 1830 and built the plantation home that is still standing. One of his daughters married Mentor Northington, son of another area planter. Today, the fifth generation of Northingtons live here and operate the farm and ranchland.

Turn right at the general store.

The store, which still retains the old-time smell of hard candy, was built about 1910, with a meat market added later. Early customers came from Wharton and Eagle Lake to visit and to buy boots, hats, and even caskets.

Turn right on the lane that intersects at the store.

The Heard-Northington family cemetery is on the right. For many years family members bricked the top of the graves to keep the Indians from robbing the burial sites. It is said that during the Texas War for Independence families hid valuables from the advancing Mexican army in freshly dug "graves" in the yards and placed furniture and food in the nearby cane breaks before they left in the Runaway Scrape.

A stage line ran from Houston to Egypt by 1839 and later was extended on to Texana. Planters began a railroad here in 1848 in an effort to get their sugarcane out of the sandy bottomland. Mules or horses pulled vehicles along hard live oak rails on the route from here to Eagle Lake and on to Columbus.

The Egypt plantation home is beyond the cemetery.

W. J. E. Heard's slaves made the pink bricks and built the plantation home in 1849. The first Methodist meeting held in the county took place here, as did important social and political events. Note the salt cedar growing in the front yard. About 1900, one of the young women in the family stuck her buggy whip in the ground as she alighted. That salt cedar buggy whip took root and has continued to flourish.

This home is a private, family museum with an impressive collection of books, furnishings, and records of early Texas and Egypt, including the original Mexican grant for this land signed by Stephen F. Austin. The home is open to group tours only, with a minimum of twelve and a maximum of one hundred guests. Advance reservations are required: write to George Northington III, P.O. Box 277, Egypt, TX 77436, or call 713/677-3562. The one-and-a-half-hour tour of the home and depot at the rear is available at 10:00 A.M. and 2:00 P.M. Adults only. Admission charge.

The plantation home faces Farm Road 1161. Drive east toward Spanish Camp.

This community got its name after Santa Anna's army camped here before moving on to Richmond and, eventually, to the Battle of San Jacinto.

Hungerford

The land to the left while the traveler is driving toward Hungerford, clear over to U.S. Highway 90A, is a big goose hunting area. Watch for the geese and Brahman cattle.

Planters settled in the Hungerford area as part of Stephen F. Austin's Colony, but a town did not develop until 1882 when the railroad came through. J. D. Hudgins came to this area in 1839 as a planter. He married Rachel Northington, sister of Mentor Northington of Egypt. In 1895 one of their sons began raising Brahman cattle. The Hudgins Partnership purchased forty head of Brahman cows from the estate of Shanghai Pierce in 1906, and other purchases of fine seed stock continued. Today, this ranch owns the largest registered Brahman herd in the United States, averaging about 2,500 head at a time. In 1980 the heifers were sold for $1,250 to $2,000, while bulls went for $1,250 to $15,000. Visitors are always welcome at this working cattle ranch.

Enter Hungerford on Farm Road 1161, turn left on Texas 60 (Loop 183), and drive into town.

The J. D. Hudgins Ranch office is on the right side of the triangle, just beyond the intersection with the flashing traffic light. Stop at the office for a guide and an opportunity to see the mounted head of Manso, the one-ton bull from whom all these prize-winning cattle have descended. The trophy collection is impressive and so is the map with pins showing cattle distribution from the J. D. Hudgins Ranch to points all over the world.

Guests are shown the sale pens, the show barn, and the process of culling and grading the stock. It has been said that a visit to this ranch is an opportunity to see several million dollars standing around waiting to be fed. The ranch office is open Monday through Friday, 8:00 A.M. to 6:00 P.M.; Saturday, 8:00 A.M. to 1:00 P.M.; closed Sunday. Call 713/532-1352 for other information. No charge for this tour.

Indian campsites dating back to the time of Christ have been found on high ground through this area, indicating that the sites were selected to avoid periodic river flooding. Skeletons, spears, animal bones, pottery shards, and other finds have been placed in the Wharton County Museum in Wharton.

Follow Loop 183 north to U.S. Highway 59 for the return to Houston.

This concludes the cattlemen's tour through the rich prairie lands prized by generations of folk who recognized the potential that lay here. The legacy left by those early adventurers is still being counted by present generations.

6. River Land Trail

This route crosses the rich delta lands of the Brazos, Colorado, and Lavaca rivers, the fertile prairies that boasted vast plantations and a social order quite different from that of the rugged interior of the state. Today, cattle graze beside chemical plants and thick palmettos grow beneath moss-draped oaks where sugar and cotton flourished 130 years ago. Once-thriving ports, which welcomed immigrants to this new land, stand as silent, neglected reminders of a past era.

Drive south from Houston on Almeda Road, Texas 288.

Arcola

In the mid-1840s, Johnathan Dawson Waters began buying land in this area for what became the largest cotton and sugar plantation in Texas. Waters owned a brick mansion, operated a shipping wharf on the Brazos River, and used a special "J. D. Waters" engine to pull trains to Columbia. The 1860 census showed that Waters had become the richest man in Fort Bend County.

Continue south on Texas 288. In Rosharon, turn right at the caution light on Farm Road 1462.

The rich bottomland along the Brazos River boasts elegant horse and cattle ranches, with manicured fields and impressive country homes. When plantations covered this countryside, the thick canebrakes and timber along the Brazos provided good hiding places for runaway slaves.

It is 3.5 miles from the Brazos River to Farm Road 762. Turn right and drive 1.8 miles to the entrance to the park.

Hale Ranch State Park

This stop is designed for birdwatchers and/or wildlife observers, especially American alligator enthusiasts. The Texas Parks and Wildlife Department projects the opening of this environmentally and biologically diversified five-thousand-acre park in the fall of 1982. Stop at the headquarters for information on screen shelters, camping areas, and the 4.5-mile trail system that is designed to accommodate wheelchair occupants, walkers, and bikers.

Return to Farm Road 1462 and turn right.

Begin watching off to the left as the trail draws near to Damon's Mound, a hill that rises ninety-seven feet above this flat prairie several miles from the road. The three-hundred-acre formation, which is a mile long, once provided all the limestone used in South Texas. Children playing on the mound discovered some water in a ravine, found that it tasted sour, and went home for sugar to make lemonade. When they told of their discovery, the word spread, and the site became known as "the medical waters of Damon's Mound." Like the limestone formation at Spindletop (Chap. 2), Damon's Mound also became a producing oil field, with a gusher blowing in in 1917. Wells are still pumping around the periphery.

At the intersection with Texas 36, turn right and drive beside the mound. Continue about seven miles to Farm Road 442 and turn left. Drive about ten miles on Farm Road 442 and turn left at the Newgulf sign. It is over two miles to the headquarters of Texasgulf, Inc.

Newgulf

Since the company, which operates the largest sulphur mine in the world, began operations here in 1928, more than 74 million tons of sulphur have been produced and much more is still available. Superheated water is pumped into the layers of underground sulphur in order to melt it. Compressed air forces the liquid sulphur to the surface through pipes, which are off to the left and easily

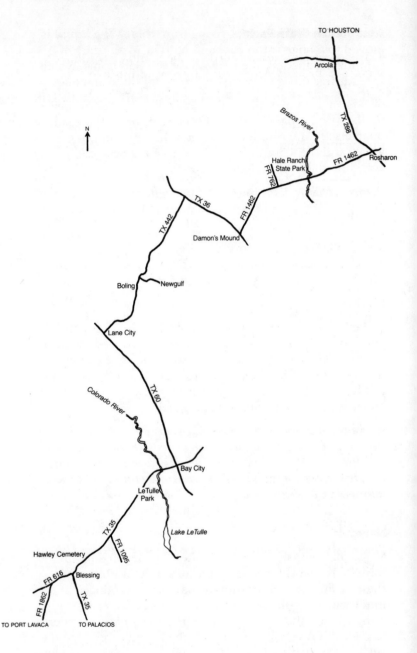

seen because of the steam rising from them. The liquid is moved to a huge vat to cool and harden. With years of sulphur production, the land above this salt dome, which spreads five miles from east to west and three and one-half miles north to south, has begun to subside. Cattle still graze contentedly over the "cap."

Raw sulphur is odorless. It is only after it is burned, producing sulphur dioxide, that the terrible rotten-egg aroma fills the air. In early times, people believed that these fumes kept away evil spirits. Later they realized that the fumes drove off insects and that sulphur could be used as a bleach and for fumigation. Around 1550 B.C. sulphur began to be used in ointments and tonics. About A.D. 1200 it was mixed with saltpeter and charcoal to make gunpowder. Today, sulphuric acid is necessary to the agricultural, paper, steel, fiber, and pigment industries.

One-hour tours of the facility are available: contact Clinton White at P.O. Box 488, Newgulf, TX 77462, or call 713/657-4481, extension 215. Because of the complexity of the operation, tours are offered only for high school age and older. Tours are conducted Monday through Friday, 9:00 A.M. to 3:00 P.M.; closed Saturday, Sunday, and holidays.

The community adjoining this plant is a company-owned town of some five hundred homes, three churches, a school, and a few businesses.

Return to Farm Road 442 and turn left into Boling.

This town began along the railroad in 1903 and remained a quiet village until the oil and sulphur boom came in 1925. Streets east of the highway are still named after oil companies.

Continue through Boling on Farm Road 442. At Lane City, turn left on Texas 60 and drive south.

Bay City

In October 1894, surveyors laid out the mile-square town of Bay City on flat land covered with abundant waving grass. Citizens had voted to move the county seat from Matagorda, the storm-plagued city on the Gulf, to this model community. Soon, tents sprang up as residents waited for lumber to arrive. Businessmen constructed fine buildings on the square, but for years cattle swam in the streets whenever the nearby Colorado River flooded. A 1908 fire destroyed all the structures on the west side of the square, but like the resilient population, the community survived and prospered.

Enter Bay City on Texas 60, Avenue F, and drive to the courthouse square.

The old Bay City Bank building (northwest corner Seventh Street and Avenue F), erected in 1903, escaped the devastating fire.

Continue around the square, turning left on Sixth Street.

The Matagorda Pharmacy (northeast corner of Sixth and Avenue G), erected in 1902 to house a drugstore, is another impressive building. Druggists have occupied the structure all these years. Look at the second-story façades on many of the buildings on this side of the square. Picture these elegant structures fronting on mud streets in the Bay City of early days.

Drive east on Sixth Street.

The Matagorda County Historical Museum (1824 Sixth Street) is housed in the old city hall–fire station complex, built in 1928. Clothing, war relics, furniture, utensils, and farm implements portraying life in early Matagorda County are on display here. The museum is open Tuesday through Friday, 3:00 P.M. to 5:00 P.M.; Sunday, 3:00 P.M. to 5:00 P.M. except holidays; closed Monday and Saturday. No admission charge. Special group tours may be arranged by calling 713/245-7502 or Mrs. C. E. Lee at 713/245-2431.

Continue two blocks to the city park.

Rallies and concerts were held on the platform of the old bandstand, which was built in 1907 on the courthouse square. When the river flooded, local citizens brought out boats they kept for the occasion and good-naturedly paddled about town. Finally, everyone gathered at the bandstand and enjoyed a concert in the comfort of their boats. In 1963, the city moved the old relic to this park.

Turn right at the next corner, Avenue J, drive two blocks to Fourth Street, and turn right. Drive to the First United Methodist Church (Fourth Street and Avenue H).

The congregation operates a Methodist Heritage Room with exhibits relating to Methodism in Matagorda County, one of the circuits followed by some of Texas' earliest missionaries. Inquire at the church office.

Continue west one block to Avenue G and turn left to the old N. M. Vogelsang Home (2416 Avenue G).

Built in 1895 for Vogelsang's bride, the nine-room house cost $2,500 and was one of the most impressive in the new town.

Turn right on Third Street and right again on Avenue F.

The large two-story home at 2400 Avenue F was completed in 1895 and served as a boarding house and as a hospital.

Continue north to Seventh Street, Texas 35, and turn left for the trip to Blessing. Cross the Colorado River bridge at the edge of town.

LeTulle Park

Victor Lawrence LeTulle owned extensive land in Matagorda County before he moved to Bay City from Columbus in 1900. He owned a mercantile store, served as president of Bay City National Bank, and bought a canal system that grew, by the 1920s, to be the largest privately owned waterway system in the world. The vast canal networks are essential for irrigating area rice crops.

LeTulle's generosity still benefits Bay Citians. In 1934 he deeded this park site to the city and gave the Bay City

Gas Company to the town. Ownership has meant that Bay City has one of the lowest tax rates in the state and has had funds for erecting a new city hall, paving streets, financing swimming pools and fire stations, and even for buying cots and blankets for the USO during World War II.

From the park, it is about twelve miles to the intersection with Farm Road 1095. Continue on Texas 35 another 2.4 miles to the marker pointing right to Hawley Cemetery. Turn right.

This road leads to the burial ground where Shanghai Pierce, the cattleman described in Chapter 5, had his life-size statue erected. The red barns on the left are all that remain of Rancho Grande, the ranch of Shanghai's brother Jonathan Pierce. In the 1860s Jonathan built a two-story ranch house with its lookout tower on the roof near those barns. It burned to the ground in 1902.

After Shanghai and Jonathan came to Texas, they both worked as cowhands and then served in the Confederate army. After the Civil War, they began buying land and rounding up cattle that had strayed during the four-year conflict. They formed the partnership of A. H. and J. E. Pierce, Stock Raisers and Cattle Dealers, with Rancho

Grande as their headquarters. Soon everyone knew that the Pierce brothers would buy cattle at the market price and would pay in gold.

Jonathan married and settled into happy family life, building the impressive Rancho Grande home, while Shanghai married Jonathan's sister-in-law and bragged years later that he only stayed home four days that first year. In the 1880s the Pierce brothers split their holdings and Shanghai built his ranch at present Pierce (Chap. 5).

It is less than a mile to the cemetery entrance. Turn left, cross the cattle guard, and watch for the big bull that grazes along here.

Shanghai's statue can be seen towering between the trees, dominating the cemetery, much the way he dominated his world as he rose from a penniless stowaway on a ship from New York to one of the largest landowners and most influential cattlemen in this part of the country.

Originally this graveyard was called Deming's Bridge Cemetery. About 1897 Jonathan incurred the ire of many in the community by changing the name to honor his friend State Senator Robert B. Hawley. It seems that Jonathan's gratitude stemmed from Hawley using his influence to get Jonathan's son Abel an appointment as a navy paymaster during the Spanish-American War.

Return to Texas 35, turn right, and drive for almost three miles to the intersection with Farm Road 616. Turn right and drive into Blessing.

Blessing

Jonathan Pierce and his son Abel laid out this town on their Rancho Grande land in 1902 when the railroad came through. With a great sense of gratitude to have the convenience of the rail line after having struggled through years of driving cattle up the trail to Kansas, and then later driving them forty or fifty miles to the nearest railhead at Wharton, old Jonathan selected "Thank God" as the name for the new town. When postal authorities rejected his first choice, Pierce settled on "Blessing."

The Blessing Hotel, on the corner with the only traffic light in town, is another Pierce enterprise. After Rancho Grande burned, Jonathan and his son Abel built this hotel, styled like the old Spanish missions except for its wood siding, in 1907. Land seekers and developers, with dreams of converting this area into citrus groves, stayed here. Both Jonathan and Abel lived here until Abel married and built his mansion a few blocks away. Jonathan lived out his life here, occupying what the family referred to as the "gold fish bowl" in the left-hand tower room on the second floor.

Chris Emmett recollected that he visited with a "long-moustached, gruff, talkative old man," rocking on the front porch of this hotel. Emmett said that his interest picked up when he discovered the old man to be the brother of, and former partner with, Shanghai Pierce, "Webster on cattle."

This twenty-five–room hotel is still in business,

owned by the Blessing Historical Foundation, which leases out the hotel and coffee shop. The "gossip shelf," on which folks can lean while visiting, still stretches across the inside of the hotel's front screen door. Plans are underway to make the hotel available to large groups for family reunions or special study seminars. The facility is not fancy, but the rooms are large and airy and the atmosphere is small-town friendly. For information regarding accommodations, call 512/588-7152 or check for a possible new listing with information.

The Blessing Hotel Coffee Shop, which occupies the old ballroom, serves a wide range of home-cooked meals. Locals pack the place: farmers, oil field workers, ranch hands, and employees at the nearby South Texas Project (STP), a nuclear generating station. Reminiscent of days when guests picked up a plate and went to the kitchen to serve themselves, the present arrangement, which is approved by the health authorities, requires guests to serve themselves from huge iron stoves that have been moved into the dining room. There are always two meats, several vegetables, homemade cornbread and rolls, as well as other fare. The steam pipes used to heat the building in past years still stretch across the ceiling. The coffee shop is open 364 days a year, 6:00 A.M. to 2:00 P.M.; closed Christmas.

At this point a choice is possible. The traveler can drive directly to Palacios, a distance of about thirteen miles, or take a roundabout route. It is thirty-five miles to Port Lavaca and another fifteen miles on to Indianola, the historic port turned ghost town. The two old port towns played significant roles in early Texas. Many of the Germans who settled in Central Texas came through Indianola, camels that served as Jefferson Davis' great desert experiment landed there, and shipping magnate Charles Morgan helped turn Indianola, "the Plymouth of the Southwest," into a port that rivaled Galveston. A sense of adventure is required—a desire to look at water and shell, fishing huts and prickly pear and imagine the thriving whirlwind of excitement that churned in Indianola and then the devastation brought by wind and water.

If the shorter route is desired, return to Texas 35 and turn right to Palacios. Take the Port Lavaca–Indianola route by following Farm Road 616 less than two miles to Farm Road 1862. Turn left, drive to Texas 35, and turn right.

Point Comfort

Just before entering Point Comfort, notice the large facility on the right, the new $100 million Formosa Plastics, U.S.A., a polyvinyl chloride plant from Taiwan, which is scheduled to open in 1982.

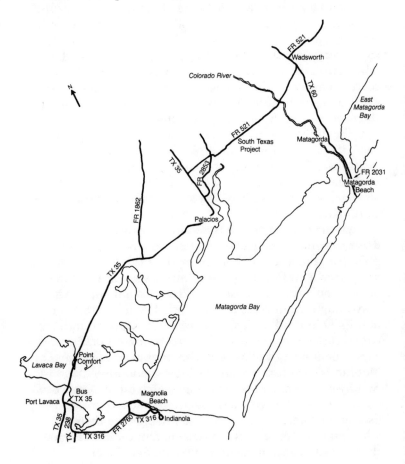

Across the highway, a huge levee encloses the Aluminum Company of America's red mud lake. Red mud is
leftover from processing bauxite, the clay substance from
which alumina is extracted. This Alcoa plant, the largest
and most versatile bauxite refinery in the Western Hemi-
sphere, begins just beyond the mud lake. Every month
about twelve ships, each loaded with forty thousand tons
of bauxite, enter the Alcoa harbor. Most of the vessels haul
their cargo in eighteen-day trips from the Republic of
Guinea in Africa with other shipments coming from South
America. Point Comfort grew up with Alcoa and provides
some of the housing for plant employees.

The point of land that juts into Lavaca Bay south of
Point Comfort served as a trading post and army supply
depot called Cox's Point during the Texas Revolution.
Juan Linn, the *alcalde* of Victoria (Chap. 5), suggested this
location as a point of refuge for citizens heading east in
the Runaway Scrape. Indians burned the town in 1840.

Port Lavaca

The 11,900-foot causeway that takes Texas 35 across Lavaca Bay was completed in 1961, just a few months before
the fury of Hurricane Carla roared across this area. The
old highway, to the left of this structure, was destroyed
during the storm, but portions of the bridge on both sides
of the bay have been left to serve as fishing piers. An old-
time Port Lavaca resident said that upon completion of
the original causeway in the mid-1920s so little traffic
passed here after dark that the young people drove their
cars onto the bridge and "spooned for hours."

The old town of Linnville, laid out by Juan Linn, lay
about three and one-half miles up the coast, northwest of
here. Linnville never recovered from the Great Comanche
Raid in 1840 (Chap. 5) and Port Lavaca became the most
logical site for a new community, sitting on this high bluff
above the bay. Called La Vaca, Spanish for "the cow," the
town soon became a shipping point for cattle, tallow,
hides, and bones. Business flourished as trade increased
with northern Mexico and South and West Texas.

The Shellfish Restaurant, on the right just beyond the causeway, is a Port Lavaca institution. Its predecessor, a French-style bakery, was started in 1894 and soon developed into a restaurant near present downtown. The reputation for good seafood continues to this day. The business was owned by the same family until 1981.

Continue along Texas 35.

The old lighthouse on the left was originally built in 1858 on the southern tip of a shell barrier in Matagorda Bay called Halfmoon Reef. This structure stood over the water on pilings. During the Civil War, Confederate soldiers extinguished the light, which enabled blockade runners to get through undetected. The federal government repaired and re-established the light in 1868, but its service ended in the 1880s. Moved first to Point Comfort, the structure was relocated here in 1979 by the Calhoun County Historical Commission.

Turn left on Business Texas 35.

This drive parallels the bayshore and passes the city harbor where the shrimp boats dock. Port Lavaca enjoyed a prosperous port facility until the authorities increased the dockage fee in 1849. Charles Morgan, the shipping magnate, promptly took his business to nearby Indianola and Port Lavaca never recovered. Travelers will remember that Galveston learned the same bitter lesson in 1874 when its wharfage was increased (Chap. 1). In that instance, Morgan immediately dredged a direct route into Buffalo Bayou and took his business to the little village called Houston.

The fish and shrimp industry is big business and big fun for this area. Each year over the Labor Day weekend, the Port Lavaca Jaycees sponsor a county-wide fishing contest. Daily winners in several categories, as well as grand prizes, are offered for adults and for children. Contact the Port Lavaca–Calhoun County Chamber of Commerce and Agriculture for more information and registration forms, P.O. Box 528, Port Lavaca, TX 77979, or call 512/552-2959.

Follow Business Texas 35 into town.

The railroad tracks that run along Railroad Street mark one of the first rail lines in the state, the San Antonio and Mexican Gulf Railroad. Chartered in 1850, the road ran five miles out into the prairie where wagons loaded with merchandise met the train. A huge volume of business took place out there at the terminus, miles from a road or a settlement. This commerce kept Port Lavaca business alive at a time when Indianola's port, with its deeper water, offered fierce competition.

During the Civil War, Confederates ripped up the track to keep Union forces from using the railroad. At the turn of the century, in accordance with the fashion of the day, excursion trains brought tourists from as far away as San Antonio to enjoy the bay at Port Lavaca. A huge pavillion, which offered a good dance floor and fine bands, stretched out over the water. After the 1919 hurricane destroyed the structure, investors hurriedly constructed another here at the end of Main Street.

Do not follow Business Texas 35 to the right at the corner of Main Street. Instead, drive straight on Commerce Street.

Landfill has been brought in at the end of Main Street and Bay Front Park has been constructed for picnic facilities. A marina has been planned along the south side of the park.

In the next block, near the old service station where Live Oak Street meets the bay, is the site of an old blacksmith shop. This is where John V. Singer, brother of the sewing machine maker, invented the torpedo mine, a land mine used extensively by Confederates during the Civil War.

On October 31, 1862, in the midst of a yellow fever epidemic, two Union gunboats anchored in the bay and demanded Port Lavaca's surrender. When the Confederate defenders refused, the Union forces allowed one hour and a half for the women, children, and sick to leave town.

The shelling began in early afternoon and continued until dark, then resumed the following day. For a time

Confederates on the shore, some of them still not over yellow fever, returned the fire, even inflicting some damage to one ship. The vessels simply moved out of range of the land batteries and kept up their attack, riddling buildings and tearing up the streets. Fortunately, no one was killed. At the end of the second day, the gunboats steamed back down the bay toward Indianola. This attack resulted in a temporary takeover, which the Union made permanent over a year later.

It is claimed that the three-block stretch between Main and Austin streets boasted sixteen saloons before Prohibition.

Turn right on Austin Street, drive one block to Guadalupe Street, and turn right beside Grace Episcopal Church.

Local tradition says that the crude iron cross hanging just inside the narthex of this beautiful chapel belonged to La Salle's expedition, which landed on the coast near present Indianola in 1685 and then traveled inland and built a fort. The location of the fort is subject to controversy but this cross is said to have been found at the old fort site. The church is open Monday through Friday, 11:00 A.M. to 3:00 P.M., and for Sunday morning services; closed Saturday.

Note the barrel-shaped concrete marker at the entrance to the church parking lot on Guadalupe Street. It came from a ship that sank in the 1875 storm off the coast of Indianola. The barrels eventually washed to shore and became foundations of a building the congregation used for worship until a hurricane destroyed the structure in 1945. This remaining barrel serves as a monument.

Drive to the corner, Leona Street, turn left, and continue three blocks to the corner of Ann Street and the Old Jail Museum.

The turbulent history of Calhoun County is related here in pictures and personal items of the early settlers who took part in building the area and watched the destruction brought by the elements. The museum is open Tuesday and Thursday, 2:00 P.M. to 6:00 P.M.; Saturday,

9:00 A.M. to 1:00 P.M.; closed Sunday, Monday, Wednesday, and Friday. No admission charge.

Retrace the route one block to Virginia Street and turn left. Drive about eight blocks to Tilley Street and turn left for two blocks to Benavides Street. Turn right.

The Methodist church bell is on the left, adjacent to the sanctuary of the First United Methodist Church. Founded in 1841, this congregation, like most on this storm-plagued coast, has lost buildings and been forced to worship on three church sites and in various public buildings.

The bell hung originally in the Indianola Methodist Church, which was destroyed in the 1875 storm and never rebuilt. According to an article by the Reverend M. A. Dunn, published in 1927 in the *Frontier Times*, Malinda Harris, a black member of the congregation, remained in Indianola. After the 1886 storm, when the Victoria Methodists repaired extensive damage to their building, men from that congregation rode to Indianola to get "the finest bell in Texas" from the old wrecked church. Malinda Harris stood up to those men and refused to let them have the bell. Later, she moved to Port Lavaca, operated a white boardinghouse, and attended Methodist worship services (old-timers remember her sitting on the back row). When the congregation built its second facility in the 1890s, "Aunt Malindy" gave the bell to the church. The Reverend Dunn says that when he served the congregation, beginning in 1901, Aunt Malindy paid $125 to paint the church building—with bills "as stiff as card boards" (as if they had been gathered from salt water and pressed). When she died in 1914, she left her property, which consisted of one-half lot worth $250 and personal property worth $25, to the church.

Go back on Benavides Street to Tilley Street, turn left to Virginia Street, turn right, and drive to Austin Street, Texas 238. Turn right for the trip to Indianola. When Texas 238 forks right, continue straight on Texas 316 for 5.7 miles to the intersection with Farm Road 2760. Turn left and follow the road to the bay.

Fannie's Magnolia Beach Cafe occupies the large metal building to the left, overlooking the bay. Diners come from as far away as Victoria to enjoy this seafood. The homemade rye bread and the broiled flounder are second to none.

Go back one-half block to Oleander Street and follow the arrows pointing to the beach.

Indianola

This county beach has designated swimming and boating areas. Because this is a shell beach, shoes feel better than bare feet even on swimmers and surf fishers. Ships using the channel to Alcoa's harbor are clearly visible from this vantage.

The point of land jutting into the bay just beyond the Indianola Park picnic tables is Indian Point, the landing spot of the first shipload of Germans in 1844. This site became known as Carlshafen to the Germans in honor of Prince Carl of Solms-Braunfels, the courtly gentleman assigned by the Adelsverein, the German emigration company, to settle his fellow countrymen in Texas. Due to poor organization, ignorance of what the emigrants would find in Texas, bungling on the part of the company and Prince Solms, no facilities awaited the new arrivals when they appeared on this barren coastline that cold December day. Four more vessels arrived on the heels of the first and tents sprang up along the shore in a vain effort to protect against the chilling wind from Texas "northers." This group actually fared better than later immigrants. The first contingent moved inland and established New Braunfels in March 1845, just one week after Prince Solms purchased the site. In a month, however, Prince Solms gave up his effort and abandoned the new townsite even before his replacement arrived.

Apparently oblivious to the primitive conditions and the inadequate provisions awaiting the new settlers, the Adelsverein continued to send shiploads of unsuspecting Germans. There were 5,247 men, women, and children who arrived in the fall, winter, and spring of 1845–46. Heavy rains and extreme cold plagued the scene, and wagons intended to haul the immigrants inland sank to their axles in the mud. In May 1846, the Mexican War broke out and all vehicles intended to transport the settlers were taken for the war effort. The wayfarers at Carlshafen faced great deprivations. In addition to crowded housing, polluted water, and no adequate sanitation, mosquitoes, green stinging flies, and house flies descended like a plague. Typhoid, cholera, and cerebrospinal meningitis claimed adults and children in epidemic proportions. The number of deaths for that summer has never been determined, but estimates range from 400 to 1,200.

Hundreds left in terror, attempting to walk to safety at New Braunfels and Fredericksburg. Over 200 died along the route. Part of that story is included in the Victoria section (Chap. 5). Despite these horrors, the Germans in Texas survived, built stable homes and communities, and offered their lives as solid citizens to their new homeland.

The beach road at Indian Point turns to the right beyond the point. It is necessary to travel for a short distance behind the beach cabins that have been constructed on the bayfront. The trail moves back onto the beach front in a short distance.

The impressive statue beside the beach is in commemoration of René Robert Cavelier, Sieur de la Salle, the French explorer who led an expedition instructed by King Louis XIV to establish a settlement at the mouth of the Mississippi River, which La Salle had explored earlier. The four ships, loaded with about three hundred, left France in July 1684. Speculation persists that La Salle deliberately passed the Mississippi delta and came into Pass Caballo, which separates Matagorda Peninsula and Matagorda Island, because he had secret plans to locate New Spain's outposts. One ship was captured by Spanish privateers, one returned to France, and the others were eventually lost in storms. The little band of survivors moved inland and built the crude Fort St. Louis on Garcitas Creek in present Victoria County (some still argue that the site was the Lavaca River in present Jackson

County). Left without a ship to carry them to safety, or to seek supplies, La Salle led an expedition in search of the Mississippi River; instead, he unintentionally headed west and explored the Rio Grande. Realizing it was the wrong river, he headed east toward the Mississippi with plans to reach the Illinois River by that waterway. As reported in the Navasota section (Chap. 4), La Salle and his nephew were killed by their own men near present Navasota, according to most scholars. Six survivors finally returned to France. Those left at Fort St. Louis died during an Indian attack except for a few children saved by the Indian women.

Continue along the beach road.

Indianola grew in this direction, especially after Charles Morgan moved his shipping business here from Port Lavaca in 1849. Known for a time as Powder Horn, the new community later became Indianola, with the Indian Point site referred to as Old Town. Long docks extended into the bay for unloading ships. Warehouses, packing plants, and businesses thrived all along this coastline.

From the La Salle statue, it is less than a mile to the historical marker noting the site of Indianola and the ruins of an old cistern.

This shallow water reservoir is made of shell concrete, which was used in much of the building construction here. These open cisterns, the shallow ponds, marshy areas, inadequate sanitation, and hordes of disease-carrying house flies made this port city a victim just waiting for an epidemic.

The port also brought excitement. In May 1856, all the citizenry turned out to see thirty-two adult camels and two calves unloaded on the docks. The strange entourage, led by three Arabs and two Turks, constituted the first shipment of Secretary of War Jefferson Davis' camel experiment. The animals were planned for use in the West for transporting army equipment in areas with too little water for horses and oxen to survive. Upon their arrival, the animals regained their land legs to the amusement of the crowd by rearing, breaking halters, kicking, and crying. Many residents, desperate for fence-building material, had resorted to prickly pear fences because cattle did not cross the sticky barriers. Neither did the camels; they ate the fences.

After three weeks, the lanky beasts walked majestically away toward duty at Camp Verde, south of present Kerrville. The camel experiment proved successful and the animals functioned very well; however, the advent of the Civil War in 1861 brought a sudden end to the endeavor. Some camels wandered away; others ended up in Confederate hands. After the war, the remaining supply was sold to private interests.

During the Civil War, Pass Caballo, the narrow inlet from the Gulf of Mexico into these bays, played a vital role to this area and to all of Texas. Goods for the Confederate army passed through here, while cotton and hides intended for Mexico and then European markets left from Lavaca and Indianola. A few blockade runners skillfully maneuvered past the Union warships at the mouth of Pass Caballo. After temporarily taking Matagorda Bay in late 1862, Union forces returned again a year later and effectively controlled this area throughout the remainder of the war. This seizure made the inland cotton route (Chap. 4) even more vital to the Confederacy.

Indianola thrived after the war. Charles Morgan's railroad used tracks laid on the docks that extended into the bay, the latest in merchandise flowed into the port, theatrical productions came to town, and restaurants even advertised service for the "elite." In the midst of the hustle and bustle, the new inventions, and the modern attitudes, the populace ignored the precarious topography: a flat terrain with a bay on one side, a lake to the rear, and smaller bodies of water around the periphery.

On September 14, 1875, the wind in Matagorda Bay gradually increased. By noon the following day, it had reached gale force. A large crowd had gathered in town for the murder trial of Bill Taylor, a participant in the infamous Sutton-Taylor Feud, which had swept South

Texas since just after the Civil War. The visitors from inland towns enjoyed the spectacle as waves pounded the
shore. The tide rose all night and by the morning of the
sixteenth sea water rushed through the streets of Indianola. The wharves began tearing loose, the tide ate away
the foundations of buildings on the waterfront, and the
swirling sea carried debris into other structures. The
roads became impassable, and the railroad was under-
mined by erosion. By evening victims who had escaped
smaller structures before they fell took refuge on the second floor of sturdier buildings and finally moved into the
attics. Wind estimates reached 145 miles an hour.

After the eerie silence of the passing of the hurricane's
eye, the wind returned with a horrible burst, driving the
water fiercely back toward the bay and ripping down
structures that had withstood the first onslaught. When
the water receded, three hundred were dead, three-fourths
of the buildings had been lost, and the remainder suffered
severe damage.

By the end of the month, residents realized that the
town must be moved to a higher location. Aware that the
cooperation of Charles Morgan would be necessary to
make a major move, representatives approached the
aging gentleman's advisors. The Morgan Line's final decision was to spend no money on a relocation project. With
that news, many businessmen left town. Others remained
and the community struggled, never again reaching the
commercial heights it had known before the storm. And
then disaster came again. On August 19, 1886, the winds
began; this time with even greater force. Buildings that
had withstood the 1875 storm collapsed. A fire broke out
and leaped from structure to structure. At least this time
the storm moved in more quickly and did not push as
much water to the low prairies behind the town, sparing
the awful damage from the outflow. As light dawned,
grief-stricken victims began dismantling the few surviving structures to move them to Victoria and Cuero. Indianola had been killed.

Today, fishing huts line this waterfront, nothing permanent, structures expected to be washed away in the

next storm. Tides have eaten away at the shore, leaving much of the old town under the bay waters. Even the bare hunks of cement piled along the beach can't stop the restless currents that chew at the land.

Return by the same route. Texas 316 intersects the beach road at the Indianola Baptist Mission. Turn left. Immediately to the right, there is a road leading to one of Indianola's old cemeteries. The road to the left, Comal Street, goes to the Old Indianola Cemetery. Follow Texas 316 back to the intersection with Texas 238 and continue into Port Lavaca. This highway becomes Austin Street and goes to the bayfront. Turn left on Commerce Street, which will join Business Texas 35 in a few blocks. Follow Business Texas 35 out of town and rejoin Texas 35 toward Palacios. Take Business Texas 35 exit to downtown Palacios, a tiny town beside the sparkling Tres Palacios Bay.

Palacios

Two tales persist about the naming of this bay. The first, admittedly a legend: Spanish sailors lost their way during a storm on Matagorda Bay. Afterward, as they drifted aimlessly, they saw in the distance three magnificent palaces amid beautiful grounds. They eagerly set sail in that direction, only to discover that the palaces had been a mirage. Grateful to again be safely on land, they named the site "Tres Palacios," meaning "place of the three palaces."

Others argue that the bay acquired its name from José Félix Trespalacios, a Mexican military leader who took part in one expedition after another, including the James Long expedition (Chap. 1), to free Mexico from Spanish rule. Trespalacios served as governor of Texas during the time Stephen F. Austin was establishing his colony. Proponents of this story argue that it would have been reasonable to honor Trespalacios in this manner.

The cement foundations to the right, after the traveler turns onto the business route, are all that remain of Camp Hulen, a summer training encampment established in

1923 for the Texas National Guard. In 1940 the site became an anti-aircraft artillery training center; the War Department declared it surplus in 1946.

In 1901, a year after Shanghai Pierce died, his estate offered this land, known as "bull pasture," for sale. Louisiana promoters purchased the site, laid off the town, and built a hotel to accommodate prospective buyers. Investors from the north bought the land, planning to use it for orchards.

In the second block after crossing the railroad tracks on Main Street, watch for Petersen's Restaurant on the left.

Known for miles for its excellent seafood, the dining room is usually filled with local families as well as tourists who have come to taste for themselves. Open Monday through Saturday 6:00 A.M. to 11:00 P.M.; Sunday, 6:00 A.M. to 10:00 P.M.

Turn right at the next corner, Fourth Street, and drive two blocks to Bay Boulevard. Turn right.

The Luther Hotel is on the right, grandly overlooking the palm trees and the bay. Originally built in 1903 on the east bay front, the huge structure supposedly was divided into three sections in 1905 and moved to this location with mules pulling the wagons. Northerners coming here to invest in land stayed at this hotel, which boasted a huge dining and ballroom, complete with a permanent orchestra.

Charles and Elsie Luther have owned the hotel since the 1930s. There are no antiques here, simply well-equipped apartments and rooms that are maintained in good condition. Northerners are still coming here, and now they winter at the Luther Hotel. Many are regular guests who return year after year. Often "honeymooners" celebrating their thirtieth wedding anniversary take the "penthouse" apartment, which opens onto a private deck overlooking the bay. For reservations or information, call 512/972-2312.

Turn around and drive east on Bay Boulevard.

Use of the lighted fishing pier is free.

Continue to the end of the street and turn left on First Street beside the Texas Baptist Encampment.

In 1906, the land company that laid out Palacios gave this thirteen-acre tract to the Baptist Young Peoples Union, provided they hold five consecutive encampments here. At the first camp in 1906, most participants stayed in tents, rented a cot for 50¢, or slept on a bale of hay free of charge. Meals were prepared outdoors. Through the years, thousands of families from all over the United States have enjoyed this beautiful facility.

At the end of the block, turn right on Main Street and then left on the boulevard that parallels the east bay, passing the boat ramp and the city park. After the route rejoins First Street, it is about three blocks to Bay Shore Drive. Turn right to continue the drive along the bayfront.

The community across the bay is Collegeport. The land once belonged to Jonathan Pierce.

*Continue straight when the road joins Farm Road 2853. This
is a pleasant shortcut through farmland that hugs Tres Palacios Bay and the Tres Palacios River. At the intersection with
Farm Road 521, turn right.*

The huge cone-shaped dome in the distance is the
South Texas Project's reactor containment building,
which towers 203 feet above ground level. The vast dirt
embankment extends for thirteen miles and encloses a
seven-thousand-acre cooling reservoir. This nuclear generating station is expected to be fully operational in the
mid-1980s and will produce over seventeen billion kilo-
watt hours of electricity each year. This plant works on
the same principle as do other generating plants using coal,
oil, or natural gas fuels. The fuel (in this case, uranium)
furnishes heat to convert water into steam, which, in turn,
drives a turbine generator that produces electricity.

The two geodesic domes on the left side of the road
house the STP Visitor Center, which offers a variety of
slides and films dealing with nuclear power for guests
with all levels of expertise on the subject. Excellent displays tell the energy story and courteous guides patiently
answer all questions. Site tours are available. Since the
STP van carries eleven passengers, groups near that number are requested. Lecture demonstrations for groups are
also available with advance arrangements. Call 512/972-
5023. The Visitor Center is open Monday through Saturday,
9:00 A.M. to 5:00 P.M.; Sunday, 1:00 P.M. to 5:00 P.M.

*Continue on Farm Road 521 to the intersection with Texas
60. Turn right for the 8.5-mile drive to the historic old town
of Matagorda.*

Matagorda

This is the location at the mouth of the Colorado River
where the group of settlers on the *Lively* were supposed to
meet Stephen F. Austin in December 1821. They mis-
takenly stopped at the Brazos River. After Austin came
overland, he traveled to this point and spent January and
February 1822 waiting for the colonists.

Drive a few blocks inside the city limits to the intersection of Fisher and Catalpa streets.

On the left corner is the yellow-and-white Dale-Rugeley-Sisk Home, a lovely example of the early houses in town.

Turn right at the next corner, Caney Street, and drive two blocks to Wightman Street.

On the northeast corner is the Culver Home, built in the late 1890s. George B. Culver donated the land and was instrumental in bringing the railroad to Matagorda in 1903. He drilled the first artesian well in town in 1904 and built a water works. He also served as a charter member of the Intracoastal Canal Association of Texas and Louisiana. For years Mrs. Lilly Culver took the responsibility of hitching horses to her buggy and driving through the community each month to collect donations for the Methodist preacher's salary.

Turn left on Wightman Street, drive one block to Cypress Street, and turn left for one block to Christ Church.

This is the first Episcopal church in Texas, organized January 27, 1839. The first church building, erected in 1841, suffered total destruction in the 1854 hurricane. The present structure, completed two years later, is fashioned from most of the original building's hand-hewn cypress timbers, some of the pews, and other furnishings. The building is still used for worship.

Continue on Cypress Street to Fisher Street, Texas 60, and turn right.

The United Methodist Church is on the right. Organized January 6, 1839, this is one of the earliest Methodist churches in Texas. The first house of worship fell to the 1854 hurricane. This 1893 structure still contains the original bell, Bible, and cypress pews.

Drive out Fisher Street three blocks to the city park at Laurel Street.

The tiny white building, erected before 1850, is a former store that also served as a post office. Until recent refurbishing, water marks stained the inside walls halfway to the ceiling, evidence of the battering this community has taken from coastal storms.

There is a Texas historical marker in the park honoring Jane McManus, the only lady empresario in Texas. The daughter of a U.S. congressman from New York and a family friend of Stephen F. Austin, beautiful and brilliant Jane Marie McManus Stolms separated from her first husband and came to Texas with the dream of establishing a colony. She received an eleven-league grant, but when finances ran short her European colonists became discouraged, broke their contract, and remained in Matagorda.

Turn left beside the park on Laurel Street, drive one block to Matagorda Street, and turn right.

The levee on the left is part of Matagorda's flood protection plan, constructed in 1961 in time to save the town from destruction during Hurricane Carla.

Follow the road over the levee, turn right beside the Colorado River, and then return into town on Fisher Street.

The Galley Restaurant at Fisher and Market (Farm Road 2031) streets specializes in seafood and steak. Open Thursday through Saturday, 4:00 P.M. to 10:00 P.M.; Sunday, noon to 8:00 P.M.; Monday, noon to 10:00 P.M.; closed Tuesday and Wednesday.

From the traffic light at Fisher and Farm Road 2031, it is about nine miles out to the beach. Turn right on Farm Road 2031.

Originally, the city of Matagorda sat beside Matagorda Bay, with the Matagorda Peninsula acting as a buffer from the Gulf waters. However, between 1926 and 1930, with the demolition of a mass of timber extending forty-six miles upstream, which had choked off the river for at least fifty years, silt moved downstream and built up this land area, which extends all the way to the Gulf of Mexico and cuts Matagorda Bay in half. In 1936 a channel was dredged across the barrier peninsula to the Gulf, but the Intracoastal Waterway, immediately beyond the levee, is now Matagorda's only link with shipping lanes.

Return to Matagorda on Farm Road 2031, turn right on Fisher Street, and follow Texas 60. Drive to Wadsworth and at the caution light turn right on Farm Road 521. It is almost 16 miles to the stop sign at Farm Road 457. Continue on Farm Road 521 about 6.7 miles to the Texas historical marker in front of the Levi Jordan Plantation Home.

This home, built by slave labor in 1854, is made of long-leaf pine brought by ship from Florida and then towed up the San Bernard River on barges. When Levi and Sarah Jordan came here in 1848 from their plantation on the Louisiana-Arkansas border, they began a sugar plantation. Brazoria County produced almost twice as much sugar as all the neighboring "Sugar Bowl" counties put together in 1852. The loss of slave labor caused a decline, which picked up again in 1871 when convict labor became available, but by 1935 production had dwindled to little more than a memory. Hurricane destruction, the 1913 flood, the import of duty-free sugar, and a plant disease all worked together to end the empire that had built opulent estates throughout this and surrounding counties.

Drive to the stop sign and turn left on Farm Road 524. Continue 4.3 miles into Sweeny, turn right on Farm Road 1459 for 4.6 miles to Texas 35, and turn right again.

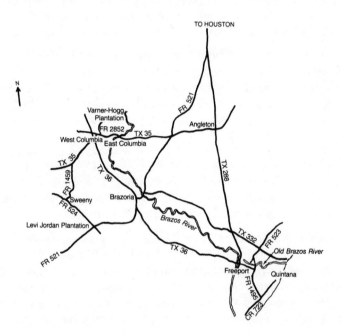

West Columbia

Josiah H. Bell, a friend of Stephen F. Austin, had served as *alcalde* (mayor/judge) at Washington-on-the-Brazos. He also took charge of the colony while Austin was in Mexico. In 1824, Bell moved to his land grant on the Brazos River. First he laid out Bell's Landing, present East Columbia. Then he built his plantation home just south of here. Next he laid out this town, known simply as Columbia at the time.

After Texas won independence from Mexico in 1836, none of the communities had facilities to house a government, but businessmen here promised rooms in various structures—enough to convince President David G. Burnet to choose Columbia for the new capital.

Follow Texas 35 into town, Seventeenth Street, turning right with the highway on Brazos Avenue.

Texas historical markers on both sides of the street designate sites where store buildings served as meeting places for the Texas Senate and House. The tiny town struggled under the influx of citizens here to do business with the new republic. Bed space sold for 50¢ and, if someone wanted privacy, he had to pay for all the bed spaces in the room.

Continue four blocks and turn left on Fourteenth Street. Drive to the block behind the First Capitol Bank.

This is a replica of the Leman Kelsey store, believed to be the building in which the House of Representatives met. The original structure had been allowed to deteriorate and the 1900 storm completely destroyed the remains. This reproduction was completed in 1979 using pictures and written descriptions as the basis for the construction. Today the facility houses the chamber of commerce. The large meeting room has been furnished in early Texas pieces, much the way historians believe the original room looked. The little shed room where Austin, as secretary of state, worked into the night and even slept on occasions has been furnished with a desk and a narrow bed. The big black pot on the lawn served during the Civil War as a kettle to distill salt water. The building is open Monday through Friday, 9:00 A.M. to noon, and plans are underway to open Saturday and Sunday, 1:00 P.M. to 4:00 P.M. Appointments may be arranged by calling the West Columbia Chamber of Commerce, 713/345-3921; Mrs. T. M. Gupton, 713/345-4213; or Mrs. Hall Griggs, 713/345-3712. No admission charge.

Because of the crowded conditions in town, or because some merchants did not actually provide the promised space, or perhaps, as the story is told, Josiah Bell discouraged the crowding because it hampered the free roaming of his hogs, the Legislature voted in 1837 to move the capital to Houston.

Drive to the end of Fourteenth Street and turn right on Jefferson Street. Turn left at the next corner on Farm Road 2852, Thirteenth Street. It is a little over a mile to the Varner-Hogg Plantation.

Varner-Hogg State Historical Park

Martin Varner, one of Stephen F. Austin's Old Three Hundred, received a land grant of 4,500 acres here and in present Waller County. He built a two-room cabin on the bank of this creek. As settlers came in, Varner felt too crowded and in 1834 sold this property to Columbus R. Patton. The following year, Patton built this mansion, enclosing, some believe, the original cabin within the first floor. Patton's slaves made the brick with clay from the nearby Brazos riverbed. He built a separate kitchen, brick slave houses, and a large sugar processing house.

After the Battle of San Jacinto, Texans moved the captured Santa Anna to Velasco, then to this plantation for a few days, and finally to the nearby Orozimbo Plantation. There is a legend that a beautiful Spanish lady who lived in the area came to visit Santa Anna while he remained here as a prisoner. She brought wine and other delicacies to the general. As she stood to leave, she dropped a glove and Major Patton picked it up for her. Again she dropped the glove and this time Patton discovered a note stuffed in one of the fingers. It said that one bottle of wine had a drug in it for the guards and that, if an escape attempt failed, the other bottle contained poison. In all the confusion, Santa Anna drank some of the poisoned wine. Patton rushed him to Dr. James Aeneas E. Phelps at Orozimbo Plantation and had his stomach pumped, saving the general for several more months as a prisoner.

The property changed owners several times until 1901, when former Governor James Stephen Hogg bought the place as a country home for his four children. Governor Hogg discovered that artesian wells on the property emitted a gas that could be ignited. Convinced that oil lay under the old cotton and sugar fields, Governor Hogg stipulated in his will that the property could not be sold until fifteen years after his death. He died in 1906 and nine years later the West Columbia Oil Field came in.

The Hogg children had this home remodeled in 1920; they added the pillars, built a new kitchen, and stuccoed the building to preserve the slave-made bricks. Miss Ima Hogg, Governor Hogg's daughter, gave the plantation to the state as a historic park in 1958. This home is open with forty-five–minute guided tours offered Tuesday, Thursday, Friday, and Saturday, 10:00 A.M. to noon and 1:00 P.M. to 5:00 P.M.; Sunday, 1:00 P.M. to 5:00 P.M.; closed Monday and Wednesday. Small admission charge.

Drive past the plantation home and go across Varner Creek to the picnic area.

The foundation of the old sugar mill is here. The beehive-looking brick mound is an old cistern. The park is open daily, 8:00 A.M. to 7:00 P.M. After leaving the park, note that the West Columbia Oil Field is still pumping on the right.

Return on Farm Road 2852, turn left on Texas 35, and drive a little over a mile to the fork into East Columbia.

East Columbia

The two towns spread all through here on both sides of the road, with East Columbia on the Brazos River bank and West Columbia on the prairie on the other side of the highway. Some of the fine homes built when this place served as a major inland port still stand vigil beside the Brazos River.

Fork to the right off Texas 35 on a road that has no street sign.

Note the large barn on the left, across Texas 35. It is the former East Columbia School.

Continue straight toward the river.

This is where Josiah Bell laid out the town that everyone called Bell's Landing. The naming of these towns still causes confusion: after the capital was moved to Houston, Columbia declined rapidly; after Josiah Bell died in 1838, this site began being called East Columbia; eventually, old Columbia became West Columbia.

This important river port received supplies intended for the interior. Warehouses, wharfs, sheds, and a store lined the river bank. Later the railroad came to the depot across the river. Freight, passengers, and mail had to be ferried across to East Columbia. This is also the place from which Stephen F. Austin's body was shipped downstream in December 1836 to be unloaded and carried to his sister's plantation for burial.

Turn left and follow Front Street, parallel to the river.

The old building on the left is all that remains of a former warehouse; in fact, trees and undergrowth have taken over the downtown area. Follow the street around to the Bethel Presbyterian Church, which was organized in 1840 with ten members.

Turn left beside the church and drive along quiet Main Street to the second block. (This route crosses the street used when the traveler entered town.)

Homes in the next block were built between the 1830s and 1850s. The Texas historical marker on the left is near the site of the Dance Gun Shop, started in 1850. It is said that, although the railroad, known as the "Sugar Road" (because it enabled planters to get their sugar crop out of the bottomland), prospered before the Civil War, Confederates tore out the tracks and used the steel for making Dance revolvers.

The next house on the left is the Ammon Underwood Home, oldest in the community. The original two-room log cabin was erected in 1835–36. Ammon Underwood, a merchant and planter, bought the property in 1838 and enlarged it to a two-story structure to serve as a residence and boarding house. Anson Jones (Chap. 4), the future president of the Republic of Texas, stayed here and is said to have left owing a bill.

Since the Brazos River makes a sharp turn here, it has continued to gnaw into the bank and has forced owners to move this home on three occasions. In 1840 the Underwoods planted the rose bush to the left of the front steps. An early photograph on display in the home shows the rose bush climbing up and across the second-floor gallery. Some of the furniture belonging to the Underwoods remains in the house. This home, listed on the National Register of Historic Places, was restored in 1981 by the First Capital Historical Foundation, Inc., West Columbia Garden Club, and First Capital Study Club. It is open to the public by appointment. Call the West Columbia Chamber of Commerce, 713/345-3921; Mrs. T. M. Gupton, 713/345-4213; or Mrs. Hall Griggs, 713/345-3712.

Each year, on the weekend nearest San Jacinto Day, historical tours are offered to interesting sites in the county as well as through several of these fine old mansions.

The last house on the right, at the end of the street, is the Weems Home, built about 1839.

To exit East Columbia, retrace the route on Main Street to the first corner, turn left on the road that enters the village, and return to Texas 35. Turn left and return to West Columbia. Turn left with Texas 35, Brazos Avenue, on Seventeenth Street. In about six blocks, turn left on Texas 36, Columbia Drive, and drive toward Brazoria. It is about 4.5 miles from West Columbia to the Prairie House on the left.

This is more than just an arts and crafts shop—dolls with porcelain heads that are signed and dated are available here as well as Raggedy Ann and Andy dolls. Homemade jams, jellies, and bread line shelves, and glass collections are arranged beside the work of many local artists. Open Tuesday through Sunday, 9:00 A.M. to 6:00 P.M.; closed Monday; bread available Friday through Sunday only.

Brazoria

Founded in 1828, this community held an important position in Texas until the advent of the railroad caused a decline in river traffic and spelled the end of this riverport city. Nothing remains to distinguish this community's early importance. Even the second courthouse, a grand three-story Victorian building erected in 1896 in a vain effort to keep the county seat from being moved to Angleton, was torn down in the 1930s and the bricks were used to construct all-weather roads.

Just after entering Brazoria, watch for the sign on the left pointing to the Masonic Oak Park.

It is two blocks from this corner to the oak, which is almost dead after being struck twice by lightning. This is where a group met and decided to petition the Grand

Lodge of Louisiana for dispensation for a lodge at Brazoria. As they waited in February 1836 for an answer from Louisiana, they held their last meeting before abandoning the town to the advancing Mexican army. Anson Jones, future president of Texas, presided and James W. Fannin, Jr., who would soon give his life at Goliad, acted as warden. The charter arrived as Anson Jones headed to the Battle of San Jacinto. He placed it in his saddle bags, where it remained throughout the fight. Mexican General José Urrea came through Brazoria on his way to Santa Anna's defense and burned everything in the Masonic lodge, except the charter riding safely with Anson Jones. General Urrea's force was still in Brazoria when the Mexicans suffered defeat at San Jacinto. The lodge was reopened in Houston in 1837.

There is a local story about Lew, a black man who made loans at midnight on the streets of Brazoria. Lew had been a slave and had run away so often that his master outfitted him in a seven-pound iron collar with projections on both sides, but Lew's "horns" did not stop his escape attempts. He even swam the Bernard River wearing the collar. To relieve the pressure on his neck, and allow him to sleep, Lew wrapped the contraption with rags at night. During the Civil War, Lew ran off and hid until freedom came. Then he returned to his former master, had the collar removed, and settled down to farming on land his master gave him. Lew prospered, eating only parched corn suspended in a bag around his neck as he worked his land. He accepted only gold in payment for his cotton and soon he went into the loan business. First he met his clients in downtown Brazoria and, if he liked them or their plan, he arranged for the midnight transaction.

The original town of Brazoria lay to the left of present Texas 36 and Farm Road 521.

Continue through town on Texas 36 toward Freeport.

About two miles out of town, the beautifully cultivated land on both sides of the road is part of the Clemens State Prison Farm.

From the main gate of the prison, it is three miles to a large white sign pointing to the right to the Gulf Prairie Church and Cemetery.

This is part of the Peach Point cotton and sugar plantation owned by Stephen F. Austin's sister, Emily Austin Bryan Perry, and her husband, James Franklin Perry. After Austin died, his body was brought to Peach Point for burial, the only place in Texas he claimed as home. In 1910 his remains were reinterred in the State Cemetery in Austin.

It is 0.3 mile to the Perry plantation home on the right, sitting among shrubs some distance from the highway.

This home is not open to the public. Stephen F. Austin came to visit his sister often and maintained his own room and office here. The house was destroyed in the 1900 storm except for Austin's two rooms, which have been restored, on the left side of the structure. The pillars, made of brick and plastered with cement, are also part of the original house. The home remains in the Perry family.

Freeport

Captain Anthony F. Lucas, the gentleman who finally brought in the Spindletop Oil Field (Chap. 2), is the one who in 1901 discovered sulphur in prospective oil wells being drilled at the salt dome called Bryan Mound just south of here. After years of setbacks, the first wagonload of sulphur in the state was hauled into the new town of Freeport on November 12, 1912.

Investors in the Freeport Sulphur Company set up the Townsite Company to form a town and port for their sulphur mining operations. After producing five million tons of sulphur, Bryan Mound was closed in 1935. The Department of Energy now uses the vast underground caverns as oil storage facilities.

The bridge over the Brazos River at the edge of Freeport was listed in Ripley's *Believe It or Not* in 1928 because engineers constructed the bridge over dry land. This is not the original Brazos River. To improve the harbor, the old river was "plugged" and a new route was channeled in a straight path to the Gulf of Mexico.

At the traffic light, just across the bridge, turn left on Brazosport Boulevard and continue one block.

The giant river plug is just beyond the **Brazosport High School.** The *Mystery*, on display at the park on the north side of the old river, is a monument to the shrimping industry in this area.

Retrace the route to Texas 36, Second Street, and turn left. Drive into town parallel to the levee beside the old river. For a closer look at the shrimp boats, turn left on Ash Street, cross the levee to First Street, and turn right.

The last weekend in April, the Freeport Shrimp Association sponsors the Blessing of the Fleet, which begins with a street dance on Friday night and ends on Sunday with a river parade of decorated shrimp boats.

Turn right on Oak Street, drive two blocks to Broad Street, and turn left.

Freeport's original post office (1912) is on the left, 118 West Broad Street. The walls are lined with early-day Freeport photographs. Open Monday through Friday, 9:00 A.M. to 1:00 P.M.; closed Saturday and Sunday. No admission charge.

Continue to the corner of Park Avenue.

The town developers laid out this esplanade park, which lends a quiet air to this industrial city.

Turn right at the next corner, Farm Road 1495. It is about 3.5 miles to historic Quintana, where the old Brazos River meets the Gulf of Mexico.

In about six blocks, note the entrance to the Port of Freeport. Often foreign cars and other goods that have been unloaded and are being held in a fenced area are visible from the roadside. The drawbridge spans the Intracoastal Waterway. It is a little over two miles east of here to the location where in 1850 the Galveston and Brazos Navigation Company began digging a fifty-foot-wide, three–and–one-half–foot deep canal to Galveston Bay. Brazoria County planters and Galveston cotton brokers used slave labor and mule teams for this project, which took from four to seven years to complete. Part of the old canal has been incorporated into the present Intracoastal Waterway.

At the intersection with County Road 723, just before reaching the Gulf, turn left.

Quintana

The levees on both sides of the road hold silt dredged from the Intracoastal Waterway. Mexican colonization laws forbade settling any land within ten leagues (about thirty miles) of the coast. However, from this vantage, it is possible to look across the river to the site of Old Velasco, a port of entry under the Mexican government (1821–1835) for over 25,000 settlers.

At the T intersection in Quintana, turn left on Eighth Street, drive one block, and turn right on Holley Street. At the end of the street, turn right on an unmarked street and drive about two blocks parallel to the river.

The Coast Guard station across the Brazos is the site where the *Lively* deposited its eighteen colonists in December 1821. They thought they had landed at the mouth of the Colorado River, where Stephen F. Austin was supposed to meet them. After waiting for several months, some of them drifted back to the United States. About three others moved on upriver, and some believe they landed in 1822 at the "bend" at present Richmond (Chap. 5).

In 1830 the Mexican government ordered the construction of forts at Velasco and Anahuac (Chap. 1). The fort at Velasco sat just behind the present Coast Guard station, surrounded by a moat and manned by a raised nine-pounder cannon. The garrison controlled river traffic and collected import and export customs.

When several Texans, among them William B. Travis, were imprisoned, anger came to a head at Anahuac, already chafing over the Mexican government's dictatorial rule. As soon as word reached Brazoria, 120 men loaded two cannon on a ship and began the trek down the Brazos. When the commander at the Velasco fort refused permission for passage into the Gulf, the Texans waited until midnight of June 25, 1832, and attacked the fort. After an all-night siege, the Mexicans surrendered, with five killed and sixteen wounded; seven Texans died and fourteen were wounded.

When five Mexican gunboats came to investigate the incident, the Texans explained that they supported the Mexican Constitution of 1824 and Santa Anna, whom they believed would free the country from the tyranny of Mexican President Bustamante. The Mexican colonel understood the Texans' sentiments, and the incident ended with a grand fiesta up the river at Brazoria. But, the basic problem did not really end. In less than four years Texans would recognize the impossibility of survival under the

"Napoleon of the West," Santa Anna. After Texas won independence at the Battle of San Jacinto, President David G. Burnet moved the capital to Velasco for a time, and it is here that Santa Anna signed the peace treaties on May 14, 1836.

Both Velasco and Quintana flourished as resort towns for wealthy planters from the time of Texas independence until the beginning of the Civil War in 1861. The completion of the early intracoastal canal in 1856 diverted shipping to Galveston and began the decline of the Velasco port. The 1875 hurricane brought terrible damage, from which both cities never fully recovered. Velasco was rebuilt as a new town up the river in 1891, and Quintana slipped into sleepy obscurity. The earthen mounds rising between Quintana and the Gulf are leftover gun emplacements built during World War I.

Return to Burnett Street and turn left. Drive to Eighth Street and turn right. Turn left again at the next intersection, Lamar Street, County Road 723. Retrace the route back to Freeport. Continue on Farm Road 1495, Pine Street, across the high bridge over the old Brazos River.

Look to the right from the top of the bridge. The huge guillotine-looking contraption that straddles the river is the Velasco Memorial Tide Gate. During storms the gate can be lowered to halt tidal waves and prevent flooding.

This street will join Farm Road 523. Turn left on Texas 332 for about 3.5 miles to the cloverleaf intersection with Texas 288.

Dow Chemical operates its Texas division headquarters just south of the cloverleaf intersection. One-hour tours leave promptly from the A. P. Beutel Building each Monday, 2:00 P.M.

To reach Dow Chemical, drive south on Texas 288 to the second traffic light. Turn right into the plant.

The A. P. Beutel Building is the three-story green structure on the left. Parking is available in the front drive.

*For the trip toward Angleton, drive north on Texas 288. The
fourth traffic light from the cloverleaf is College Boulevard.
Turn left for less than a mile to the first entrance to the
Brazosport College.*

Parking for the Brazosport Center for the Arts and
Sciences is available near this entrance. This facility has
an impressive display of ivory and jade, as well as one of
the finest public shell collections in this part of the country. Many of the naturally colored shells rival the elegance
of any jewelry store display. Some of the shells are for
sale. The museum is open Tuesday through Saturday,
10:00 A.M. to 5:00 P.M.; Sunday, 2:00 P.M. to 5:00 P.M.;
closed Monday. No admission charge.

*Turn left on College Boulevard, return to Texas 288, turn left,
and continue north.*

Angleton

In 1890, after the town of Velasco decided to move up the
Brazos River to a site less vulnerable to Gulf storms, a
huge land boom began with developers trying to induce
residents in the Midwest to buy in the new Velasco "garden of Eden." It proved difficult to reach the "garden"
because travel required a train into Houston, transfer to
Columbia on the Tap Line (the Columbia Tap Railroad),
and then a trip by riverboat to their destination. As an
inducement to get the Velasco Terminal Railroad to come
through this way, the developers gave the railroad a half-
interest in their new town of Angleton. With Angleton
being centrally located in the county and Brazoria disad-
vantaged by not being on the railroad, a close election
named Angleton the new county seat in 1897.

Continue into town on Texas 288.

Kelley and Sons Antiques is at the intersection with
Texas 35. This shop features clocks, furniture, and leaded
glass. Open seven days a week, 9:00 A.M. to 6:00 P.M.

It is about five blocks north on Texas 288 to the old Brazoria County Courthouse.

Built soon after Angleton became the seat of government, this facility houses the Brazoria County Historical Museum. In addition to exhibits of county interest, including old newspapers, and a research room, the museum receives traveling exhibits. Open only on Wednesday, 10:00 A.M. to 2:00 P.M.; Saturday, 9:00 A.M. to 1:00 P.M. No admission charge.

Return to Houston on Texas 288.

This concludes the river land trail through the heart of the rich river bottoms and the stories of the growth and change that shaped this region. Southeast Texas claims its own bold beauty and offers a special heritage to the state. As travelers explore the locales where history has been made and hear the stories behind those human acts, events that have lain dormant in history books take on a new dimension. Texas is big; its history is exciting. The people who settled this land made it so.

Sources

The hundreds of sources used in preparing this book included personal interviews; on-site investigations; state and county histories, some of which are rare books and are on deposit at the state archives in Austin; historic and current newspapers; historical quarterlies; and the extensive files pertaining to Texas historical markers and national register listings at the Texas Historical Commission in Austin. For the traveler who wishes to read further, the following publications are listed under the chapter to which they pertain:

1. Ports Trail

Charnley, Mitchell V. *Jean Lafitte, Gentleman Smuggler*. New York: Viking Press, 1934.
Department of Highways and Public Transportation. *Texas Trails*. Austin: Travel and Information Division, [on-going series].
Handbook of Texas. Edited by Walter Prescott Webb. 2 vols. Austin: Texas State Historical Association, 1952.
———, *a Supplement*. Edited by Eldon Stephen Branda. Austin: Texas State Historical Association, 1976.
Lewis, Carroll. *Treasures of Galveston Island*. Waco: Texian Press, 1966.
Lighthouses and Lightships of the Northern Gulf of Mexico. Washington: U.S. Coast Guard, Department of Transportation, 1976.
Malsch, Brownson. *Indianola, the Mother of Western Texas*. Austin: Shoal Creek Publishers, 1977.
O'Connor, Kathryn Stoner. *Presidio La Bahía*. Austin: Von Boeckmann-Jones Co., 1966.
Partlow, Marian. *Liberty, Liberty County, and the Atascosita District*. Austin: Jenkins Publishing Co., 1974.
Robinson, Willard B. (text), and Todd Webb (photographs). *Texas Public Buildings of the Nineteenth Century*. Austin: University of Texas Press, 1974.

Sibley, Marilyn McAdams. *The Port of Houston*. Austin: University of Texas Press, 1968.

Smith, Ashbel, M.D., A.M. *Yellow Fever in Galveston, Republic of Texas, 1839: An Account of the Great Epidemic*. Edited by Chauncey D. Leake. Austin: University of Texas Press, 1951.

Turner, Martha Anne. *The Yellow Rose of Texas: Her Saga and Her Song*. Austin: Shoal Creek Publishers, 1976.

Weems, John Edward. *A Weekend in September*. New York: Henry Holt and Co., 1957.

2. Industrial Trail

Black, W. T. *A History of Jefferson County, Texas, from Wilderness to Reconstruction*. Nederland: Nederland Publishing Co., 1976.

Clark, James A., and Michel T. Halbouty. *Spindletop*. New York: Random House, 1952.

East, Lorecia. *The History and Progress of Jefferson County*. Dallas: Royal Publishing Co., 1961.

Federal Writers' Project in Texas. *Beaumont*. American Guide Series. Houston: Anson Jones Press, 1939.

————. *Port Arthur*. American Guide Series. Houston: Anson Jones Press, 1940.

Stewart, William Ford. *Collision of Giants: The Port Arthur Story*. San Antonio: Naylor Co., 1966.

Stilwell, Arthur E., and James R. Crowell. *I Had a Hunch*. Port Arthur: LaBelle Printing Co. and Port Arthur Historical Society, 1972.

Tolbert, Frank K. *Dick Dowling at Sabine Pass: A Texas Incident in the War between the States*. New York: McGraw-Hill, 1962.

3. Big Thicket Trail

Abernethy, Francis E., ed. *Tales from the Big Thicket*. Austin: University of Texas Press, 1966.

Foreman, Grant. *The Five Civilized Tribes*. Norman: University of Oklahoma Press, 1934.

Loughmiller, Campbell and Lynn, comps. and eds. *Big Thicket Legacy*. Austin: University of Texas Press, 1977.

Martin, Howard N. *Myths and Folktales of the Alabama-Coushatta Indians of Texas*. Austin: Encino Press, 1977.

4. Heritage Trail

Allen, Irene Taylor. *The Saga of Anderson.* New York: Greenwich Book Publishers, 1957.

Barker, Eugene C. *The Life of Stephen F. Austin: Founder of Texas, 1793–1836.* Austin: University of Texas Press, 1969.

Gambrell, Herbert. *Anson Jones: The Last President of Texas.* Austin: University of Texas Press, 1964.

Jordan, Terry G. *German Seed in Texas Soil.* Austin: University of Texas Press, 1966.

Kilpatrick, A. R. "Brief Historical Sketch of Navasota, Texas." *Examiner Review,* 1876.

Puryear, Pamela Ashworth, and Nath Winfield, Jr. *Sandbars and Sternwheelers: Steam Navigation on the Brazos River.* College Station: Texas A&M University Press, 1976.

Ramsdell, Charles William. *Reconstruction in Texas.* Austin: University of Texas Press, 1970.

Winfield, Judy and Nath. *All Our Yesterdays.* Waco: Texian Press, 1969.

5. Cattlemen's Trail

Boethel, Paul C. *The History of Lavaca County.* San Antonio: Naylor Co., 1936.

Dobie, J. Frank. *Tales of Old-Time Texas.* Boston: Little, Brown and Co., 1928.

Emmett, Chris. *Shanghai Pierce, a Fair Likeness.* Norman: University of Oklahoma Press, 1953.

Reese, John Walter. *Flaming Feuds of Colorado County.* Edited by Lillian Estelle Reese. Salado: Anson Jones Press, 1962.

Rose, Victor M. *History of Victoria County.* Edited by J. W. Petty, Jr. Laredo: Daily Times Print, 1961.

Sowell, A. J. *History of Fort Bend County.* Houston: W. H. Coyle and Co. Stationers and Printers, 1904.

Wharton, Clarence R. *History of Fort Bend County.* San Antonio: Naylor Co., 1936.

Williams, Annie Lee. *A History of Wharton County.* Austin: Von Boeckmann-Jones Co., 1964.

6. River Land Trail

Calhoun County Historical Survey Committee. *Indianola Scrap Book.* Austin: Jenkins Publishing Co., 1974.

Creighton, James A. *A Narrative History of Brazoria County, Texas*. Waco: Texian Press, 1975.

Emmett, Chris. *Texas Camel Tales*. Austin: Steck-Vaughn, 1932.

Jeter, Lorraine Bruce. *Matagorda, Early History*. Baltimore: Gateway Press, 1974.

Johnston, Eleanor. "Victor L. LeTulle, the Philanthropist." *Texas Historian* 41, no. 2 (1980): 24–26.

Stieghorst, Junann J. *Bay City and Matagorda County History*. Austin: Pemberton Press, 1965.

Strobel, Abner J. *The Old Plantations and Their Owners of Brazoria County*. Historical Scrapbook of West Columbia, Texas, 1926.

Weddle, Robert S. *Wilderness Manhunt: The Spanish Search for La Salle*. Austin: University of Texas Press, 1973.

Index